AN UNCERTAIN FUTURE

AN
AUSTRALIAN BIRDLIFE
UNCERTAIN
IN DANGER
FUTURE

GEOFFREY MASLEN

Photography by Dr Rohan Clarke

hardie grant books

Published in 2017 by Hardie Grant Books,
an imprint of Hardie Grant Publishing

Hardie Grant Books (Melbourne)
Building 1, 658 Church Street
Richmond, Victoria 3121
hardiegrantbooks.com.au

Hardie Grant Books (London)
5th & 6th Floors
52–54 Southwark Street
London SE1 1UN
hardiegrantbooks.co.uk

A Cataloguing-in-Publication entry is available from the catalogue of the National Library of Australia at www.nla.gov.au

An Uncertain Future
ISBN 978 1 74379 323 7

Cover design by Sandy Cull
Text design by Patrick Cannon
Typeset in 11/16 pt Minion Pro by Cannon Typesetting
Printed and bound in China by 1010 Printing International Limited
Photography by Dr Rohan Clarke, except where specified

'Magpies' by Judith Wright published with the permission of the Estate of Judith Wright and HarperCollins Publishers Australia

Foreword

GEOFFREY MASLEN'S WONDER for Australian birds is inversely matched by many species' horrifying spiral towards extinction. Twenty-two species have been eradicated since 1788 and hundreds more are on the way out because of logging, land clearing, urban sprawl, marsh drainage, feral predators and weeds. The biggest killer is habitat destruction.

Whereas in the United States strong habitat protection laws are helping birds recover, Australia's state and federal governments aid and abet the continuing destruction of habitats. As Maslen points out, if Australian politicians spent as much on rare bird recovery as they claim in expenses each year, scores of these birds could be saved.

Yet, far from complete gloom and doom, his book is a celebration of our avian cousins. Not only did songbirds spread throughout the world from Australia, but our birds were also the most intelligent creatures in the world just 20 million years ago. Nowadays we humans, out of Africa, claim the highest-order intelligence. Yet birds also have remarkable brains: they were playing, singing, sharing food, making tools and mating for life long before we took on these qualities (and unlike us, birds are not sending humans into oblivion).

Maslen's anecdotes about birds – including shearwaters, magpies, lyrebirds, chooks and swallows – are delightful and finely balanced with the rapidly evolving scientific studies that give this book such authority.

As I write this, critically endangered swift parrots have arrived back here in southern Tasmania from their winter stay on the mainland, to nest and breed in old tree hollows. Each year fewer return. Mainland woodland clearing and Tasmanian logging are just two of the hazards to their continued existence. But in Maslen all our birds have a champion – for to read this book is to want to come to their aid and defy the government's latest plans to submit millions of hectares of forests and woodlands to the chainsaw.

Maslen's book is a clarion call for Australia's brilliant but disappearing birds.

Bob Brown
Former Senator and Parliamentary Leader of the Australian Greens

Contents

Author's Note

WITHOUT THE UNTOLD decades of work by numerous biologists, this book could not have been written. Tireless in their efforts to uncover the secrets of birdlife, these remarkable scientists happily spend much of their lives in the field, often under the most trying of conditions. I am enormously grateful to every one of them for their help in freely giving me the time to interview them and to report on their findings.

I extend particular thanks to Professor Jane Hughes, of Queensland's Griffith University, whose work I have seen first-hand in the field in Victoria and have reported on at various times since 1996. Jane concluded a remarkable 25 years of on-the-ground research into the Australian magpie in 2017 – one of Australia's longest studies devoted to a single species. But further papers on the work she and her team have carried out will continue to appear. As she says, 'We now have the long and exciting task of pulling all the 25 years' worth of data together.'

I also pay a special tribute to Dr Rohan Clarke at Monash University, not only for his help with the chapter on Ashmore Reef and his several studies on the grey-crowned babbler, which are described in Chapter 7 *Giving New Life to the Babbler*, but also for providing most of the beautiful photographs in this book. These include the dramatic cover shot of the seriously endangered helmeted honeyeater.

Two other people were also crucial to this publication making its appearance: former publishing director Fran Berry, who championed this book from the beginning, and editor Allison Hiew, who was masterful in clarifying unnecessarily dense passages.

Finally, all of the scientists whose work is described in these pages, along with the leaders of Birdlife Australia and the thousands of volunteers who contribute to its efforts to save endangered birds, are in no doubt that too many Australian birds are under threat of extinction. A dramatically changing climate coupled with governments that permit the ongoing destruction of bird habitats have brought too many species to the edge of the abyss.

This disaster is happening around the world and unless something is done, humans will bring an end to a 100-million-year-old history of the most wonderful creatures to have evolved on our planet. We can only reverse what seems inevitable if enough people act to force their governments to respond immediately. In saving Earth for birds, remember, we will be saving all other life forms as well. And that includes us.

Introduction

BIRDS ARE THE closest we have to angels on this planet, to paraphrase the poet Robert Adamson. Light as the air itself they swoop and dive, flit and flutter, hover, glide and soar around us, not only adding their wonderful songs and beauty to our lives but also playing an essential role in sustaining Earth's ecosystems. The 10,000 species of birds that fill niches in the great web of life on this planet number in the billions, yet they face an uncertain future. Climate change and the ever-rising tide of humanity have already affected billions of birds – and many more seem certain to be tipped into the abyss of extinction.

Long ago, Australia sent its songbirds out into the world. Today 898 officially recorded bird species are spread across this continent, as well as on its offshore islands and territories.[1] Of these, 165 are 'vagrant' – accidental visitors – and nearly half of the remainder are classified as Australian endemics: that is, they are found nowhere else on Earth.[2] Officially, twenty-two bird species have become extinct in the wild since the British illegally occupied this land in 1788, although the true figure is certainly much greater. Worse still, almost 150 species – a staggering one in six of those that remain – are now classed as critically endangered, endangered or vulnerable to extinction,[3] and the number rises as the years pass.

This is a book about birds and their complex lives, and about their intelligence – some species are smarter than most of the great apes, our nearest relatives. Most crucially, this book focuses on the threats to birds' survival and on the researchers who are working to prevent their extinction and uncover their secrets. These are the scientists whose discoveries reveal how complex bird life is, how clever birds are, and how essential this avian array is to our own existence. These biologists are committed conservationists with a passionate concern for birds – people who are prepared to spend years, sometimes studying just one species, in their efforts to protect birds, their environment and, ultimately, all other living beings.

Investigators with the national organisation BirdLife Australia note that native birds provide vital information about the state of the environment – and that what is happening to them may soon affect all humanity: 'Birds are highly sensitive and responsive to change, and often a decline in bird numbers is an early indicator of wider problems.' In other words, birds are the canaries in the coalmine and the plummeting populations of so many species is a warning that all living creatures, including us, are in danger. So, as both the top predators and the protectors of all life on Earth, humans should start taking action now – before it is too late.

The alarming threats confronting Australia's birds are described in a major report, *The State of Australia's Birds*,[4] where the BirdLife researchers reveal that the effects of climate change on birds will be profound across almost every region, though different species are already being affected in different ways. Pointing to northern Queensland, the biologists glumly predict:

> The Fernwren that lives in the moist montane forests will suffer as the moisture-laden clouds of these forests rise to ever higher altitudes, eventually occurring above the level of the mountains. When the mists no longer shroud the forests, the habitat will die, and so will its inhabitants.

When the mountain mists have gone, so too will the fernwren.

Then there are the birds that nest on beaches. Their habitats will be destroyed by rising sea levels, as will those of other species, including vast flocks of shorebirds living in low-lying coastal areas. Once, these waders and migratory seabirds numbered in the billions, but their populations have plunged by up to 90 per cent over the past thirty years as a result of human actions, even before the effects of climate change began to take their toll. That shocking decline has been caused partly by the overfishing of the seabirds' food sources and the rising sea levels that force shorebirds off the world's beaches, but also because human developments are destroying their stopover resting places along the coasts of China and Korea.

Meanwhile, the melting of pack ice is already causing devastation among the species that live in Antarctica. Adélie penguins, the cutest-looking of all Antarctic birds, are facing sharp falls in their numbers because of the warming earth. Biologists estimate their population could plunge by 30 per cent over the next few decades and they fear

Adélie penguin: cute, but facing extinction

the entire Adélie species will be extinct before the end of the century.[5] Inevitably, birdlife in the Arctic and around the North Pole is being seriously affected as well, with millions of migratory birds experiencing increasing difficulty finding the right places to breed – a situation that will only worsen.[6]

Of all the species of birds, amphibians, reptiles, mammals and plants that have disappeared from our planet over the past five centuries, 70 per cent were wiped out by human over-exploitation as a result of hunting and agricultural activities. Often their destruction also occurred with the introduction of invasive alien species;[7] however, climate change is now the dominant problem. The looming biodiversity crisis will affect all life on Earth, not just birds. Urbanisation and a continuing rise in human populations, combined with all these other forces, will only dramatically increase rates of extinction.

The State of Australia's Birds draws on a mass of information to present a disturbing account of declining populations for many of

Australia's most charismatic birds, including magpies, kookaburras and willie wagtails. A key factor behind the falling numbers of many species is habitat loss due to Australians' penchant for clearing land on a massive scale. Since the first British convict picked up an axe in 1788 and began chopping down a tree, more than a million square kilometres of Australia's most fertile bushland has been cleared for agriculture and enlarging towns and cities. Across the entire continent more than half of the original forested areas have been demolished or extensively modified while much of the remaining bush, scrub, grassland and open woodland ecosystems are now degraded or severely fragmented. The inevitable effect of this wholesale destruction has been to push increasing numbers of bird species to the edge of extinction – and beyond.

The first birds on this planet preceded humankind by more than a hundred million years. Yet it is now we who are responsible for preventing their ultimate demise – and ours as well, for that matter.

The charismatic willie wagtail: numbers are declining

1

The Sixth Mass Extinction

At least five mass extinctions of living creatures have occurred on Earth over the past 450 million years. The last one – until now – happened 66 million years ago when a 10 kilometre-wide asteroid struck the Yucatan Peninsula in Mexico and the explosive after-effects killed off all the non-avian dinosaurs (then the dominant animal species) and wiped out two-thirds of all plant and animal life across the entire globe. That left the ancestors of today's birds to roam the skies while also opening the world to the rise of mammals and the eventual appearance of Homo sapiens*: us!*

MYRIAD BIRDS, ANIMALS and plants are being driven to extinction on this planet and it is we humans who are responsible. Regrettably, Australia has one of the worst animal extinction records among all developed countries, so the ultimate fate of the birds that still survive on the continent is uncertain. The global organisation BirdLife International estimates that about one in eight of Earth's 10,000 bird species will soon face the end of their time here, while 217 species are at an extremely high risk of imminent extinction in the wild.[1] Worldwide, nearly 1400 bird species could vanish, either because their numbers are tiny, they occupy ranges that are too small or fragmented, or their populations are already in rapid decline.

'Without any doubt, Earth's sixth great mass extinction is upon us,' is the grim conclusion reached by a team of American scientists.[2] Extinction rates on Earth today, they say, have reached levels unparalleled since the last of the dinosaurs died. Among these senior biologists from top universities across the United States is the renowned biologist Professor Paul Ehrlich of Stanford University. He flatly declares: 'There are examples of species all over the world that are essentially the walking dead – they have no future.' Ehrlich has been researching extinction rates for more than forty years and has called for immediate action to save the world's threatened species, warning that the window of opportunity is rapidly closing.

Even using conservative estimates, this research shows that animal and plant species are now disappearing up to *one hundred times* faster than would have been predicted even a decade ago: 'We emphasise that our calculations very likely underestimate the severity of the extinction crisis, because our aim was to place a realistic lower boundary on humanity's impact on biodiversity,' the scientists say.

> The long list of impacts includes land clearing for farming, logging and settlement; introduction of invasive species; carbon emissions that drive climate change and ocean acidification; and toxins that alter and poison ecosystems. The spectre of extinction hangs over amphibians, mammals and birds.

The evidence, in other words, is incontrovertible: extinction rates have never been so high in human history, and probably not since that massive asteroid struck Mexico 66 million years ago. If the currently elevated rate of extinction continues, we will soon – 'in as little as three human lifetimes,' the biologists warn – lose the benefits bestowed on us by the great diversity of life on this planet. In human time scales this loss would be effectively permanent: after previous mass extinctions, life on Earth took hundreds of thousands to millions of years to rediversify.

Australian birds are under threat not only from climate change but also as a result of the excessive land clearing that began with the British invasion in 1788 and has continued unabated for more than 200 years – often with the active endorsement of state governments. A disturbing example of a species on the brink of extinction is the delightful swift parrot, a small green bird that is one of only three migratory parrots on Earth. The swift parrot (*Lathamus discolor*) flies from its nesting sites in Tasmania to mainland Australia in the winter months, as it has for tens of thousands of years. In May 2016, the federal environment department raised the parrot's listing from endangered to critically endangered, meaning their numbers have fallen so low they are rapidly heading for annihilation.

This is a direct outcome of decisions made by the Tasmanian government, and approved by its federal counterpart, to allow destruction of more of the forests where the parrots breed – even though both governments are obliged by their own laws to protect threatened species. As spring arrived in 2016, with the swift parrots soon to return to their Tasmanian nesting sites, the species was dealt yet another blow when a number of its most important nesting trees were illegally cut down for firewood.

'This site is one of the most important locations for swift parrots in Tasmania and on the mainland,' as Australian National University biologist Dr Dejan Stojanovic said of the area.

> Since 2010, of the eighteen nest trees that I've been monitoring with motion-activated cameras, ten have been cut down. It might seem like a trivial matter to cut down a tree that happens to have a swift parrot nest in it, but when you consider that these birds are literally that close to extinction, there's not really any leeway here.[3]

The end looms for the migratory swift parrot – and humans are responsible.

Another problem confronting the swift parrots is predation by sugar gliders that eat the birds and their eggs, greatly affecting their overall breeding success. With such a small population, any hurdle the species faces is serious and adversely affects their chances of survival. Other bird species are suffering in similar situations across Australia, the threatened Carnaby's black cockatoo in Western Australia among them.

A quarter of the birds that once lived on Earth have now disappeared as a direct consequence of human actions. Populations of birds in the world's tropical forests could be losing 144 million individual birds annually so that by the year 2100, 14 per cent of all bird species may be extinct and one in every four could be functionally extinct, the numbers within a species so low it can no longer play an important role in the ecosystem.[4]

One of the key problems facing many species in Australia is that there are no alternative places for them to go if their existing environment becomes too hot or too dry to support them. More alarmingly,

Too few places to nest: Carnaby's black cockatoo in disastrous decline

the climate on this continent is expected to change beyond anything most species have known in their entire evolutionary history. That is, many birds, mammals, plants and insects will be unable to adapt to the changes because they have never experienced anything like them, even over their long past. Equally worrying is that the areas expected to suffer the greatest climatic changes are also some of the most important biodiversity regions in the nation. These include the northern wet tropic rainforests, the south-west and east coast wet forests, and the tropical far north of Cape York and the Northern Territory.

Biologists also warn that endemic species, those found nowhere else on Earth, face a 6 per cent higher risk of extinction in these regions.[5] They predict that, under current high carbon emission rates, a third of all rainforest birds, mammals, reptiles and frogs will be either critically endangered or extinct by 2085. Likewise, 60 per cent of the endemic species that were intended to have full protection when Australia's World Heritage Area was declared over the Gondwana rainforests in

New South Wales and Queensland are now at high risk of disappearing forever if current emissions rates continue:

> These numbers are conservative as they are based on species being able to freely move and does not account for increasing habitat fragmentation. If species can't move, their extinction risk doubles.[6]

BIRDS PLAY A crucial role in maintaining our living environment because of the numerous crucial tasks they perform: 'Birds pollinate and disperse the seeds of many plants, including crops important to humans,' University of Queensland biologist Professor Hugh Possingham points out.

> They help in controlling crop pests while scavenger birds such as crows and vultures help with the decomposition of organic material. All of these benefits to humans and other organisms will decline along with bird numbers. Because birds have an important role in controlling other organisms, their decline may even encourage the spread of disease.

Possingham, director of the ARC Centre of Excellence for Environmental Decisions (CEED) at the University of Queensland, says one small piece of good news is that the actions of conservationists around the world are slowing the path to extinction for many species. More and more concerned people around the globe are becoming involved in local conservation initiatives by helping count, track and protect the birds in their communities, 'And their efforts can make a significant difference!' he says. But the question is whether the efforts of these committed individuals have come too late to reverse the downward path to extinction facing many species – even our own.

Australian scientists have strongly backed the findings of Ehrlich and his colleagues, agreeing that mass extinction of native species means the time needed to re-establish Earth's rich biodiversity would effectively take forever in human terms. As Melbourne ecologist Dr Sarah Bekessy says, 'It will be more than a million years for the current diversity of species to recover. So the behaviour of humans is equivalent to the Earth being hit by a massive meteorite.' Bekessy, a researcher and biodiversity specialist at RMIT University, is also a chief investigator with CEED. She says biodiversity underpins the cultural and economic prosperity of Australia, yet government interventions to protect this natural inheritance are hopelessly inadequate. Founded in 2011 with a $12 million, seven-year grant from the Australian Research Council, the centre brings together researchers from five Australian universities, as well as others from around the globe.

The findings by the centre's researchers appear in its free publication, *Decision Point Online*, as in the September 2015 edition where Dr Claire Runge and colleagues report on the disastrous collapse in many populations of the world's migratory birds. Runge says that designing solutions across a complex global network of sites is a major challenge. Conservation planning has tended to assume that the targets of management, such as species or ecosystems, are static in space and time – but this is simply not true for migratory birds, whether they be ocean-crossing travellers or they simply fly from one region to another. But the waterbirds that cross the hemispheres are not alone in confronting a threat to their future on this planet. Land birds such as magpies, kookaburras, willie wagtails and many other icons of birdlife are as familiar to Australians as a nightly view of the Southern Cross – yet sightings of these species are also increasingly rare in many regions.

IMAGINE NEVER AGAIN hearing the musical warbles of a magpie as dawn breaks or the maniacal laughter of kookaburras as the sun goes down. Yet the birds are already being silenced, as BirdLife Australia's *The State of Australia's Birds* shockingly reveals. Significant numbers of Australian birds that are widely believed to populate most places around the nation and to be under no threat are actually experiencing serious declines. In compiling the report, the BirdLife research team analysed data collected over many years from hundreds of thousands of surveys taken around Australia by bird-loving volunteers dubbed 'citizen scientists'.

The analysis found that, among Australia's terrestrial bird species, only a mere 10 per cent appear to be in a healthy state, while the startling majority, including populations of magpies and willie wagtails, are falling in many regions. Magpies and willie wagtails occupy territories across most of the continent, yet each shows variability in different areas.

Will the maniacal laugh of the kookaburra be silenced?

Magpie numbers are suffering from a consistent slump over time, and the birds' main population along the east coast has already nosedived; meanwhile, sightings of willie wagtails have also been on a downward slide in coastal regions and in the eastern Mallee.

Apart from these drops in numbers, the BirdLife report points to a near 40 per cent plunge in the average detection rate for kookaburras across southern Australia. Equally troubling is the fact that there have been fewer sightings of birds of prey: reporting rates for the brown goshawk, for example, have dropped by 50 per cent in the last fifteen years while the southern boobook and tawny frogmouth owls both show marked population falls in all but one region.

Sean Dooley, editor of BirdLife Australia's quarterly magazine, *Australian Birdlife*, told the ABC that habitat loss, climate change, and predators, such as cats, could be to blame, but that more research is needed before more species are classed as under threat:

> While they're still not endangered, it's basically the first step to them becoming endangered, so we really need to use this as a wake-up call and start looking at what we're doing across landscapes to try and figure out what's going on.

The first edition of *The State of Australia's Birds* was produced in 2003 and nine volumes had been published up to 2015. The aim from the start was to track trends in bird numbers while exploring some of the greatest challenges facing Australian birdlife. The 2015 edition is the gloomiest in terms of recording widespread drops in population, as counted by the bird-lovers and biologists who do the spotting, with fewer sightings of twenty-two out of thirty-nine Mallee woodland-dependent species.

In the case of the Mallee regions, the data show that the number of birds sighted dropped sharply between 2001 and 2006, when a decade-long drought was in progress, began recovering up until 2011, as was expected, but then began falling again even after the drought broke.

These are regions with big national parks where populations of birds would normally be expected to be flourishing.

The State of Australia's Birds draws from information that has been collected by thousands of the volunteer 'citizen scientists', who have amassed more than 14 million records since 1998, in addition to work by researchers. Wildlife surveys on this scale are rare, and have never been conducted in Australia before. The report gives a clear if alarming picture of what is happening to different species across the nation. The 2015 edition also displays a new feature: *The Australian Terrestrial Bird Index*, a series of indices for Australia's major land-based bird groups that maps the health of bird populations using globally endorsed analytical methods.[7]

By providing a national health check for Australia's birds, and biodiversity in general, the index helps identify which bird groups and particular species are in trouble across Australia, as well as in specific regions. This doesn't mean that every species at every site within a region follows the same pattern; rather that the index represents the average trend for a set of bird species in a particular area. The researchers who devised the indices point out that they function as a health check for the state of Australia's bird populations:

> Just as a cholesterol test does not directly tell you why you are unhealthy, the bird indices can only measure the state of health of bird populations, not provide analysis of the causes.

Unfortunately, this 'health check' for birds highlights the decline of many species in most regions, starkly revealing the worsening state of Australia's biodiversity as reflected in bird numbers.

The survey of the Carnaby's black cockatoo (*Calyptorhynchus latirostris*) that began in 2010 is a good illustration of this volunteer-based research at work. Hundreds of BirdLife Australia's citizen scientists responded to a call to accurately count how many Carnaby's black cockatoos there were at more than 250 sites across several thousand square kilometres of Western Australia.[8] Carnaby's black cockatoo is one of just two species of white-tailed black cockatoos in the world – the other is the Baudin's black cockatoo (*Calyptorhynchus baudinii*) – and they both live only in Western Australia's south-west.

But the surveys by bird-lovers show that the Carnaby's numbers are collapsing, again largely because of the loss of habitat: in some parts of the state's wheat belt where the birds used to number in the thousands, less than 5 per cent of the original native vegetation remains, the rest having been cleared for farming. Even where nesting trees have survived, the cockatoos often have to fly too far to find food, making it impossible for them to successfully raise their chicks.

On the Swan River coastal plain, where many of the cockatoos spend the non-nesting season, urban development and introduced pine plantations have replaced much of the natural bushland. Hundreds of cockatoos are now dependent on the pine trees for food, but the plantations are being harvested and not replanted, causing another important food source to disappear. This places even more importance on the remaining native vegetation, which continues to be cleared as Perth expands ever outwards. The state parks and wildlife department published a 'recovery plan' for the cockatoo in October 2013 that aimed at stopping further falls in the distribution and abundance of the parrots. According to the plan, this would be achieved by:

> protecting the birds throughout their life stages and enhancing habitat critical for survival throughout their breeding and non-breeding range, ensuring that the reproductive capacity of the species remains stable or increases.

The wildlife officials who drew up the plan clearly lacked any predictive abilities, because evidence collected by 'the Great Cocky Count' shows their projections have turned out to be badly wrong. Far from the cockatoos gaining protection, they have become even more endangered as revealed by surveys where the number of parrots at known night roost sites is counted by hundreds of volunteers on a single evening each April. While the number of these surveys and the area covered has increased each year, the actual number of birds recorded has fallen by around 15 per cent at every annual count for the past six years.

BirdLife Australia researchers warn that the Carnaby's cockatoo population in Perth, and in the rapidly expanding Peel region south of the capital, could plummet by a further 50 per cent under a government-proposed 'Green Growth Plan'. This will lead to the loss of half of the cockatoos' known habitat and, despite supporters claiming the growth plan is the 'absolute best opportunity for the bird's survival', it will destroy 14,000 hectares of the cockatoos' native feeding habitat – including beautiful jarrah and banksia woodlands – and raze 8500 hectares of a vital food source for the Carnaby's cockatoo at the Gnangara pine plantation. A paltry 5000 hectares will be retained to replace all this destroyed habitat.

HUMAN-DRIVEN LOSS OF habitat has long been one of the major causes behind the collapse in bird numbers. A warming planet is another, while in Australia researchers have discovered that bird and animal species are also being pushed to the verge of extinction by changing fire patterns.[9] The International Union for the Conservation of Nature's (IUCN) Red List of Endangered Species warns that fire and 'fire suppression' in Australia are creating severe threats to more than a hundred types of birds and animals living there. During the 2015–16 summer, bushfires in Victoria, Western Australia and Tasmania took a devastating toll on birds that were already under duress – and on unique ecosystems located in national parks across the nation.

Among the worst hit was Cape Arid National Park on WA's south coast, home to the only known population of the critically endangered western ground parrot, which survives in unburned heathland. The bird's distribution has shrunk rapidly in recent decades and, before the 2015 fires, a mere 140 birds were thought to be alive. Then, in October and November that year, a series of bushfires destroyed 90 per cent of the bird's known habitat. It is not certain if any birds survived that fire, although a small group of parrots was discovered early in 2016 in another region where it had been thought the species no longer existed.

Late in 2015, fires at Western Australia's Two Peoples Bay Nature Reserve burned the habitats of the critically endangered Gilbert's potoroo – the world's rarest marsupial – as well as those of the threatened noisy scrub-bird, the western bristlebird, the western ringtail possum and the quokka. Equally alarming is a report by BirdLife Australia researchers that the mallee emu-wren may have become extinct in South Australia after the 2014 bushfires. Today, only small populations of the emu-wrens remain in the Murray–Sunset, Hattah–Kulkyne and

Bushfires threaten the survival of the tiny mallee emu-wren.

Wyperfeld national parks in Victoria. Likewise, the red-lored whistler most likely died out in South Australia's Billiatt Conservation Park after the fires, with a few left in the Ngarkat Conservation Park. As well, the black-eared miner, an endangered honeyeater endemic to Mallee woodland in south-eastern Australia, lost up to a third of its breeding habitat during fires in 2006 and 2014.

The establishment of a Mallee Birds Conservation Action Plan, however, should help the survival of these threatened species as well as other woodland birds, including the western whipbird, regent parrot and malleefowl. BirdLife Australia's chief executive, Paul Sullivan, has called for donations to help the organisation develop a full-scale, science-based scheme to tackle the threats facing all of Australia's woodland birds. This would involve multiple partners working across state borders to create more connected habitats and larger and better-quality remnants of the bush that remains, work that should surely also involve state and federal governments.

But why are bushfires across the nation causing such problems today when Australia's native species have evolved in fire-prone environments over tens of thousands of years? The answer, of course, is that bushfires are now more severe and more frequent in many parts of Australia because of the changing climate. There is also the fact that environmental destruction due to fire and human activity has left too little habitat where numerous species can survive. For birds and marsupials whose numbers have already declined, and who rely on bush that has not been burned for a long time, a single fire can now wipe out entire populations. These events create complex ecological challenges for land managers and conservationists – especially if regular 'prescribed burning' is used to reduce fire risk to people and their property, as was the case in Victoria,[9] where 5 per cent of the state's bush used to be regularly burnt off each year.

Other threats such as habitat destruction, disease and introduced predators may also have triggered population declines and thereby made bird species more vulnerable to fire. This is why it is essential that any conservation plan take account of the interactions between the various threats. As well, if a species has only a few individuals remaining, then captive breeding and the establishment of 'insurance populations' may be necessary, as is already occurring with many threatened birds.

Looking beyond land birds, though, consider whether any rescue scheme could overcome the serious problems facing tens of millions of the world's migratory seabirds and shorebirds. They have already suffered massive population falls as they make their annual cross-continental journeys. Tackling this real and present danger is one of the great challenges facing the world's biologists, who are desperately trying to save more of these amazing species from extinction.

2

Catastrophic Collapse of Seabirds

Tens of millions of seabirds and shorebirds make extraordinary long-distance migrations as they fly from one side of Earth to the other and back again every year. The lives of these itinerant aerial travellers are spent nesting in one hemisphere for some months and then spending a second, often longer, summer feeding and resting on the opposite, warmer side. Today, however, the populations of these migratory waterbirds are in freefall, having plummeted by a startling 70 per cent in the past six decades.

THE AWESOME JOURNEYS undertaken by the world's ocean waterbirds can involve annual round trips of 50,000 kilometres or even more each year. But these long-distance champion flyers have suffered fearful population collapses – and the situation is becoming worse. Millions of shorebirds heading to the Arctic to nest and rear their chicks are finding it increasingly difficult to find the right conditions.[1] By 2070, biologists estimate the breeding areas for 80 per cent of all migratory bird species could shrink by more than half, while five species – the Pacific golden plover, stilt sandpiper, curlew sandpiper, white-rumped sandpiper and red phalarope – may have no suitable place at all even to lay their eggs. They will, before long, simply cease to exist.

As our planet warms, birds and animals are starting to adapt to the changing climate by moving north or south towards the cooler polar regions. Species that breed in the Arctic, however, are already at the 'top of the world' so they have nowhere left to go – unless they head to the Canadian and Russian Arctic islands as their last refuges to rear their young. With the birds' habitats shrinking, countries around the world will see even larger falls in the numbers of migratory species reaching their shores. According to biologists Hannah Wauchope and Richard Fuller, writing in *The Conversation*,

> In a double whammy for Australian shorebirds already struggling with habitat loss along the Yellow Sea, our results predict that their breeding regions in western Alaska and eastern Siberia are going to be hit hardest by climate change too, with little or no habitat left for many species.

A REMARKABLE EXAMPLE of a species making these vast flights is a tiny songbird called the northern wheatear. Each year, this diminutive bird flies from the Arctic to northern Africa and back. To follow the wheatear's movements, an international team of researchers attached tiny geolocators to the legs of forty-six birds and tracked them as they travelled from Alaska and from Baffin Island in north-eastern Canada.[2] The scientists discovered the wee birds were making one of the longest to and fro flights of any songbird in the world – covering a total distance of 29,000 kilometres. Now, a wheatear tips the scales at just 25 grams (equivalent to just two tablespoons of sugar), so the biologists who electronically equipped these tawny-and-white insectivores were amazed by their flight endurance.

But even that feat pales beside the long-distance annual migrations of Australia's short-tailed shearwaters, which have also been tracked as they leave the east coast, head down towards the Antarctic continent and then travel north to the equator. These remarkable seabirds fly 800 kilometres a day for more than a month as far as the Arctic Circle, where they spend the northern hemisphere summer sailing the sea and feeding on krill, before making the return trip home to breed a new generation of long-distance travellers. The population of breeding short-tailed shearwaters in eastern Australia is estimated to be about 23 million birds – a huge number, yet way down from the *100 million* that Matthew Flinders calculated he saw in flocks when the great explorer was sailing through Bass Strait in 1798.

Shearwater numbers, however, look set to fall even further with the effects of climate change and a warming of the world's oceans. This has already led to sharp drops in the number of fish that the birds rely on for food, with disastrous consequences – as happened in late 2013, when a massive die-off of short-tailed shearwaters and other seabirds occurred along the coasts of eastern and southern Australia. Such a mass death is called a 'wreck', and this one was linked to unusually warm sea temperatures at the time. Early in 2016, the same sort of disaster struck the northern hemisphere when more than 22,000 common guillemots were found dead around the coast of Alaska, the largest wreck ever recorded. Like the shearwaters, the guillemots had starved to death: they usually forage underwater to depths of 100 metres, with each bird daily consuming as many as 300 small school fish such as herrings. But the fish prefer a narrow band of cold water and, if the sea temperature rises, they go much deeper or disappear into other parts of the ocean, leaving nothing for the birds to eat.

THE SHORT-TAILED SHEARWATER is one of more than 1450 species of avian migrants that travel along nine different freeways in the sky, known as 'flyways', during their annual flights from one side of the planet to the other and then back home again. The birds that make their journeys to and from Australia follow the East Asian–Australasian Flyway, one of the world's great migratory routes for avian migrants. The twenty-two countries that the birds cross established a global conservation zone in 2006. The aim was to create greater protection for migratory waterbirds, their varying habitats and the livelihoods of the people dependent on them. Although the decision was woefully belated, it was still an incredible achievement by the organisations and individuals who managed to persuade thirty-seven groups within the different nations to sign up.

All countries along the flyway agreed to take part, including their national governments, intergovernmental and non-government agencies, as well as private enterprise groups, with all participants backing the objectives and prepared to support any actions taken under the partnership. Such a degree of cooperation offers some hope for the survival of the numerous species of birds that use the flyway – except for one crucial fact. Despite the involvement of all the nations and hundreds of individuals, the dreadful collapse in seabird and shorebird populations continues a decade after the creation of the conservation zone.

More than fifty-five migratory bird species travel along the flyway, making the route crucially important to millions of waders and seabirds. Every species of shorebird using the flyway, however, is affected by the increasing human pressures on the coastal spots where they have long stopped to rest and replenish. This is especially the case around the Yellow Sea in East Asia where, over millennia, millions of shorebirds have rested during their migrations. Along China's 32,000 kilometre–long coast, tidal flats where the birds once stopped to feed are being converted to land by coastal engineers; river mouths no longer exist and seawalls are kilometres from where the sea used to be.

Then there is the problem of the over-heating planet, which has a serious impact on some birds, including one of the world's iconic Arctic-breeding shorebirds: the red knot (*Calidris canutus*). Rapid warming of the red knot's high-Arctic breeding grounds is causing its young to hatch smaller than previous generations – presumably because of the reduced quantity and lower quality of the food their parents are providing.[3] The young birds also suffer higher mortality rates because of a distinctly unusual fact: they have shorter bills. So when they reach their tropical wintering grounds along the African and Australian coasts, the bills of these latter-day shrunken red knots cannot reach the best shellfish buried deep in the mud and sand. Instead, they are forced to rely on far less nutritious seagrass and any other food they can find, often resulting in malnutrition and death.

Ecologists fear this climate-induced body shrinkage and lower survival rate may soon extend to other Arctic migrants, as even the offspring

A cloud of red knots: climate-induced body shrinkage is slashing their numbers

of land bird species are also becoming smaller. Ecologists analysed the timing of snowmelt within the red knot's Arctic breeding grounds over a period of thirty-three years and found that, each year, the snow had begun to melt about half a day earlier. On one occasion, they captured nearly 2000 juvenile red knots on their way to West Africa and measured their body sizes; the results showed the birds were indeed much smaller than their predecessors had been before the snow had started to melt earlier every year.

On top of these climate-related threats to shorebirds and seabirds, human actions are continuing to deplete their food sources through overfishing and increases in oceanic pollution, including the insidious effects of plastic. Then, when the surviving birds land to rest along the flyways, they are likely to find their habitats destroyed by human developments or they face invasive, often predatory animals. Researchers have called on countries along the flyway to make greater efforts to protect these colonies and allow their populations to grow, with the benefit not only of improving the birds' wellbeing, but also that of the marine ecosystems as a whole.

In one of the first detailed surveys of the various species and numbers of birds using the East Asian–Australasian Flyway, Western Australian ecologist Dr Mike Bamford and four colleagues prepared a report[4] giving population estimates for each species and listing the almost 400 internationally important sites where the migratory birds rest and replenish their intake of food. Australia has the greatest number of sites with 181, followed by Japan with eighty-nine and China with fifty-one. 'Migratory shorebirds present a particular conservation challenge because their patterns of movement take them across international boundaries, in some cases almost spanning the globe,' the report states.

> They utilise different sites in different countries at different times of the year, and conservation of these species therefore requires management of the suite of sites that are important to them.

Populations of the Far Eastern curlew have plunged.

Typical among the summer visitors to Australia is the Far Eastern curlew, the largest of the shorebirds that visit Australia. Yet these spectacular-looking birds are becoming harder to locate here because their population has plunged by 85 per cent over the past thirty years due to habitat loss, and they are now listed as critically endangered.

THE UNITED NATIONS established World Migratory Bird Day in 2006. Held on the second weekend in May, the day is celebrated each year to raise greater awareness of the wonders of bird migration around the globe. As a UN spokesperson said at the time, these annual journeys 'are often challenging and sometimes perilous but tens of millions of birds undertake them every year'. A decade later, in May 2016, the chief executive of the East Asian–Australasian Flyway Partnership,

Spike Millington, sent an e-newsletter from his base in Korea to its members and to bird-lovers everywhere:

> The last few days have seen the numbers of migratory waterbirds build up on Songdo mudflats to 25,000 individuals, mostly shorebirds, literally a ten-minute drive from the secretariat office here in the Republic of Korea. Among them are familiar friends: Bar-tailed Godwits from Australia and New Zealand, and Great Knots from Australia and China bearing personalised coloured and engraved flags and bands, the same individuals turning up year after year. One New Zealand–banded Godwit arrived on 22 March and was still here yesterday, making it 48 days since arrival – the Songdo lugworms must be good this year![5]

Of course, although the Songdo mudflats provide a respite on the birds' arduous journeys, hazards also loom: illegal mist nets are stretched across favoured mudflats, farmers who fear for their crops spread poisoned bait in known feeding areas, and illegal hunters wait with shotguns for passing birds. Licensed and controlled hunting is permitted in some countries but most shorebirds and especially threatened species of wildfowl are protected. The vast areas that migratory waterbirds cross, however, are impossible to monitor by authorities and illegal killing has become an increasingly serious problem. The encouraging news, according to Millington, is that more and more concerned citizens are calling on national authorities to take action and the calls are being backed by critical reports in newspapers and other media:

> This indicates that many people are taking the problem seriously and feel the need to do something about it so that perpetrators are being caught and punished. In another encouraging sign, birdwatchers and local groups in southern China are now working with local authorities to identify illegal trapping and mist-netting … Record

numbers of spoon-billed sandpipers were recorded on the mudflats the previous winter and although that may have been a coincidence, illegal trapping is down and spoon-bill numbers are up – so that is something to celebrate.

A much greater international collaborative effort is needed to save the world's migratory birds given how many are facing the risk of extinction, according to a team of biologists from Australia's Centre of Excellence for Environmental Decisions.[6] They warn that more than 90 per cent of migratory birds are inadequately protected by poorly coordinated conservation schemes around the globe. Their study found huge gaps in public knowledge about conservation of migratory birds, particularly among people in China, India, and parts of Africa and South America.

Although the majority of migratory birds have well-protected areas in some countries, they receive little protection in others. A report of the study says:

> More than half of migratory bird species travelling the world's main flyways have suffered serious population declines in the past thirty years. This is due mainly to unequal and ineffective protection across their migratory range and the places they stop to refuel along their routes. A typical migratory bird relies on many different geographic locations throughout its annual cycle for food, rest and breeding places. So even if we protect most of their breeding grounds, it's still not enough – threats somewhere else can affect the entire population. The chain can be broken at any link.

The biologists found that of the 1451 migratory bird species whose migration routes had been mapped, more than 90 per cent had inadequate protection for at least one section along their migration pathway. Eighteen species had no protection in their breeding areas and two species had none at all along their entire path. For migratory birds listed as threatened on the IUCN Red List, less than 3 per cent had appropriately protected areas.

Establishing new reserves to extend coverage of the unprotected sites – and more effectively managing all protected areas for migratory species – is critical to ensure the survival of these iconic species, the team says. The study results underline the urgency of coordinating designated protected areas along all parts of the seabirds' and waders' migration routes. Moreover, the scientists say, it is not just a case of neglect by poorer nations: many Central American countries meet the targets for more than 75 per cent of their migratory species, yet these same species have less protection along the coasts of Canada and the United States.

Those that visit Australia, including shorebirds, seabirds, raptors and songbirds, are subject to protection laws under the federal *Environment Protection and Biodiversity Conservation Act*. It is intended to provide a framework for the conservation of migratory shorebirds and their habitat in Australia, with an outline of national activities to support their conservation throughout the flyway. This laudable aim, however, has been seriously compromised by a number of foreign governments that have differing goals or that ignore the destructive activities of their citizens.

IN 2016 AUSTRALIA'S premier bird journal, *Emu Austral Ornithology*, devoted an entire issue to the East Asian–Australasian Flyway, with thirteen papers prepared by biologists from Australia, China, Europe and New Zealand. In the papers, the scientists discuss population trends, threats, and what the future is likely to hold for the flyway travellers. In the opening commentary, editor Katherine Buchanan points out that

> Despite the crucial international importance of the Chinese coastline to shorebirds, economic development is having massive and diverse

> effects on their coastal habitats ... Most of the Chinese coast is not managed for shorebirds and even protected areas are subject to land claim. The problems are daunting but it is encouraging that in 2013, China's central government proposed an Ecological Protection Red Line to protect critical sites.

The key problem is that economic incentives for development coupled with a lack of resources for those managing the rest sites in China are the strongest drivers of habitat loss. As the researchers say in the issue's final paper:

> A growing understanding that China's long coastline provides in excess of US$200 billion per year in ecosystem services [is countered by] the huge financial incentives for local governments to promote reclamation over protection. Local governments can make two and a half times more on US$100 million building projects compared with the cost of reclamation. From a purely economic perspective, it is therefore not surprising that economic development takes precedence over conservation within the flyway.

The editors conclude their opening comments with a celebration of the shorebirds' superb adaptations to their specialised lives:

> Tiny sanderlings [migrate] from South Australia to the Arctic in only forty days; Red knots ... migrate up to 10,000 kilometres from their non-breeding grounds to one small but high-quality staging area in Bohai Bay, [in] the gulf of the Yellow Sea in north-east China, before undertaking another huge flight to breeding areas that they unerringly locate ... The ability of shorebirds to make these remarkable movements is testimony not only to their flight abilities but also to their ability to locate foraging grounds across huge areas and exploit them efficiently enough to refuel on a tight schedule.

In an effort to tackle the 'suite of threatening human activities' causing the massive fall in migratory seabird and shorebird numbers, BirdLife Australia co-hosted the nation's first Migratory Shorebird Summit, bringing together stakeholders from government, research institutions, NGOs, business, the general public and the international community. Among the key issues was a discussion regarding implementation of the federal government's Wildlife Conservation Plan for Migratory Shorebirds,[7] which was intended to identify what should be done by Australia and its regional neighbours, including Japan, China and Korea, to safeguard migratory species.

Acknowledging that populations of the shorebirds are falling, the summit discussed the growing need to reduce the threats to the birds' habitats. The latest conservation plan also includes a highly critical review of the former Howard government's original scheme, released in 2000, concluding that the conservation plan had totally failed to meet its objectives and apparently had not reduced the rate of decline among any of the listed species.

Australia's first Threatened Species Commissioner, Gregory Andrews, was introduced at the summit, where he was also named as the nation's first Emissary for Migratory Shorebirds, to coordinate with countries along the shorebirds' migration route. The current plan calls for further international engagement and bilateral talks with Japan, China and Korea to discuss engaging local communities to help manage threats to migratory shorebirds in the Yellow Sea region. It encourages those countries taking part 'to act globally, and find ways to tackle the threats to shorebird habitats around the Yellow Sea'.

OF ALL MIGRATORY shorebirds, one of the most mysterious is the grey plover, the largest member of the four species in the *Pluvialis* genus to visit Australia each year. Classed by the IUCN Red List as vulnerable to extinction, this global migrant settles and feeds along the world's coasts when it is not nesting in the Arctic regions. More than 11,000 of these 30-centimetre-long birds feed beside Australia's coastlines from September each year to the following March before migrating thousands of kilometres back across the equator to breed in Siberia and Alaska during the northern summer.

In a truly odd twist, though, almost the entire plover population that flies to Australia is female, adding to the many unanswered questions about the birds and where they go on their travels. Most migratory shorebirds leave Australia in March and April, travelling in very large groups and using well-known routes and stopover locations such as those along the Yellow Sea in China. But not *Pluvialis squatarola*: The grey plover is believed to head back to the Arctic either alone or in small numbers – 'believed' being the operative word, because very little is known about the bird. So no-one knew, at least until a satellite tracking experiment began, where the plovers' refuelling sites were north of the Yellow Sea, what threats they faced, or exactly where they nested in

The mysterious grey plover is now vulnerable to extinction.

the Arctic regions. What was known, however, was that the number of plovers arriving in Australia had been falling rapidly.

In a novel scheme to raise money for a project to track the cross-hemisphere journeys of the grey plover, a group of local researchers resorted to crowdfunding. Australian researchers Inka Veltheim, Ken Gosbell and Danny Rogers used the crowdfunding site Pozible and raised more than $25,000 in donations to discover where the plover goes on its journeys and where its breeding places are. With the support of the Wader Study Group, a special interest offshoot of BirdLife Australia, the researchers used satellite tracking technology to find answers to several perplexing questions.[8]

Lacking the money to track more birds, they captured five on the Western Australian coast, fitted them with transmitters and began receiving satellite position downloads every two and a half days.[9] The first position download showed that four of the birds remained close to the area where they were originally caught until the first bird, dubbed Ecosure, decided it was time to head north. The transmitter on the fifth bird failed to send any signals after an initial transmission, possibly because the harness attachment fell off or the bird was caught by a predator. Within a week, the team reported that three of the plovers fitted with satellite tracking devices – Ecosure, Nad and Charlie – had taken off from Broome on their annual migration north, with the fourth, Mymi, still presumably building up her strength.

Ecosure left Australia and touched down along the coast of the city of Shantou in China four and a half days later, after a non-stop flight of 4700 kilometres. Her average speed of 44 kilometres an hour was similar to that of other species of waders on this leg of their northern migration and indicated satisfactory wind conditions. She was then expected to rest for a few days before moving up the coast into the Yellow Sea. The other two birds, Nad and Charlie, took different routes, with Nad making a stopover in Indonesia. By early June, Ecosure and Mymi were still based along China's coast while Nad and Charlie had crossed Inner

Mongolia and landed in northern Russia within the Arctic Circle. There they stopped and were assumed to have begun breeding, having flown more than 10,000 kilometres in a little more than forty days.

The researchers hoped to continue locating where each of the plovers landed to feed and refuel. By this stage of the migration, however, signals from Ecosure and Mymi were no longer being received and the researchers feared that the birds had become so thin the devices had fallen off. The path taken by each of the birds, up until transmission ended and the last two of the birds had settled to nest, is shown on the BirdLife webpage.[10]

THE FACT THAT the grey plovers visiting Australia are almost exclusively female highlights the differing gender roles migratory species play in rearing their young. Three European scientists reveal the extent of this variation in a report comparing the parental care patterns of various shorebirds with those of the spur-winged plover.[11] This species was chosen for its socially monogamous coupling, where the male and female form a pair bond and share the rearing of their offspring. In other species, such as a sandpiper called the ruff, the female incubates the eggs and looks after the chicks on her own while the male, having fertilised her eggs, wanders off to try someone else. Then there are birds where the gender roles are reversed and the female deserts the eggs as soon as she lays them, with the male taking over the incubation and care for the chicks on his own.

After comparing data from eighteen different shorebird species, the researchers found that the pattern of parental care was strongly correlated with the sex ratios among the adults. In species where males outnumbered the females, males took more care of their offspring; if females were more numerous, they assumed the primary parental role.

The overall ratio of males to females in the different populations varied significantly, ranging from fifty-fifty for the spur-winged plover to seventy-thirty for the species where males were the main carers. It was these gender biases that seemed to affect the differing forms of parental care: for species where males are more common, a male lucky enough to find a mate is unlikely to win another one and therefore needs to devote all his efforts to maximising his reproductive success from the eggs produced with that female.

Conversely, his female mate would have no problem finding a new partner because of the male surplus in the population. Where males are more common, females tend to desert their first partner once they have laid a clutch of eggs and then take up with a new male they can produce a second clutch of eggs with, thereby doubling their own reproductive success. This strategy works for females because the deserted male will still care for the eggs he helped produce, given this is the only way he can reproduce little birds that carry his genes.

The same process works in reverse in populations where females are more numerous. Hence, the sex ratio among adult seabirds affects male and female roles, the investment that the different sexes will commit to parental care, and the way they treat their partners. The researchers argue that such basic evolutionary dynamics are likely to be universal across sexually reproducing animals, including humans. In which case, they say, such research might help predict the social consequences of sex-biased human populations in China and India, where males outnumber females, as their current young people mature and reach reproductive age.

MEANWHILE, A CRISIS is also confronting Australia's collapsing populations of waterbirds, not just those that migrate to the coasts but also the inland species of pelicans, ducks, swans, cormorants and other birds found along the rivers, lakes and swamps. Over the past three decades, the total inland waterbird population in Australia is estimated to have dropped by 30 per cent as the ponds, lagoons and billabongs where they once nested have dried up or been emptied. Since British occupation began, half of Australia's wetlands have disappeared, along with untold numbers of the birds whose survival relied on them. Worldwide, wetlands are also under threat from water resource developments, agricultural activities and climate change. The loss of these swamps has serious implications for wildlife given that many species are wetland-dependent throughout their lives while others, such as various species of waterbirds, rely on wetlands to breed – and this is where Dr Kate Brandis comes in.

Dr Brandis is a research fellow in the Centre for Ecosystem Science at the University of New South Wales, and also at the Australian Nuclear Science Technology Organisation. Concerned by what has been happening to Australia's inland waterbirds, Brandis has developed a neat method of using nuclear physics to create an Australia-wide map of where waterbirds go to find their food and to raise their young.[12] Knowing which wetlands the birds frequent when they aren't breeding could help ecologists work out the places that need protection – and she says this could be done with a new technique to analyse the birds' feathers:

> Traditional tracking methods such as leg-banding and satellite trackers have had limited success and can be expensive. So we looked for a cheaper and more effective method – and what could be easier than collecting bird feathers: These are made of keratin (the same material as human hair and nails) and as they grow, they record the diet of the bird in the chemical elements they consume. Once fully grown, feathers are inert – they no longer change.

Chemical elements such as carbon, hydrogen, nitrogen, oxygen and so on exist in a number of different forms known as isotopes.

The isotopes of some elements are radioactive while others are stable and non-radioactive, but this means the relative proportion of the different isotopes can be linked to a specific location, as has been done with monarch butterflies in North America. To test whether the use of isotopes could be applied to Australian wetlands and waterbirds, Brandis did a pilot study in 2010–11 when widespread flooding in the Murray–Darling Basin resulted in waterbird colonies breeding at a number of wetlands across New South Wales. These included the Gwydir Wetlands, Macquarie Marshes and Lowbidgee Floodplain, which are geographically distinct and spread across the basin from north to south.

The Gwydir Wetlands are located north-west of the town of Moree and are among the most significant inland systems in the state. Since records began in the 1920s, at least seventy-five waterbird species have been recorded there, fifty of them breeding at the location, with species such as the straw-necked ibis, intermediate egrets, glossy ibis and nankeen night herons nesting in large colonies when heavy upstream rainfall causes floods to extend across the wide plain. The wetlands once spread out over 100,000 hectares but are today reduced to a remnant covering only 15 per cent of its former area. Still, in a move that has parallels in other regions, four local landowners had portions of the wetlands they owned listed under the Ramsar Convention in 1998 and these are now preserved as part of the greater Gwydir Wetlands State Conservation Area.

In her study, Brandis and her colleagues analysed feathers from chicks and juveniles from these wetlands because they were eating food from only the wetland where they were hatched and so provided a unique signature for that area: 'Results from these analyses showed that we were able to distinguish between the three wetland sites based on the elemental composition of the feathers and their isotopic composition.'

Brandis decided to expand the project nationally to generate a Feather Map of Australia as a citizen science project by obtaining the 'signatures' of as many wetlands across the country as possible. Interested members of the public have been asked to collect feathers from their local wetlands and send them to Brandis for analysis. She then plans to have an isotopic map of the wetlands against which waterbird movements can be tracked; meanwhile, feathers collected from chicks and birds that do not move large distances will also provide a 'signature' for that particular patch of wet ground. Feathers of birds that travel long distances can be analysed and the signature in their feathers matched against those of the wetlands to identify where the birds have been. As Brandis says:

> The signature will not tell us all the movements a bird has made, but it will tell where it was when it grew the feather. And this will also give us information about the health of the wetland based on what food the bird has eaten and how long it took to grow the feather … Knowing the movements of waterbirds helps identify wetlands that are important habitats, as well as providing information to policy-makers and water managers for improved water delivery, wetland management and ultimately protects wetlands and waterbirds.

Many more such projects are underway across Australia as biologists try to capture as much information about wetland birdlife as they can before it is possibly lost forever. Back on the world's oceans, however, seabirds face yet another threat to their survival: a secret, silent killer that destroys them from the inside, slowly and horribly …

3

Secret, Silent Killer of Sea Life

Throughout the world's oceans lurks a silent killer that will outlive us, outswim us and even undo us. This predator is plastic. And it is floating in an ocean near you, choking sealife, including many of the world's billions of seabirds. As the Australian Marine Conservation Society warns, untold tonnes of rubbish enter the world's seas each year and its load of plastic pollution rides the ocean currents until it reaches the farthest shores.[1] *Plastic has now invaded even the Antarctic wilderness.*

THE INCREASING SPREAD of plastic throughout the oceans of Earth is causing huge numbers of seabird deaths. Research into this problem has been going on since the 1970s, yet more and more species are becoming seriously affected. Once swallowed, plastic debris can cause serious damage, including blocking a bird's digestive tract, reducing stomach volume and leading to impaired growth and even starvation. Toxic chemicals such as polychlorinated biphenyls, or PCBs, and polybrominated diphenyl ethers, or PBDEs, may also be released from plastic debris and, when consumed by birds, cause subtle effects that become evident often only after long periods.

Unlike naturally based paper or glass, plastic never truly goes away; it just breaks down into smaller pieces. That means that every piece of plastic you and I have ever used is probably still around today. The vast majority of the plastics floating in the world's seas is from urban areas. As the Australian Marine Conservation Society notes on its website:

> Almost 90% of the marine debris found on Sydney's beaches is plastic, mostly bottles, caps and straws. Australians buy 600 million litres of bottled water a year. We use 10 million plastic bags a day (that's 3.9 billion plastic bags a year)! This is a global problem, with a truly local solution. We can turn our plastic addiction around. Plastic packaging is a recent craze – a fast fix. It's unnecessary, unsustainable and must become unacceptable. We must change our habits and break the deadly cycle.

Dr Mark Carey is a scientist who has spent years studying seabirds and he says ingestion of plastic debris has hugely increased since the 1970s, particularly among birds that roam long distances, such as petrels and albatrosses, resulting in lethal and sub-lethal side effects:

> The Laysan Albatross on Midway Island [in the middle of the north Pacific Ocean] are just full of plastic material, mainly user plastic like cigarette lighters, bottle tops, but also industrial resin pellets ... used for moulding plastic. And that's having serious consequences on a birds' breeding condition and they often die because of it.

Carey conducted research over many years into Australia's most abundant seabird, the short-tailed shearwater, that mostly breeds on islands in Bass Strait (chapter 5 covers his work there). In one project[2] he investigated the effect of plastic on short-tailed shearwater chicks on Phillip Island in Victoria, just as the chicks were fledging and preparing for life in the air and on the ocean. He collected data on the amount of plastic in the gizzards of young shearwaters that had died in the sea after failing to take off on their first flight. The little mutton-birds had an average of more than seven particles of plastic per bird, weighing a total of 113 milligrams, that must have been part of the food the parents had regurgitated to the chicks. Such a load could affect the life cycle of the birds and their reproductive success, ultimately causing long-term harm to entire populations. The most common type of debris Carey found was widely used plastics, followed by industrial pellets and a small proportion of other refuse, such as polystyrene and plastic bags.

Seabirds swallow plastic because they confuse it with prey such as squid, and it can cause physical damage, perforations, mechanical blockage or impairment of the digestive system so the birds die of starvation even when food is plentiful. Some plastics are also a source of toxic pollutants that are released during digestion, which seems to affect chicks more badly than adult birds. When plastics are regurgitated by parents to their chicks, survival rates are likely to worsen. The young birds Carey collected from the beach had never been out of their burrows before, so the parents were bringing back plastic in the food they fed to their chicks, plastic collected during their own hunt for seafood. If a bird ingests enough plastic, it can cause PCB and PBDE concentrations to go up, affecting its body condition or growth, and its reproductive biology.

Subsequent to Carey's research on this topic, a team of researchers from the University of Tasmania and the state department of primary industries also investigated how much plastic material was present in pre-fledged shearwater chicks and what its effects were on their body condition. They conducted post-mortems on the bodies of 171 chicks that had been confiscated from illegal poachers and measured the amount of plastic debris in the little birds' proventriculus, a glandular part of the stomach where digestion of food begins before it enters the gizzard. The researchers were checking to see whether there was a correlation between body condition and the quantity of plastic ingested; they also discovered that the chicks had swallowed more than a thousand plastic particles consisting of 31 per cent industrial plastic and 69 per cent user plastic.[3] None of the chicks had left their burrows before being dragged out by the poachers, yet almost all had pieces of plastic inside them. Although the total mass of ingested plastic was not significantly related to body condition, the study highlighted the prevalence of plastic pollution in apparently healthy shearwater chicks.

The shocking discoveries by Carey and the Tasmanian researchers were confirmed on a national scale when the Commonwealth Scientific and Industrial Research Organisation (CSIRO) conducted a three-year investigation[4] into the effects on wildlife of marine debris, which, as expected, consisted mostly of plastic. This involved a remarkable survey of marine debris conducted at sites roughly every 100 kilometres along almost the entire Australian coastline.

The scientists also developed a national marine debris database where the public could contribute information they had collected about local beach litter online. Around the coastlines, about three-quarters of the rubbish collected was plastic and, although most came from nearby sources, some had drifted to Australian shores from overseas. In coastal and offshore waters most floating debris was plastic, with the density ranging from a few thousand to more than 40,000 pieces for every square kilometre. Not surprisingly, the debris was more highly concentrated around major cities, which points to local sources for the pollution.

A global risk analysis of nearly 200 seabird species and the amount of marine debris they were swallowing found that 43 per cent of species and two in every three individual birds within a species had plastic in their gut. Plastic intake is estimated to reach 95 per cent of all species by 2050, given the ever-rising amount of plastics in production.[5]

Even today, two in every three short-tailed shearwaters are believed to have swallowed plastic litter in the ocean. Juvenile birds swallow more than the adults, presumably because they do not yet know what to avoid. The birds eat anything that resembles food, from balloons and glowsticks to industrial plastic pellets, rubber, foam and string.

Tiny plastic particles called microbeads, widely used in cosmetics, are also ending up in the oceans. Following widespread concern about the impact of microbeads, Australian supermarkets agreed to phase out products containing them – although not until July 2018. That will be too late to save an untold number of seabirds affected by the beads, as researchers from RMIT University and Hainan University in China have shown: up to 12.5 per cent of the chemical pollutants on the microbeads pass into the fish that swallow them, and then into birds that prey on the fish.[6] This study provided the first conclusive evidence that microbeads were capable of leaching toxic chemical pollutants into fish. Scientists already knew that plastic attracts and concentrates toxic chemicals when in water, but the problem is compounded with microbeads because of their size and surface area. This research shows how organic pollutants accumulate in the tissue of fish that eat microbeads and that if a person or a bird eats the fish, they risk consuming the pollution absorbed by the fish. This includes PBDEs, pollutants known to 'biomagnify up the food chain' in marine animals, becoming increasingly concentrated at each step.

Other researchers have discovered a different kind of microplastic in the stomachs of seabirds and other marine animals, coming from synthetic fibres after clothes made from them had been washed; the wastewater then carried the fibres through sewerage plants and down to the sea. Dr Mark Browne, a researcher at the University of New South Wales, calculates that washing a single polyester garment could add more than 1900 plastic fibres to wastewater, while using facial scrubbers added millions of granules of microplastics. Browne found the quantity of microplastics was often nearly twice that of larger plastic debris, yet the chemical contaminants they contained had been largely ignored.

Having tiny pieces of foreign matter in an animal's body is bad enough, but plastic also behaves like a sponge in absorbing chemicals that are already in the sea, including pesticides, flame retardants and industrial chemicals. Dr Chelsea Rochman, an ecotoxicologist at the University of California, said on ABC's *Catalyst* program that the pieces of plastic she had tested 'hyper-concentrate these chemicals to levels sometimes a million times more than what was once in the water':

> [I find] PCBs which were abandoned in the early '80s, and DDT which was abandoned in the early '70s ... on every single piece of plastic I take out of the ocean [as well as] metals like copper, lead, nickel, cadmium.

As Rockman says, the problem for seabirds or animals such as humans in consuming fish full of toxic chemicals is that these may also be absorbed by the predators with serious side effects.[7]

Lives cut short: like most seabirds, too many short-tailed shearwaters die needlessly after swallowing pervasive plastic.

As a result of his research, Browne concludes current policies regarding plastic debris are outdated. If countries classified the most harmful plastics as hazardous, their environment agencies could have the power to restore affected habitats and prevent more dangerous debris from accumulating. Policies aimed at slashing the amount of plastic in the world's oceans, however, cannot come quickly enough to save some seabird species. For short-tailed shearwaters, one of the world's most remarkable seabirds – capable of marvellous 60,000-kilometre cross-hemisphere feats of migrations – a slow and painful death as a direct consequence of human habits seems horribly cruel and unjust.

4

Ashmore Reef: A Tropical Paradise for Seabirds

A huge tear drop-shaped reef on the edge of Australia's continental shelf, far out to sea from the mainland's north-west coast, is a paradise for tens of thousands of birds. Dozens of different seabirds, such as boobies, frigatebirds and terns – including all eleven species of the latter – jostle for space on four small islands inside the reef rim while herons, egrets and water rails patrol the shorelines together with plovers, sandpipers and godwits. In the air above the reef, occasional visitors such as buzzards, goshawks and peregrine falcons soar, sharing that vast space with migrant songbirds, including shrikes, fantails, magpie larks, barn swallows, tree martins, Arctic warblers and even a chestnut-cheeked starling.

DESPITE THE WORLDWIDE collapse in populations of seabirds and shorebirds, some protected regions around the globe still have expanding numbers. This is occurring on Ashmore Reef, where a vast area under the protection of Australian authorities has become a resting and breeding place for hundreds of thousands of birds. Named after an Irish

Ashmore Reef: a tropical paradise, but only for birds

sea captain named Samuel Ashmore, who on 11 June 1811 was the first European to record the reef's existence, the reef and its surrounding seas are proof of how myriads of bird species will flourish given the right conditions and the absence of human plunderers.

Itinerant biologists from Monash University in Melbourne have also been lured to this avian wonderland. But for them it requires a plane trip from Melbourne to Broome and then a two-day boat ride to the reef in a vessel that will also serve as their base for two to three weeks. They are equipped with high-tech devices aimed at uncovering secrets about the birds breeding on the islands, as well as the thousands of migratory shorebirds that use the reef for stopovers on their way to and from Australia.

Small portable telescopes called 'spotting scopes' are essential instruments for these professional birdwatchers, as are binoculars and clickers (hand-held counting machines). These are conventional tools for ornithologists, but recently small drones have been added to the arsenal.

The drones gather high-resolution images of the nesting seabird colonies from above without disturbing their inhabitants. These images from the drone flights are literally giving the biologists a new perspective on the nesting birds while also streamlining the process of counting bird numbers. Also, for the first time, the drones enable the team to assess the accuracy of the more traditional, on-the-ground counts using clickers. After all, some mistakes must surely occur when nesting numbers are in the tens of thousands and the yearly total exceeds 110,000.

'Another first for our research is the way we use small GPS devices attached to frigatebirds, boobies and tropicbirds to find out where they go to obtain their food,' says Monash ecologist Dr Rohan Clarke, who heads a team that has been conducting research on the reef since 1996.

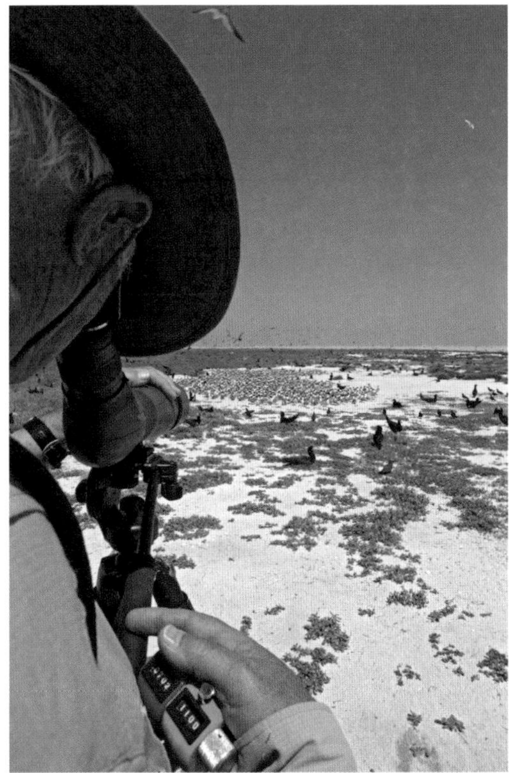

Seabird counting: individual birds are identified according to their species and counted. Here a team member counts using a clicker.

Brown boobies fly up to 140 kilometres to catch food for their young.

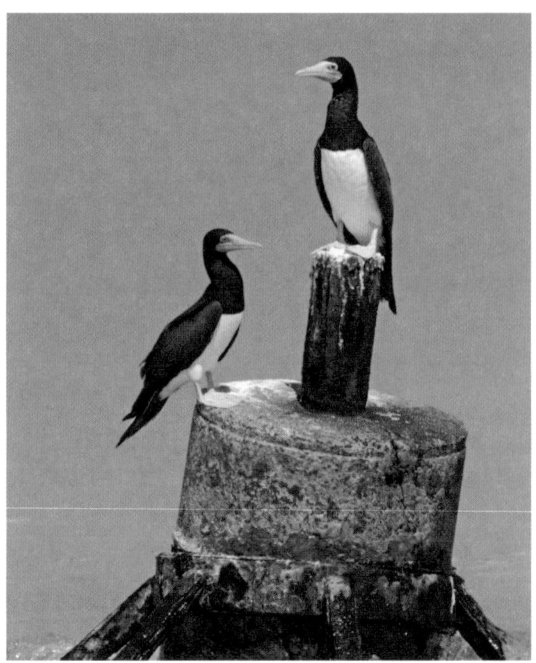

The data we've obtained from the birds' GPS tags show that most boobies make daily foraging trips involving flights of up to 140 kilometres from the breeding islands. Frigatebirds, though, go on journeys lasting up to ten days that take them as far as 400 kilometres from the nesting site before they return.

ASHMORE REEF IS within a Commonwealth marine reserve way out in the Indian Ocean – about 840 kilometres west of Darwin and 610 kilometres north of Broome – but also a mere 140 kilometres from the Indonesian island of Roti. Although the reef encompasses an area of 155 square kilometres, the reserve itself, including the nearby Cartier Island reserve of 172 square kilometres, covers an astonishing

538 square kilometres. This would be almost enough to enclose the city of Canberra. Within Ashmore's encircling reefs are two extensive lagoons, shifting sand flats, seagrass meadows, and the four islands that support shrubs, seasonal herbs, and grasses – with one providing a tropical touch with two palm trees.

Regular monitoring of seabird numbers has confirmed that more than 110,000 now breed at Ashmore Reef each year, with thousands of others making use of the islands as a night-time spot to roost, together with shorebirds that visit from as far away as the Siberian tundra.[1] The data collected has been especially valuable in identifying seabirds that breed elsewhere yet routinely forage in the oceans surrounding the reef. While a pair of frigatebirds is nesting on an island inside the reef, one will keep the egg warm while the other goes off foraging for three to eight days. As a result, the biologists now know that most of that foraging occurs in the Indian Ocean towards Indonesia. Once the breeding is over, though, they go much farther and head into the Java Sea for most of the wet season.

Among Australia's external territories, the reef is the closest point to Indonesia and Indonesian fishermen routinely visit Ashmore, as they have for centuries. Under a memorandum of understanding signed by the Australian and Indonesian governments in 1974, the fishermen were allowed to traverse the sea around the reef without the need for Australian visas. With no government agencies closely monitoring the reef, at least until recent years, the fishermen could do whatever they liked – and that included plundering seabird colonies for eggs and chicks, and even killing breeding birds as well.

Then in 1995, people smugglers in Indonesia began dumping asylum-seekers on the reef because, once they had landed on Ashmore, they could claim to have entered Australian territory and request to be processed as refugees. By 2001, when the numbers of these 'boat people' started rapidly rising, they became a major political issue. Later that year, the Howard government excised Ashmore Reef and Christmas Island from the Australian migration zone so the newcomers would no longer be entitled to be processed as refugees. This was the beginning of an endless saga of different Australian governments trying to stem the flow of refugees, dubbed 'illegal immigrants' by some politicians to denigrate them and provide a rationale for locking them up within Australia but also in nearby countries.

The federal government assigned a permanent team of Customs Department officials – now known as 'Border Force officers' – to keep watch over the reef and advise of any new arrivals. Rohan Clarke says the year-round presence of the officials aboard dedicated vessels has improved protection of the 'biodiversity assets within the reserve and, in that way at least, the asylum-seekers have done the seabirds a good turn'. Ashmore Reef was designated a Ramsar Wetland of International Importance in 2003 thanks to the significant role that the reef and its islands play in providing a resting place for migratory shorebirds, as well as supporting large colonies of nesting seabirds.

Anything a researcher might spot on Ashmore Reef has the potential to be a discovery, Clarke says. Not just identification of birds from far-off places that have not been recorded on the reef before, but even common Australian birds that unexpectedly turn out to be migrants. The team now has data on a large number of other birds that are just visiting Australia – a fact that was unknown before the Monash studies on Ashmore began. One exciting discovery involved peregrine falcons. Although young peregrines move from place to place on the Australian mainland, the adult birds are basically sedentary. Yet in 2009, the Monash researchers started seeing falcons flying around the reef even though they were 140 kilometres from Indonesia and 350 kilometres from Australia. Because the reef does not have the right environment to support falcons, Clarke realised the visitors must have been 'birds on the move'.

This means it is a stop-off for falcons from the northern hemisphere – some from as far away as Siberia. Clarke says biologists could not make these sorts of findings in the Kimberley or anywhere else on the mainland, given the vastness of those areas:

> we're only encountering the birds because the tiny islands act as magnets to draw them off a large area of ocean as they fly past. The visiting falcons usually spend only a day or two on the reef and then they're gone.

The birds have been seen in April, when the raptors leave Australia for the northern hemisphere summer, and again in November while heading south to the mainland during the Australian summer. Although European ornithologists knew their falcons were migratory, no-one had any idea European birds travelled as far south as Australia until Clarke spotted one on Ashmore. When he realised the peregrines seen on the reef were actually migrating birds, he screened photos of falcons on the web and identified several birds that had been photographed in Australia but were overlooked by local ornithologists who must have assumed they were residents:

> One had been photographed by a mate who told me he had taken the photo at the Healesville Sanctuary outside Melbourne. I chased that up with the keepers and it turned out the falcon had been found injured only about ten kilometres from where I live, and then held at Healesville for a few years before it died. They thought it looked 'odd' but nobody had twigged it wasn't an Australian bird!

So why would a raptor such as a falcon set off on an immensely long migratory journey twice each year to fly a total distance of more than 50,000 kilometres? Clarke says earlier exploring falcons had probably come across good feeding grounds far south of the equator and passed the information back to their offspring. Of course, this makes the falcons no different from any of the other migratory birds that cross the equator with the ease of modern-day aeroplane travellers.

BECAUSE OF THE extensive oil and gas developments along the north-west shelf of Australia, the Monash scientists have been monitoring population trends at the Ashmore breeding sites, locating the birds' foraging ranges and their essential food resources. While the Indonesians were increasingly using the seabirds on the reef as a food source, the bird populations were falling. Since regular monitoring began, however, bird numbers are on the rise. The researchers also maintain continuous records of marine fauna on their way to and from the islands within the reef, including seabirds, whales, dolphins, turtles and sea snakes. As well as the nesting bird populations, the islands have significant marine turtle nesting areas. Dugongs breed within the reef lagoons and various types of whales are frequent visitors, as are whale sharks.

Although the reef is a tropical paradise for the seabirds and shorebirds that stay there, for the biologists it is more like spending weeks working full time in a particularly hot sauna. With humidity nearing 100 per cent and temperatures rarely falling below 30 degrees, few escape heat stress. Clarke and his colleagues are usually at the reef 'on the shoulders of the wet' in November, when the weather is at its hottest. The team goes ashore at 7 am: by the time they arrive on one of the islands, they are soaked in sweat. West Island, one of the four islands inside the reef, is also covered in long grass. Clarke describes pushing his way through as 'like spending time in hell'. Yet it is all worth it, because they are

> on one of the remotest, least known corners of Australia. To experience that in so many different ways, to be immersed in it over the years and see the changes that occur around the reef is amazing. When we are there at the end of the dry season, almost all the vegetation on the islands has turned to dust. Then, when we come

back in March or April after a decent wet season, the vegetation is waist-high and there may be 100,000 seabirds nesting.

The point of going to Ashmore at different times in the year is to take account of the changes that also occur among the birdlife. The main purpose in November is for the researchers to obtain a reasonably stable summer population count of the migratory shorebirds that live on the mudflats at a time when seabird migration to the south has mostly finished. The birds number up to 15,000, most having left the northern hemisphere's wintry conditions behind to spend a summer on the reef. In the past, various scientific reports claimed that Ashmore was simply an important stopover site for shorebirds on their way to the mainland. But the data collected by the Monash researchers show that it is, in fact, a significant wintering site on its own and the birds do not fly on to Australia; rather, they stay at Ashmore.

'There is no evidence shorebirds use Ashmore Reef as a stopover site on the way to Australia,' Clarke says. 'If they did we would expect hundreds of colour-banded birds to arrive in September to early November then a decline as they fly on to the mainland. But we don't see this.'

Of all the research trips Rohan Clarke has made to Ashmore Reef since 1996, one stands out in his mind as the greatest challenge he has faced on the reef. The year was 2009 and on 21 August Australia's worst oil disaster began.

An oil well on the Montara platform, located on the Sahul Shelf 105 kilometres west of Ashmore, blew out, resulting in a vast volume of oil and gas being ejected over the next seventy-four days. This was the biggest oil spill in Australian history, creating an oil slick that spread out over 6000 square kilometres across the Timor Sea. Not until 3 November was the leak stopped by engineers pumping mud into the well and cementing the wellbore – which was also two days after the platform had caught fire as engineers were trying to stop the leak. The Thai-owned company that was working the well platform, PTTEP Australasia, later estimated it had spent $170 million to stop the leak, with another $5.3 million spent on the environmental clean-up. In 2012, the company pleaded guilty to charges under Australia's *Offshore Petroleum and Greenhouse Gas Storage Act* and was fined $510,000.

That was a pitiful sum compared to the almost US$19 billion – the largest corporate settlement in United States history – that the giant oil company BP finally agreed to pay in fines and other charges in July 2015 for its massive spill of oil in the Gulf of Mexico five years earlier.[2] But then, the BP spill had caused the deaths of eleven people working on the rig, affected the lives and livelihoods of tens of thousands of people along the United States coast, created enormous ecological damage, and killed or badly affected untold millions of birds and animals.

The Australian government and PTTEP commissioned Clarke to undertake a five-year study assessing the impact of the spill near Ashmore on the populations of seabirds and other avian species. His report was based on a pre-impact assessment and a post-impact field survey in April 2010.[3]

The Monash team's initial survey of the reef's islands counted more than 75,000 breeding seabirds and 4200 shorebirds, providing a post-spill baseline. In the report, Clarke warns that breeding seabirds might have been exposed to the oil via a number of pathways. Surface-plunging species, such as terns and boobies and those that rest on the sea surface as shearwaters do, were most at risk. Clarke explains the risks in the report:

> Because seabirds are top order predators any impact on other marine life may disrupt and limit food supply both for the maintenance of adults and the provisioning of young. Any direct impact of oil on terrestrial habitats within the reserve, including the shorelines of islands and sandbanks, has the potential to contaminate birds present at the breeding sites.

Crested terns are among the 100,000 birds that breed on Ashmore Reef.

Complete island-wide counts of breeding seabirds were also undertaken each year from 2010 to 2014 on all the islands. In Australia, starting in 1990, tabs were secured to individual shorebirds' legs with small coloured plastic bands. This 'leg flagging', as it's called, led to a flagging protocol for the East Asian–Australasian Flyway, setting out how the marking of shorebirds should be done. During the counts at Ashmore Reef and the nearby Cartier and Browse islands, the flocks of birds were routinely scanned to identify leg-flagged individuals.

The colour combinations of any birds that carried the tags were recorded and these were sent to the Australian Wader Study Group flag database so that their origins could be determined. Sixteen species of seabird and four species of heron breed at Ashmore Reef, and the largest colony of eastern reef egrets as well as relatively small numbers of wedge-tailed shearwaters and tropicbirds can also be found there.

Eastern reef egrets add to Ashmore's enormous diversity of birdlife.

'The diversity of seabirds across the small islands is exceptional in an Australasian context,' Clarke notes.

> It has been speculated that this diversity may have arisen because of the isolated nature of this island group, the diversity of available habitat on the three vegetated islands and the proximity of Ashmore Reef to the Indonesian 'Through Flow' – a potentially nutrient-rich current linking the Pacific and the Indian oceans that is active in the vicinity of the reef. Up to 54,000 common noddies, 45,000 sooty terns, 5000 brown boobies and more than 2000 lesser frigatebirds have been reported breeding on Middle Island and East Island prior to the commencement of this study.

Some of these bird colonies are among the largest in the Australasian region: Ashmore Reef supports the largest colony of sooty terns in Western Australia and the second largest colony of common noddies in the entire nation. Although earlier researchers had concluded the reef could support up to 50,000 breeding seabirds, recent data indicate the total number of breeding seabirds exceeds 100,000 during a twelve-month cycle. This was confirmed during the Monash team's 2013 visit to the reef when 107,800 seabirds were counted.

Clarke says the absence of any serious oil contamination detected on the birds and other wildlife in the aftermath of the spill was probably because the oil was light and fluid, with a consistency close to diesel rather than the black sludge that leaked from the BP well in the Gulf of Mexico. As a result, the impact of the spill on the environment and the animals and birds appears to have been far less significant. Nevertheless, he calls for further monitoring to provide 'a defensible measure of population trends and opportunities to detect trends and any points of significant change in total seabird and shorebird numbers within the reserves'. The federal government and PTTEP agreed and the research continued until the project concluded at the end of 2014.

The reef attracts the largest colony of sooty terns in Western Australia.

The available evidence now indicates that although there may have been some slowing in the population growth among the breeding seabirds around the time of the Montara oil spill, the populations continued to grow in the years afterwards. In 2013 and again in 2014, more than 100,000 breeding seabirds were on Ashmore during a single survey visit:

> With ongoing growth of seabird colonies, at some point the breeding seabirds will either occupy all of the available breeding space on the islands or the food resources such as fish and squid around the island will place a cap on the number of birds that can be supported there. So, given continuing protection of the reef, the population growth will slow and eventually stabilise. When that happens we'll finally have a good understanding of just how many birds this amazing place can support.

Unfortunately, it is only in a small number of places on Earth that seabird and shorebird numbers are showing such welcome increases. On the contrary, in too many regions their populations are falling with increasing rapidity, even among the amazing short-tailed shearwater, Australia's most abundant seabird.

5

Traversing the Globe: The Bass Strait Mutton-Birds

Giant tiger snakes with heads the size of a fist live on Great Dog Island in Bass Strait, along with copperheads that are almost as big, and the much smaller white-lipped snakes. So it was always with some trepidation that Mark Carey pushed his arm down the burrows where the mutton-birds nested.

'I HAVE A fear of snakes,' Dr Mark Carey says. 'And if students are with me on the island, the one rule is that the "s" word is not to be spoken unless there's actually one of them nearby.' Just to be sure, though, before Carey shoves his arm down a burrow he puts a leather glove on his 'catching hand' and, because a snake had once crawled up the sleeve of a previous field worker, he also wears two long-sleeved shirts and tapes the cuffs to the glove. 'I [have] never met a snake down a burrow. There are dozens of them on the rookery and I've watched them go down burrows but never seen one come out.'

I first spoke with Carey in June 2010 when he was based at La Trobe University's department of environmental management and ecology.

He was teaching and also conducting research for his PhD into the short-tailed shearwater, to give the mutton-bird its official name, as he had been for the previous six years. He would spend up to four months on Great Dog Island every year and, by the time of our first interview, reckoned he had spent more than a year of his life down there. On that occasion, I asked him what he thought of the little shearwater after years closely studying the birds: 'I love them,' he promptly said, expressing the feelings of many ornithologists who devote huge amounts of their time to a single species. 'I think they're amazing birds. They are long-lived, they form life-long bonds with their mate, they migrate extraordinary distances every year – they are an incredible species.'

It would be hard to dispute that assessment about the small, dark-brown bird that spends its annual holidays flying to Arctic regions in the northern hemisphere at a top speed of more than 800 kilometres a day, then floating around the Pacific Ocean eating krill for a few months before making the return journey home later in the year. Or that it happens to be Australia's most abundant seabird.

Carey obtained a PhD for his research into the life of the short-tailed shearwater, the wonderful Latin name of which, *Puffinus tenuirostris*, was first proposed in 1835 by a Dutch ornithologist, Jacob Temminck, because of its slender bill (*tenui* meaning 'slender', *rostrum* meaning 'bill'). The genus name *Puffinus* is actually a 'new Latin' loan word based on the English 'puffin', although the birds called puffins are actually auks, a completely different species to the shearwaters, which comprise a variety of about twenty different small- to medium-sized species. The short-tailed shearwater is still called *Puffinus* in most countries but taxonomic changes in Australia led to it being renamed *Ardenna tenuirostris*. Carey says he still uses *Puffinus* in correspondence with international researchers but that it makes for difficulties when a species has two scientific names 'depending on who you are talking to around the world'.

As for the mutton-bird name, that term was first applied to providence petrels (*Pterodroma solandri*) by starving prisoners on Norfolk

Island in the late eighteenth century. These transportees had been sent to the island from Sydney as punishment. When supplies ran low, the hungry prisoners resorted to 'harvesting' adult petrels for food. Dubbed 'flying sheep' by an officer in the Royal Marines (hence the origin of 'mutton-bird'), the petrels live in burrows and are similar to short-tailed shearwaters. So heavy was the 'harvesting', however, that they were ultimately wiped out on Norfolk and now only survive on Lord Howe Island where their status is listed as vulnerable to extinction.

That is not likely to happen in the near future to short-tailed shearwaters, given their current population is estimated at around 23 million breeding birds with possibly a further 11 million non-breeding birds – which is why it is the most abundant of all Australian seabirds. And also why a northern rivers observer on the New South Wales coast wrote to me early in September one year to say she had just spent days watching the amazing sight of 'vast clouds of the short-tailed shearwaters flying in great V-shaped flocks the size of Boeing 747s' making their way south over the ocean.

MATTHEW FLINDERS WOULD have agreed. The great explorer was sailing through Bass Strait in 1798 when he also saw huge numbers of shearwaters and estimated their population then at *100 million*. That figure, however, implies the current population of these shearwaters could have plummeted by 45 million in some 220 years. Since most of that decline would have occurred in the last fifty years, the future of this seabird, as with most others, could not be said to be rosy. Still, as they have for millennia, from September to April each year millions of the shearwaters breed in nearly 300 colonies on small islands dotted along the coast, from the Great Barrier Reef, south to New South Wales, Victoria and Tasmania, and across to Western Australia. But their stronghold is in Bass Strait, where an estimated 18 million arrive on the islands off Tasmania each year to form 167 colonies and to re-occupy or remake 11 million burrows.

As the Tasmanian Wildlife Service notes:

> The short-tailed shearwater is a member of a group of sixty medium to large seabirds in the family *Procellariidae* whose members have tube-like nostrils on the top of their upper beak. They are believed to be one of the few bird families with a well-developed sense of smell and almost all breed in burrows while also being, like the albatrosses, truly impressive oceanic fliers. They are often seen floating in large 'rafts' while feeding off the shores of Tasmania.

The statement about a bird's sense of smell, however, is outdated and many birds are now known to possess a sense of smell. In his book *Bird Sense: What it's like to be a bird,* Tim Birkhead, a distinguished British ornithologist and professor of animal behaviour, has a chapter on the capacity of birds to smell. He says the evidence gathered over more than fifty years indicates that many species of birds can smell and they use this sense with others, such as sight, in detecting and obtaining their food. This includes the common pigeon, which appears to use a sense of smell as well as its magnetic sense to navigate.

Adult shearwaters have a wingspan of about a metre – not bad for a bird that weighs a mere 500 or so grams. Naturally, they are excellent swimmers with webbed feet and legs placed well back on their body, while their wings are long and narrow for efficient high-speed gliding. Although these features are nicely adapted for life on and above the ocean, the shearwater has problems moving on land and taking flight in windless conditions. That's one reason, the wildlife service says, why the colonies are often found on headlands that allow the birds an easy take-off and landing, although they also choose islands covered with tussocks and succulent vegetation such as pigface. The largest colony in

Bass Strait is on Tasmania's Babel Island, which, with 3 million burrows, you would think had been almost hollowed out by now.

Conservationists object to humans continuing to kill the birds and their chicks, although mutton-birds have been hunted by Aboriginal Tasmanians over thousands of generations. Many Indigenous families continue the practice, and commercial operators also 'harvest' them: the shearwater is one of the few Australian native birds said to have sufficient numbers to be commercially harvested without threatening its survival. At the peak of hunting in the early 1900s, a million birds were said to be taken each year, whereas today up to 300,000 chicks are still killed for their feathers, flesh and oil. This occurs during an annual open season that was imposed by the state government after hunting the birds became an industry. In early times, European sealers and Aboriginal families freely took large numbers, whereas today, hunters must obtain a state government mutton-bird licence first before they can take part.

GREAT DOG ISLAND, where Mark Carey spent so many months for his research on the shearwaters, is part of the Furneaux group off Tasmania's north-east coast. It covers 370 hectares but the island is uninhabited – apart, that is, from the snakes, silver gulls and little penguins that breed there. Not to mention the 950,000 shearwaters living in their burrows for six months or so, making the island Tasmania's third largest mutton-bird rookery. The birds arrive every year to breed. Then the female lays one egg in the same burrow every year, in a leaf-lined chamber, as the species may have done for millennia. Despite the huge number of birds and the way they are spread out over the island, their laying seems almost synchronised; as Carey discovered, 85 per cent of eggs are laid by the birds within three days around 25 to 26 November.

The chicks hatch from the 10th of January onwards and, after fifty-three days, they fledge in the last half of April to the first week of May. They remain in their burrows for three and half months – provided they survive the tiger snakes, although the snakes have to grab them early because the chicks grow fast and two weeks after hatching are too large for even a big tiger snake to swallow. 'There is always a glut of these beautiful chicks and the snakes go crazy trying to eat as many as they can,' Carey says.

> But the great majority survive and then they are abandoned by their parents and have to learn to feed and to fly by themselves. Yet somehow they know how to migrate to the northern hemisphere and back home again in one of the world's great mass avian movements.

On his trips to the island, Carey was always accompanied by at least one other member of the La Trobe department or one or more students. They lived in a hut during the four-month breeding season, although to get there required a plane trip from Essendon Airport in Melbourne to Flinders Island – and then a twenty-minute boat ride with a local fisherman. The fisherman also brought fresh food and other supplies when needed. Carey recalls:

> The hut was well-equipped with a gas stove, a gas fridge and rainwater tanks. But all food supplies and fuel for the generator had to be brought in by boat; a radio was our only source of news from the outside world. The shearwater burrows come almost to the back door so it really is their island. At night when the birds come in, you can actually hear them scratch out their burrows and call to their partners. It's quite noisy and it takes a couple of weeks to get used to before you can sleep through.

Because of the months he spent on the island, Carey learned a great deal about the shearwaters, their individual characteristics and their behaviour as a group. He found that each bird forms strong bonds with its mate: they dig out a burrow together and defend it against intruders. The pair return year after year to the same burrow unless death or some other catastrophic event separates them. The female lays the one egg but both parents take turns at incubation until it hatches. Then, together, they carefully nurture their one chick. Says Carey of the shearwaters:

> Every bird has its own personality. You can get really quiet, gentle birds and then hit a really aggressive one that would absolutely tear your hands to bits – I've got scars to show how aggressive these birds can be. Because the adults only produce one egg a year, they put a lot of investment into their chick-rearing and they also need to provision their chick for up to three months so it can survive.

Shearwaters do not start breeding until they are five or six years old and their colonies always contain a mixture of breeding pairs of adults and non-breeding youngsters. The latter are the first to leave the colonies, early in March, followed by the breeding adults in April and May, and, finally, three or four weeks after the last of the adults have gone, the fledglings take off to head into the unknown. Until Carey and three international colleagues decided to find out for themselves, little was known about where the short-tailed shearwaters went on their travels around the world, what they did in the northern hemisphere and whether the route they took north was the same as the one they followed to return home.

To collect the evidence they wanted, Carey attached tiny electronic data loggers to the legs of twenty-seven mutton-birds before they began their overseas trip.[1] The 1.8-gram loggers were developed by British scientists at the survey's headquarters in Cambridge University, and were devised to record the times of sunset and sunrise each day as well as how long the bird was in the air or on the water. These remarkable recording instruments measure light levels every sixty seconds, storing the maximum value in ten-minute intervals, thereby identifying times of sunrise and sunset based on light-curve thresholds. The bird's longitude could be calculated from the time of local midday relative to Greenwich Mean Time, and the latitude estimated from the length of that day, thereby providing two locations each day.

Of the twenty-seven shearwaters that Carey had fitted with loggers, ten males and ten females were recaptured the following year on Great Dog Island in November and December. The condition of all twenty birds was as good as that of the non-equipped adults and, of the tagged birds, fourteen were members of a pair while the rest had presumably lost their partners along the way. Twelve of the twenty recovered loggers provided complete records, while another seven had partial details. Carey then flew to Cambridge to analyse the information collected about the shearwaters' remarkable travels with the other scientists.

Their research revealed that after the birds left the Furneaux islands in Bass Strait, they headed south to below the Antarctic Convergence – a huge region rich in Antarctic Ocean krill that the shearwaters fed on, presumably to build up enough reserves to undertake the long-haul flight to the northern hemisphere. Between 15 April and 9 May, all the birds departed on a northerly migration through the South Pacific, passing the equator within a few days of each other. The birds then flew north-west towards the east coast of Japan until they reached the 30th parallel north, where seven birds diverged north-east towards the Bering Sea around the Aleutian Islands, and the remaining group continued to the east coast of Japan.

They stopped their northward passage at about the 40th to 50th parallels north, and began moving across the Pacific basin after travelling more than 11,000 kilometres in thirteen days at a speed of 840 kilometres a day! This was an incredible feat, not only because of their speed but also because the short-tailed shearwaters make a round trip of nearly 60,000 kilometres on their annual migration journeys. Given that some of the birds can live for forty or more years, a typical shearwater might fly more than 2 million kilometres in its lifetime – or nearly six times the distance to the moon and back again. A short-tailed shearwater was found in 2015 at Port Fairy in Victoria with leg bands that had been attached to the bird in 1968; that is, it was nearing almost a half-century of long-distance flying. That record was broken when a great egret was captured in South Australia fifty-one years after it had been banded. On top of that, the world's oldest banded bird is believed to be a Laysan albatross that is at least sixty years old – and still laying eggs.

Carey and the team in Cambridge found the monitored seabirds remained north of the 40th parallel throughout the sub-Arctic summer, spending an average of 148 days in the North Pacific. The birds were based in one of two major regions: either around northern Hokkaido in Japan, or west of the Pribilof Islands in the Bering Sea, areas also characterised by cold, highly productive waters. They then began their return migration to the Australian breeding islands in mid September to early October, travelling in a south-westerly direction through the central Pacific, west of the Hawaiian Islands. Passing the equator in early October – all within a few days of each other, as on the outbound journey – the birds continued flying south-west towards the east coast of Australia and then travelled south down the coast, passing my northern New South Wales correspondent until they reached the Furneaux islands in mid to late October.

The average time taken for the southward migration was eighteen days, with the birds covering nearly 700 kilometres a day. The mean distance travelled during their migration and the non-breeding period cruising around the northern hemisphere totalled 59,600 kilometres. While the tracked shearwaters selected one or another of the two major areas to spend their time up north, some migrated initially to waters off Japan and later moved to the Bering Sea before the return migration south; in contrast, birds that travelled first to the Bering Sea did not cross to the Japanese waters. The researchers say this change in distribution before the return migration has also been observed in flesh-footed shearwaters and may have been a response to retreating sea ice in the Sea of Okhotsk causing a bloom of ocean plant growth, 'leading to enhanced foraging opportunities'.

SUCH BEHAVIOURAL VARIATION within species and between individuals has implications for their ability to cope with environmental change. Those species exhibiting what the biologists call 'behavioural plasticity' – those that do not stick rigidly to the age-old routes on their travels – are likely to be more resilient in coping with global climate change than birds saddled with 'inflexible migration strategies'. Rising global temperatures and the severity and frequency of El Niño events affect major ocean ecosystems, including those of the North Pacific. A drop in the availability of food or shifts in the distribution of key fish species could lead to population collapses among migratory birds.

After years studying the shearwaters at close range, Carey completed his PhD and began work with the Trust for Nature, a not-for-profit organisation set up to protect native plants and wildlife in cooperation with private landowners. In 2012, he moved to Canberra to take up a position in the federal environment department's migratory species section, where he has responsibility for Australia's three migratory bird agreements with Japan, China and the Republic of Korea, as well as domestic migratory bird policy. Short-tailed shearwaters are listed on all three agreements, he hastens to explain. His focus has shifted, however, to birds that are in dire trouble, as well as to the Far Eastern curlew.

The Far Eastern curlew (*Numenius madagascariensis*) is not only the largest curlew but also the world's largest sandpiper and the largest migratory seabird. The species is classed as critically endangered in Australia, and evidence points to the bird suffering significant declines over the past twenty years – a result, unsurprisingly, of habitat loss, human disturbance and possibly hunting. Biologists say successful conservation of this increasingly rare bird requires urgent collaborative action across its full geographical range, including at breeding locations, important migration stopover sites, as well as in non-breeding areas.

At the eighth meeting of the East Asian–Australasian Flyway Partnership in Japan, Carey notes Australia proposed the formation of the Far Eastern Curlew Task Force and also sought a commitment from all other partners, including governments, to develop an international action plan. The task force was officially endorsed by the partnership 'to restore the species to a favourable conservation status and remove it from the threatened categories on the IUCN Red List'. Only time will tell if this goal is achieved but the prospects, unfortunately, must be considered slight given the past few decades of devastating falls in global seabird numbers.

6

Saving Australia's Threatened Species

At least twenty-two Australian birds have been driven to extinction since the British began to colonise the country in 1788 – officially, that is, although the number is certainly higher because obtaining an accurate count across the entire nation prior to or at the time of the invasion was impossible. Regardless of how many birds are no longer alive, when any species is lost from an ecological community the functions it performed in the great web of life are also lost – and there will be some impact on the survivors. Every bird species contributes to the maintenance of its environment and, if one disappears, an effect will be felt on its ecosystem – minor, sometimes, but also deadly serious on occasion.

OF THE AUSTRALIAN birds known to have been wiped out since the arrival of Captain Arthur Phillip and his flotilla of convict-laden vessels, the majority were on Norfolk and Lord Howe islands. Others include the Kangaroo Island emu, hunted until the last bird in the wild was killed in 1805, the dwarf emu of King Island that vanished in 1822, and the Tasmanian emu that survived until 1850. Today, almost 1800 Australian animal and bird species are facing similar death sentences, and many more are likely to be condemned unless prompt action is taken.

Then again, very occasionally, a bird comes back from the dead. Widely known as 'the world's most mysterious' bird, the Australian night parrot or *Pezoporus occidentalis*, was thought to have died out in 1912. But then one of the curious little creatures, nocturnal and ground-dwelling, was sighted seventy-five years later and, by 2013, others had been briefly captured and tagged (the extraordinary story of which is recounted in the final chapter of this book).

Another fourteen birds were added to the National Threatened Species List of the vulnerable, endangered or critically endangered birds[1] in May 2016, bringing the total to nearly 150, compared with more than a hundred similarly threatened mammals. Despite these disturbing and rising numbers, the state of Australia's environment and its threatened species barely rates a mention in national political debates and discussions. Nor, for that matter, have the consequences of climate change been highlighted in political coverage by the media across the country. No surprise there: following the electoral disasters of the Gillard and second Rudd governments, where climate change received much negative attention, successive Coalition governments made little attempt to take that topic seriously.

Nevertheless, in one brief interlude, the Abbott government released a Threatened Species Strategy Action Plan[2] in 2015 aimed at tackling the rising extinction rate among Australian birds and animals. The government committed $6.6 million 'as a down payment on delivery' to boost the national profile of threatened species, explore solutions and promote 'practical and effective ways of tackling the rising threats to the nation's animals and plants'.

Three major conservation organisations, however, delivered a savage critique of the action plan in their report, *Recovery Planning: Restoring Life to Our Threatened Species*.[3] In their blistering attack BirdLife Australia, the Australian Conservation Foundation and Environmental

Justice Australia noted that the nation had earned itself 'the shameful title of a world leader in extinction', losing more native mammal species to extinction than any other developed country. Of course, it's not only marsupials that have been pushed over the extinction cliff; the government's own list of species lost forever has more than a hundred entries that, along with twenty-seven mammals, include twenty-two birds, four known frogs, one invertebrate and thirty plants. As the conservation groups declare in their report:

> In reality the number is higher than this, with species such as the Christmas Island pipistrelle, a bat which disappeared forever when the last of its kind passed away in 2009, and the Bramble Cay melomys, a small rodent not seen since 2007, yet to be formally categorised as extinct.

In preparing their report, the three groups were responding to the belated decision by the federal government to take the extinction crisis more seriously than it or its predecessors ever had. As part of its action plan, the government declared war against the nation's 2 million or more feral cats, deadly enemies of birds and small mammals – and almost certainly responsible for killing off many species. Also under the plan were moves to create safe havens for species most at risk, as well as improving and enlarging their habitats, and intervening in emergencies to avert extinctions. These seemed to be highly significant developments but the conservation groups were deeply sceptical about the seriousness of the government's intentions. Not just because of the half-hearted attempts previous governments had made, but because the key factor needed for birds and mammals to survive – their habitat – barely rated a mention or an acknowledgement in the Coalition's five-year program.

Even the Department of the Environment and Energy, in its summary of the government's threatened species strategy, notes that since European settlement at least 130 species have become casualties of the spread of white people across the land, while the list of animals and plants threatened with extinction continues to grow.[4] As part of the plans for birds, the strategy proposes that 'twenty priority birds will have improved population trajectories by 2020', with actions underway to launch each trajectory by 2018. Now, depending on how they are counted, Australia has nearly 900 species of birds, apart from the twenty-two officially recognised as having become extinct in the wild, but also including twenty-seven that were introduced or simply arrived uninvited. Not all of Australia's native birds are threatened with extinction, but with only twenty species allocated a 'priority survival chance' this seems an inadequate response.

The initial list of twelve birds requiring intervention included the seriously threatened plains-wanderer and the hooded plover, while the others were the helmeted honeyeater, eastern bristlebird, regent honeyeater, mallee emu-wren, the newly discovered night parrot,

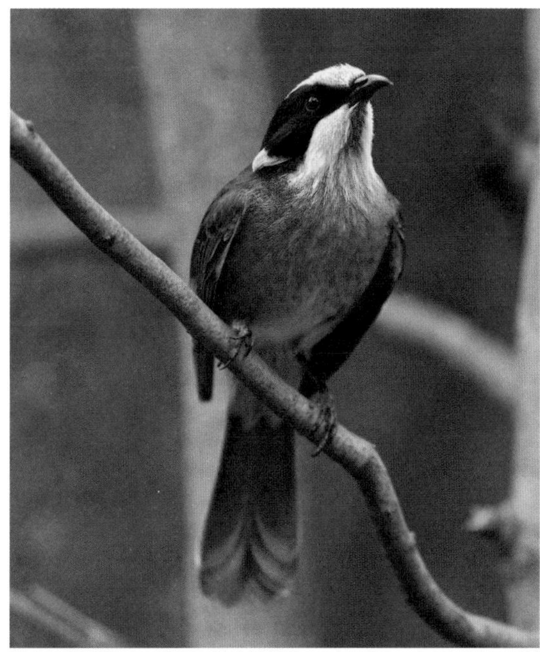

Helmeted honeyeater: threatened with extinction

Alligator River yellow chat, and, on Norfolk Island, the indigenous green parrot and the boobook owl. Another two birds were singled out for emergency intervention: one is the orange-bellied parrot, a small grass parrot about the same size as a budgerigar with an orange patch on its belly that, like its cousin the swift parrot, migrates between the Australian mainland and Tasmania, spending the summer breeding in Tasmania and winter in coastal Victoria and South Australia. But fewer than fifty of these parrots exist in the wild, making it one of the world's rarest and most endangered species; in fact, it is listed as critically endangered. The second bird is the western ground parrot, unique to Western Australia and another of the world's rarest species, although it may already be extinct.

The names of the remaining eight birds listed for urgent attention under the Threatened Species Strategy were announced a couple of months later. The Environment Department's document boasts that the

Orange-bellied parrot: fewer than fifty survive in the wild

Boobook owls: yet another declining species

action plan has built-in monitoring and reporting requirements while regular measurements 'will show whether investments are improving the status of threatened species and will encourage learning from what has been done'. Great, except that the *Recovery Planning* report reveals how poorly thought-out the government's actions were because they failed to offer any protection of the threatened species' habitats. Without tackling this crucial element, the strategy plan seems impotent in saving any of the threatened species from oblivion.

Despite an 'active protection of habitat' recommendation in the strategy's introductory section, only one in ten of the schemes affecting the most endangered birds and other animals imposes clear restrictions on the loss of their surroundings. Yet destruction of their natural environment is the most significant threat to the survival of the great majority of endangered animals. The conservation organisations highlight how the national plan consistently avoids prescriptive measures to save the habitats of threatened species, and note that successive governments have avoided their responsibility to protect the habitats of birds in danger, thereby entrenching the process of extinction:

> The four case studies in our report – Carnaby's Black-Cockatoo, Swift parrot, Proserpine rock wallaby and the Southern cassowary – illustrate that failure. And, by failing to articulate clear and unequivocal limits on the loss of habitat, most of the recovery plans allow habitat loss to continue.

The recovery plans, developed under the *Environment Protection and Biodiversity Conservation Act*, are meant to be the federal government's key instruments for bringing threatened species back from the brink – but instead will help push them over the edge.

THE SCALE OF environmental destruction in Australia was revealed in a nation-wide study by five senior ecologists.[5] They found that six regions had lost 50 per cent or more of their original forests and bushland and that, when combined, the total destroyed area amounted to almost a million square kilometres – about a seventh of the entire Australian continent! The worst hit are some of the mallee ecosystems in southern Australia that have suffered losses of up to 97 per cent of their original trees, shrubs and grasses. Likewise, the temperate eucalypt woodlands of south-east Australia, which previously covered more than a million square kilometres, now occupy less than half that, the rest having been cleared for agriculture and urban development.

Yet these areas include some of the most biodiverse woodland communities on Earth, including the critically endangered box-gum grassy woodland, which has been reduced to less than 10 per cent of its area in pre-colonial times. As a result of all this devastation, Australia has been named by the World Wildlife Fund as among Earth's greatest deforesting nations, hardly enhancing Australia's global standing as avid conservationists. One chapter of the World Wildlife Fund's *Living Forests Report* series singles out eleven regions around the globe for all the wrong reasons: as the places on Earth where forests are most likely to suffer destruction between now and 2030.[6] Australia scores a prime spot alongside Papua New Guinea and the Democratic Republic of Congo – neither are renowned for their commitment to saving trees or wildlife.

'More than 80 per cent of deforestation between 2010 and 2030 is likely to happen in just eleven places. These are the "deforestation fronts",' the *Saving Forests at Risk* report states.

> Without action to change current trends, up to 170 million hectares of forest could be destroyed in these places by 2030 – more than 80 per cent of total projected forest losses globally. Imagine a forest stretching across Germany, France, Spain and Portugal – wiped out in just twenty years …

The report's writers use projections of recent rates of forest loss to estimate how much each of the eleven regions is on track to lose in the years up to 2030. For eastern Australia, the estimated losses are up to 6 million hectares – although the WWF also refers to changes to environmental legislation in Queensland that, under the one-term Newman government, removed protection from more than a million hectares of bushland in that state alone. Back in 2012, the Council of Australian Governments signed off on a series of goals to provide a 'native vegetation framework' that included increasing 'the national extent and connectivity of native vegetation by 2020'. What a wonderful aim! Except that land clearing today exceeds the replanting and restoring of bushland by 100,000 hectares every year, with Queensland the main culprit in its brigalow region, and New South Wales seemingly eager to follow.

THE VAST BRIGALOW region is an appalling example of how governments allow widespread habitat loss to occur, so much so that 180 or more species of plants and animals in that area now appear to be doomed. The brigalow has been dubbed 'a national hotspot for wildlife', especially for birds and reptiles, such as the black-throated finch, golden-tailed gecko and the brigalow scaly-foot, that are found nowhere else in the world. The Brigalow Belt, as it's called, extends inland along the Queensland coast from Townsville in the north down to New South Wales, covering an area of about 6 million hectares or slightly less than the entire state of Tasmania. Despite its size, however, only about 2 per cent of the belt is protected in conservation reserves and the whole region has been called one of the most transformed and contested areas in Australia.

Land clearing is the greatest current threat to Australia's biodiversity while also being a major contributor to greenhouse gas emissions, to degradation and reduced water quality in waterways and estuaries, and to dryland salinity, says Martine Maron, one of Queensland's top senior academics and environmentalists:

> For wildlife, land clearing means smaller and more fragmented populations, and such populations are more vulnerable to extinction. This is basic ecology. As habitat is lost, animals don't simply move elsewhere or fly away. It is time to think about the end-game of land clearing in Australia, and what we are willing lose along the way. If we genuinely want to achieve a reversal of deforestation by 2020, then we need to see significant policy changes. And they need to happen now – sooner rather than later.[7]

In further damning commentary on land clearing in the brigalow region, other scientists point out that Queenslanders want to use the brigalow for many different purposes.[8] While these include conservation, they also include grazing, agricultural production, and mineral and gas extraction – given that the region also overlaps with Australia's largest reserves of coal and coal seam gas. 'Together, these economic activities bring land clearing, changes to water sources, invasion of exotic species and changed fire patterns, which threaten the region's unique biodiversity,' the scientists say. But none of this is particularly new: back in the early 1970s, hundreds of environmentalists across the nation protested at the vast clearing then taking place across the brigalow forests by Queensland farmers furiously expanding their holdings – and being paid by the state government to do so. Despite the protests and the subsequent publicity, the mass clearing continued almost up to the present day, paid by grants to farmers from the state government.

Yet the brigalow ecosystems once formed extensive open-forest woodlands across Queensland, as was the case over much of the Australian continent – apart from the arid interior – until the British invasion began. Dominated by a species of silvery wattle called

Acacia harpophylla, commonly known as brigalow, the Queensland forests covered nearly a third of the state's southern region. Since the mid nineteenth century, however, 90 per cent of the original forest has been cleared, mostly for farming, while the remaining 600,000 hectares consist of relatively small, isolated and fragmented remnants that are now protected as endangered ecological communities. That protection, though, came too late for eight animal species. Some were local species, such as the eastern quoll and northern bettong, while others were more widespread, including the Darling Downs hopping mouse.

In their report, the scientists say there are many ways of dealing with the impact on the brigalow's extent and biodiversity. They worked with forty 'key stakeholders' to find 'the most bang' for our conservation buck. Although the simplest solution would be to stop all development, the scientists recognise the reality is that the brigalow's native plants and animals are threatened by an accumulation of past, current and future land uses, and all these need to be addressed if threatened species are to be saved.

THE SAME COULD be said, of course for all the other areas in Australia that have endured or are experiencing widespread land clearing. Those involved in the brigalow project added a 'common vision' strategy because they saw this as vital to achieving their other aims. The vision would identify shared goals that balanced environmental, social and economic considerations, such as the extent and nature of future developments: 'We discovered that managing fire and invasive plant species would provide the best bang for our buck in terms of protecting the Brigalow Belt's threatened plants and animals,' the scientists say. 'Protecting remaining stands of vegetation offered high benefits to native wildlife, but came at high economic costs.'

The experts estimated it would cost about $57 million each year to implement all twelve of the proposed management strategies arising from the project, at a rate of about $1.60 per hectare every year. The scientists warn that if the money isn't spent then twenty-one species could disappear over the next fifty years – and, if the strategies were adopted, twelve of the species would likely survive, including the threatened regent honeyeater, northern quoll and bridled nail-tail wallaby, while the outlook for many other species would also be brighter.

Extinction of birds and animals in the brigalow or anywhere else in Australia is not inevitable, as BirdLife Australia's head of conservation, Samantha Vine, says:

> Where we have tried in the past, Australia has been remarkably successful at recovering threatened species and, in many cases, averting extinction has been straightforward and relatively inexpensive. Securing and improving existing habitats for threatened species remains one of the most powerful and cost-effective conservation tools at our disposal. It is essential that Australia makes protecting endangered species' habitat a key focus in combating the current extinction crisis.

Back in Canberra, the federal government offered a $100,000 contribution to tackle the pressing environmental problems that plague the plains-wanderer in southern New South Wales and northern Victoria. A small, ground-dwelling bird, the wanderer (*Pedionomus torquatus*) is unique, being the only representative of its family, but it has also been elevated to the most serious conservation status: critically endangered. The species occurs nowhere else on Earth yet its population has fallen alarmingly – by 90 per cent in recent years. The government also promised that an 'insurance population' of plains-wanderers would be established to ensure their survival into the future.

Some good news, however, came from Parks Victoria chief conservation scientist Mark Norman in June 2016. He reported that seven of the birds had been spotted during a night survey in a national park near the central Victorian city of Bendigo – the greatest number of plains-wanderers detected in a single survey for many years: 'In a sea of discouraging news on conservation issues and battles, it was very encouraging to find a trend turning the other way,' Norman told *The Age* newspaper.

> The plains-wanderer is … the 'Mr Bean' of endangered birds. They're strange-looking, awkward birds that live in strange and difficult habitats. And they don't have an easy time, particularly with invasion of weeds and land management practices and changing climates. But they are special creatures that are part of the unique Ark that Australia is in terms of the animals that have evolved here …

Plains-wanderer: the 'Mr Bean' of endangered birds and very special

Grant funding has been allocated to save the beach-nesting hooded plover.

Meanwhile, the hooded plovers of the New South Wales south coast are also likely to benefit from the government grants, with $40,000 set aside for an intensive examination of their overall ecology, including their movements, interactions and genetic makeup. This data will enable biologists to better understand what these beach-nesting birds need to survive. Although this announcement was welcome, questions were also raised about the survival of other beach-nesting birds, such as the lesser sand plover. With its numbers down 84 per cent, this plover is also facing a decline into extinction, as are many other migratory shorebirds unless the crisis is tackled.

The *Recovery Planning* report says Australian authorities have consistently failed in their duty of care to protect animal life:

> Actions by our predecessors in clearing and degrading the Australian bush have left present generations with an extinction debt – thousands of species of plants and animals are on an extinction

pathway because of the threats already unleashed and because the area of habitat left for them is insufficient to support viable populations into the future: Our national environment law, the *Environment Protection and Biodiversity Conservation Act*, currently lists 1,839 species and ecological communities as being on this path to extinction. But it is not a one-way route. One of the very reasons the Act exists is to prevent extinction – to identify the species at risk and the actions that must be taken to turn their fate around. Yet, for the majority of species, it is failing at this most fundamental task.

This is not because the task is impossible, conservationists would argue. Extinction need not be inevitable for the vast majority of Australia's threatened species, although it becomes increasingly likely because of the inaction of successive governments. As Samantha Vine says:

> For every step forward there are too many steps back. A fundamental problem with Australia's state and federal environmental laws is that they are riddled with loopholes and escape clauses, allowing ministers to permit inappropriate developments that inexorably push threatened species closer to extinction.

THE NAMES OF the remaining eight priority birds to be saved were announced in January 2016, including the swift parrot, white-throated grasswren, eastern bristlebird, helmeted honeyeater, plains-wanderer, and the orange-bellied parrot.

Efforts were also to be made to save the Christmas Island frigatebird, one of the most evolutionarily distinct and globally endangered birds in the world. This is a species that Australia shares with Indonesia,

The helmeted honeyeater, Victoria's only endemic bird, is critically endangered and survives is a single, small conservation park outside Melbourne.

Christmas Island frigatebird: globally endangered but evolutionarily distinct

although the forest canopy of Christmas Island is the only place where it breeds and nests. The male frigatebird is famous for its bright red throat pouch, called a gular, which it blows up like a fancy balloon to attract females during the mating season. A mating pair take at least fifteen months to raise one chick and, if the baby survives, it can live as long as fifty years. Frigatebirds primarily forage in the ocean for food, scooping up marine organisms such as fish and squid, but overfishing in its south-eastern habitat has slashed the food availability and is contributing to the species' decline.

As part of its efforts to tackle extinction rates on the island, the government also allocated $500,000 to begin an ambitious feral cat eradication program to reduce predation on the bird. Parks Australia staff are also working with researchers to monitor the spread of yellow crazy ants and are conducting extensive baiting to reduce the introduced ants' impacts on the frigatebird and other island species. Staff are collaborating with the Christmas Island community to develop a long-term recovery plan to manage and protect all of the island's unique threatened species, including the frigatebird.

All these decisions offer a slightly more optimistic future for Australian birdlife, although the nation's grim past is a gloomy reminder of the dangers still facing its native birds and other animals.

7

Giving New Life to the Babbler

The original range of the grey-crowned babbler was once so vast it extended from southern Papua New Guinea across Torres Strait to cover two-thirds of the Australian mainland. The babblers (so-called because they chatter all the time) occupied territories across much of the northern and eastern states – at least until Europeans arrived and began devastating the land and its original inhabitants, including the Indigenous peoples, most birds and every other native animal. Since 1788, more than 30 per cent of Australia's woodlands overall, and 80 per cent of the wonderfully diverse temperate woodlands, have been cleared. Because a third of Australia's land birds are woodland-dependent, a deplorable outcome of this destruction is that at least one in five of these species is now threatened with extinction – while many more may have gone before they were even known to exist.

THE GREY-CROWNED BABBLER (*Pomatostomus temporalis*) is the largest of Australia's four babbler species: a dark brownish-grey bird with a distinctive grey crown stripe and a dark face mask that contrasts with its white eyebrows, making it look perpetually cross. Its bill is long and curved, while it has short rounded wings with cinnamon-brown patches and a long tail tipped with white; the eyes are pale yellow in adults and bright brown in the young. Researchers use these eye colour changes to calculate how old the babblers are.

As has happened to untold numbers of other Australian birds following Captain Arthur Phillip's arrival at Sydney Cove, widespread land-clearing has left the surviving babblers' habitats fragmented. When groups of birds become isolated, their numbers may drop below a critical threshold – at which point they cannot maintain a viable population, so they die out, or genetic problems arise from inbreeding. Degraded habitats are a factor in the decline of many bird populations: a consequence of weed invasion, removal of timber, grazing by cattle and sheep, along with 'fuel-reduction burning' by firefighters, which contributes to a loss of leaf litter and thereby reduces the amount of invertebrate food available for insect-eating birds such as the babblers.

Across eastern Australia populations of the babbler are listed as near threatened, although in Victoria the species is classed as endangered.

Populations of the grey-crowned babbler have collapsed. In southern regions, the species has completely disappeared.

In South Australia and Victoria's southern regions, however, the species has become locally extinct, with overall numbers of the birds in those two states having plummeted by 95 per cent since white settlement. Their survival today is not being helped by harassment from noisy miners as well as attacks by avian predators such as pied currawongs and kookaburras. In 1994 the state government of Victoria initiated a habitat restoration program, as the estimated babbler population consisted of only 260 family groups and even that low number was rapidly falling.

Subsequent studies suggested the babbler population and average family group size had increased in areas where restoration works had taken place. A follow-up investigation by a team of Melbourne researchers is a good example of the careful methods biologists use with birds that are facing 'death by a thousand cuts' and the efforts they make to devise solutions. Those who conducted the study included Monash University lecturer Dr Rohan Clarke, head of the Ashmore Reef research, and Professor Andrew Bennett, one of four biologists from Deakin University.[1]

Southern populations of grey-crowned babblers have plummeted because of the loss and fragmentation of box and ironbark woodlands. In these landscapes the birds have just managed to survive by breeding in roadside plantings or in small adjacent remnant woodland patches within farmland, as well as along the edges of the few existing large conservation reserves. The babbler is noisy and gregarious and is sometimes called 'happy family' or 'yahoo' because the latter call sounds like the song a mating pair makes, with the female singing 'Yah!' and the male replying 'Hoo!' as a kind of duet. The birds are collaborative breeders and the dominant breeding pair is assisted by 'helpers', usually offspring from previous nestings that can assist with rearing chicks for up to four years. Egg laying and hatching occurs over an extended season, from June to the following March or April.

But the places where the birds can breed are often so limited that, in the more populous states, babblers have had to take refuge in the patches

Researcher Kate Stevens measures a grey-crowned babbler as part of her PhD studies.

of bush planted alongside roads by local councils. The Melbourne biologists wanted to discover how the babblers were managing to survive when their numbers were falling throughout their range. So they focused on babbler territories in three regions to see how isolated each group of birds was from neighbouring groups, the size of each group, and the type of vegetation in the three territories – including how large individual shrubs and trees were. They used the presence of chicks in the birds' nests and the size of the family group as 'surrogates of quality' because both are strong indicators of successful reproduction among babblers. They also looked into what factors might influence the quality of the territories. Did the complexity of the bush, and the availability of resources such as food, shelter and nest sites affect their success?

BABBLERS CONSTRUCT NUMEROUS large communal roost nests in their territories and at least one brood nest is used each breeding season by the leading female. In the south, the birds survive in remnant woodland patches separated by unsuitable areas of cleared farmland. The researchers were certainly not half-hearted in selecting the size of the three study areas, opting for a massive 22,250 square kilometres in northern Victoria, where the state's largest remaining babbler population survives. In each of the three large test areas they chose twenty-four separate sites, although the seventy-two tests sites still only represented about 4 per cent of known grey-crowned babbler territories.

To confirm the presence of birds at each site, the researchers played a recording of the babblers' calls. Any babblers that were there responded by calling back. They also made an on-ground search using this 'call playback' system in areas of suitable habitat within a 2-kilometre radius of each study territory to determine the distance to adjacent groups. More than half the territories were located on linear strips of roadside vegetation 40 to 60 metres wide – a dramatic example of the effects land clearing has had in destroying the birds' traditional homes.

In his splendid book *Australian Birds, Their Nests and Eggs*,[2] Gordon Beruldsen describes the babbler's nest as being in the shape of a rounded bottle lying on its side, with the spout-like entrance near the top and sloping slightly downwards. Constructed from sticks and twigs woven together, the nest is lined with soft grass, fur and sometimes feathers in which the eggs are buried if a parent bird is away. Beruldsen says nests are located either in an upright fork of a smallish sapling, or in the fork 'at the extremity of a limb of a substantial tree'. The researchers assessed the babblers' breeding successes by visiting every territory at roughly eight-week intervals over the entire breeding season to determine whether recently fledged young were present. That meant many long-distance trips from Melbourne to the seventy-two sites. Apart from their smaller size, the newly fledged young could be distinguished from the adults by their dark-brown eyes and begging behaviour – both characteristics they maintain for up to six months or until the adult birds tire of waiting on them.

Along with collecting data about the breeding success of each group, the biologists also recorded information about how many shrubs greater than a metre in height there were, the number of logs larger than 30 centimetres in diameter, how many tree stumps were about, and the number and types of live trees classified into different sizes. The breeding success of individual groups, as indicated by the number of fledglings, and the size of the groups were the two indicators the scientists used to assess the babblers' response to their site. Group size was included as an additional hypothesis to determine whether this was an important predictor of breeding success. Two-thirds of the monitored babbler groups produced fledglings and the team found that group size in a territory was the only variable that had an important influence on their presence. Once a group had seven or more adult birds, the likelihood of fledglings surviving exceeded 90 per cent, evidence of how much helper birds boost breeding success.

The researchers say the results highlight the importance of conservation actions that help increase the size of babbler family groups and boost breeding rates 'for a declining species'. Several management projects subsequently begun in the study areas showed promise of achieving this goal. These involved restoration of the original bush by protecting and maintaining woodland suitable to the babblers, particularly by retaining numerous large old trees.

The biologists also suggested that the total area of wooded land be expanded by revegetation and regeneration, while treed corridors between islands of wooded habitats be increased. Where such work was subsequently carried out, the number of babbler groups either stabilised or increased.

IN AN UNUSUAL coincidence, a month after a report of this study was published a second report concerning the grey-crowned babbler was also published.[3] It was undertaken by six other researchers, four from the University of Melbourne; this time the biologists built on an extensive historical study from the early to mid 1990s by conducting surveys thirteen years later at 117 sites, divided between those where earlier bush restoration works had been undertaken and the rest, where there had been no revegetation. The researchers counted the number of babblers in the social groups in each area and compared these with the numbers that had been found in the first survey in 1995.

The researchers discovered that babbler group size had decreased over the survey period at sites where restoration works had not been carried out but, where it had, this had been effective in stemming population declines. In fact, restoring the babblers' habitat was responsible for adding an additional one bird to a group of three to five babblers. While that might seem insignificant, one additional bird had an important effect in boosting the groups' reproductive success. So while grey-crowned babblers were detected at 58 per cent of the 117 sites in 1995, this had increased to 74 per cent of the sites in 2008. Group sizes during all surveys ranged from one to ten birds, but where restoration works had been carried out there were fewer sites with no birds in 2008, and more groups of larger sizes compared to the sites without restoration.

OTHER STUDIES HAVE found that when native birds learn to survive in cities, they sometimes prosper to an excessive degree: for example, rainbow lorikeets and crows. In yet another investigation into grey-crowned babblers, Dr Kathryn Lambert and colleagues from the University of New England (UNE) discovered that groups of these normally bush-dwelling birds were living and breeding happily in the New South Wales rural city of Dubbo, along with magpies, crows and other birds that had adapted to urban life. Lambert's team found the Dubbo babblers were feeding on lawns and in playgrounds and were even searching for insects in leaf litter along a train track at the back of a housing estate, visiting the backyards along the way. This indicated the birds were sufficiently adaptable to survive outside their woodland habitat – and, as long as they continued to find enough food, were able to disperse between nearby groups and also had access to native nesting trees.[4]

> We found that during one breeding season, one group contained nine birds whereas six years earlier there were seven – suggesting that the babblers were indeed raising chicks, particularly since at least one of them did not have any bands on its legs,

Lambert says.

> These birds remain in a territory and do not move during the breeding season and the only time they do is if individuals disperse to other groups or colonise new areas, but this is rare. The ones in Dubbo have been in the same territory for at least seven years that I know of and were still foraging in the local park and returning to their same nesting area as they were in 2009. The size of this group suggests they are doing well in this habitat, even with a dog park nearby and a sporting oval!

As well as studying the babblers in Dubbo, the researchers also surveyed those in altered remnants of bush 'in natural open forest 19 kilometres east of the centre of Dubbo' and in continuous areas outside the city. Their hypothesis was that if babblers were coping poorly with a city environment and the population was declining, then when compared with babblers living in their natural surrounds they would show an imbalanced sex ratio with an excess of males, small group sizes, few young birds, and low average body weights, or at least the presence of some 'very light individuals'.

The UNE researchers located forty-five babbler groups in the study area, although, because of time constraints, only twelve came under close scrutiny, with four groups living in typical bushland and the other eight in 'altered habitat'. Although the sample size within Dubbo was small, the biologists found no evidence of imbalanced sex ratios, smaller groups, or fewer young birds compared with those in the bush. There was also no indication that groups in and around Dubbo were smaller than those in any other studies where the habitat was continuous.

So how and why had the babblers opted for Dubbo? Lambert suspects they may have been living in the area before the town was built around them:

> Either that or they colonised the city area after some had left a group in the bush nearby. There's one group in an old area where plane hangars have been since the 1940s that are surrounded by native trees. The group may have stemmed from there and formed their own site over time or there may have been other groups too, depending on how the vegetation changed in association with development. Based on the size of the trees, though, I'd say they've colonised the area after the removal of vegetation and housing construction.

THESE THREE PROJECTS are among many that have been undertaken across Australia by committed biologists attempting to turn back the tide of extinction that is sweeping away many animal and plant species. Another earlier and even larger-scale study than the babbler investigations took place in Victoria over three years.[5] The research was conducted across a 1.2 million hectare area of western Victoria and it confirmed the intuitive belief that re-creating a forest ecosystem will attract the creatures that once lived there, and even birds and animals that weren't present before.

After the first Europeans began occupying Victoria in 1835, vast areas of the state were cleared for farms and towns and, eventually, for big cities. Nowhere is this so obvious as in the grazing and wheat farm region of the western district. This was the area that researchers from Deakin University investigated – a region stretching west from the Grampians to the South Australian border, north to Balmoral and south to Portland on the Victorian coast. It was across these sweeping plains that Dr Rohan Clarke, coordinator of the project, spent three years leading researchers in a detailed study of the effects of revegetation on biodiversity.

In this case, the project was financed by the Glenelg Hopkins Catchment Management Authority after the researchers had proposed the study. Rohan Clarke, who has been involved in several of the research projects described in this book, says the catchment authority and farmers in the region have a good history of revegetating cleared land going back decades. So the team had little difficulty finding 120 landholders who gave their approval for their properties to be used as part of the study and where forty-three 'landscapes' of 800 hectares each were selected.

'We started by poring over aerial photographs looking for places that were potentially suitable for our landscapes – particular types that varied between zero and twenty per cent revegetation,' Clarke says. 'Then we went round and knocked on people's doors to get permission to work on their properties.'

Almost all the landholders who agreed were sheep and grain farmers. Clarke says the response was really positive:

> Ecologists and farmers aren't always recognised as seeing eye to eye but the response and dialogue was very encouraging. Some of the areas had been replanted with trees forty to fifty years before and,

in those early days, many were Western Australian flowering gums that farmers had planted to reduce erosion and improve the view. More recently, indigenous trees have been put in with the aim of boosting the region's biodiversity.

Having gained the farmers' permission, the researchers set out to map each landscape. Every patch of trees, whether remnant bush or a revegetated area, and every big solitary paddock tree in the study landscapes, was mapped – a time-consuming task completed on a computer by hand digitising. The forty-three areas of 800 hectares each were mapped to within plus or minus 5 metres of accuracy for all the trees they held and this amounted to thousands of individual plants, with mostly red gums, a feature of the region, being mapped. Each of the forty-three landscapes had a dozen one-hectare survey sites marked out, a total of 516, and each was surveyed four times over the following twelve months.

Birds were systematically counted at the twelve sites in each landscape. At each season, the researchers surveyed all the sites looking for birds, spending fifteen minutes on each site to identify every one they could see and hear in that one hectare. 'The two bird surveyors knew birds really well and identified lots of them by call and by sight,' Clarke says.

> We ended up with a measure of all the birds present on every site in terms of species and number, and we eventually obtained 22,500 bird records – the baseline data we then used to analyse the responses of birds in each clearly defined area.

By surveying so many sites repeatedly, the researchers had an accurate measure of the number and location of the birds and the presence or absence of different species in a particular area over time. A typical scientific study published in a reputable journal might rely on surveys of a hundred sites, whereas the Deakin researchers had five times that number. So they were confident of their results, although the time and effort involved was considerable.

In fact, it took the researchers six months to set out all the sites, another year full-time to survey them all, and a further six months to enter the data in the computer. The findings, however, confirmed the researchers' early hypothesis that if re-planted trees are there in sufficient numbers and not so close as to form thickets, then most of the original bird species will return. Revegetated areas that have a different structure, such as flowering trees, will attract different species. The project proved that revegetation of farm landscapes does benefit wildlife: not only are revegetated sites used by a wide range of species, including birds, mammals, reptiles and butterflies, but revegetation also reverses the loss of native plants.

Of the sixty species dependent on forests or woodlands, forty-eight, or 80 per cent, were recorded in revegetated areas. Clarke says the number of woodland bird species was most strongly influenced by the total amount of wooded cover in the landscape. Also, as the extent of revegetation increased, so did the number of bird species, demonstrating that rural restoration can attract species back into the landscape:

> We were very pleased with the outcomes. It was a huge project but now we have some really nice results and they are certainly a cause for optimism. We also feel we've had a very positive impact in the region by working directly with so many supportive landholders, presenting our findings to hundreds of additional landholders and promoting the value of revegetation.

Biologists involved in large studies such as this have demonstrated how species of birds, mammals, amphibians and insects can be brought back from the brink of extinction by re-creating their original environment, even more so when carried out on a large scale.

Unfortunately for the grey-crowned babbler, they were not among the range of birds that now inhabit this large experimental area in the western district. Clarke says the babblers seem to have disappeared from south-western Victoria sometime before the mid 1980s. The birds may have last been recorded in the Little Desert in 1993 and, on this basis, he says babblers now appear to be extinct across most of western Victoria.

8

A Multicoloured Mob of Angels

They arrive early in the morning, a shouting, kaleidoscopic crowd, as noisy as if all the schoolteachers in the district had sent their classes out to play at the same time. The effervescent flock flits about the tops of the big banksia trees in the backyard, scrambling among the branches to get nectar from the drink can-sized blossoms and bellowing to each other at the tops of their voices.

THE RAINBOW LORIKEET makes more noise in a group than almost any other parrot. It is also one of the most wondrously coloured birds, and its name fits perfectly: the head is a royal blue with a greenish-yellow collar, while the wings, back and tail are an almost luminescent deep green. In sharp contrast, the chest is red with blue-black barring while the belly is deep green, and the thighs and rump are yellow with deep green bars. It is difficult for an observer to distinguish between the sexes, although juveniles have a black beak that gradually brightens to a startling orange as they grow to adulthood.

Unlike so many other species facing population declines or even extinction around the world, the rainbow lorikeet (*Trichoglossus haematodus*) is one of a number of birds that has dramatically expanded

The rainbow lorikeet has expanded its range to cover much of the nation, but in Western Australia it is classed as a pest and shot.

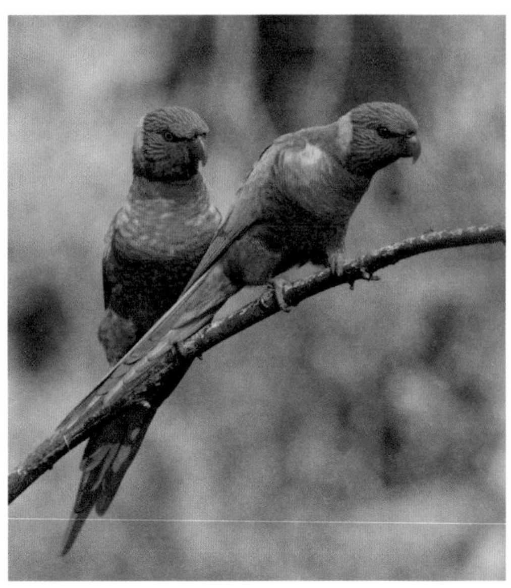

its range across Australia, particularly in the capital cities, where the populations of these small, colourful creatures are growing larger by the day. So much so in Western Australia that the rainbows are classed as a serious pest and tens of thousands have been shot. In Tasmania, the state's invasive species branch is running a control program to try wiping them out while warning the public to be 'on high alert for this species and report all sightings – early detection and rapid response to incursions is vital'.

Intrigued researchers are unravelling the causes of the rainbow lorikeets' mass invasion of much of the continent. Thousands of bird-lovers and the 65,000 supporters of BirdLife Australia are assisting them in their research.

WHEN I FIRST saw rainbow lorikeets en masse I was with my children. We were travelling north from Melbourne late in 1970 and stopped off at the Currumbin Wildlife Sanctuary, just across the New South Wales border in Queensland. The kids were little and they were startled as thousands of these vivid birds gathered in huge noisy flocks in the park's main area. Visitors competed to feed them specially prepared nectar and the birds, to my children's alarm, settled on their heads and arms to consume the liquid. Much the same happened at the Lone Pine Koala Sanctuary when we drove to Brisbane, and again, much later, in Sydney, where semi-tame lorikeets would arrive to be fed on the balcony of a friend's high-rise apartment in Paddington, where we often stayed. I only realised much later that each occasion demonstrated how humans can so enhance the survival prospects of a bird species that its population explodes.

Even in a small group raiding flowering gums, rainbow lorikeets are incredibly noisy – as Brisbane's citizens know only too well. Researchers there have observed roosting flocks of 60,000 or more. They rarely shut up except to sleep: imagine the row a mob that size makes as the birds

Aggressive rainbow lorikeets take over nesting holes and drive other birds away.

wake at first light! Back in Melbourne, there were none of these flashy creatures around my neighbourhood when the children were growing up; now there are hundreds – although where they came from in only a few years was a mystery. The reappearance of rainbow lorikeets is of particular interest to biologists in Melbourne because the birds had disappeared from the city in the 1920s. They are said to have been common when British colonists from Tasmania first crossed Bass Strait in the 1830s, yet, less than a century later, the lorikeets were gone.

The parrots began to return in the 1970s and are now believed to be more abundant in the area than before John Batman landed on the banks of the Yarra River in 1835. Scientists at the Australian Research Centre for Urban Ecology suggest one reason is that these tropical and subtropical birds were attracted by the 'heat island' effect of the city's environs. The skyscrapers, cement footpaths and bitumen on the roads absorb the sun's rays and radiate the day's heat back into the night, keeping the city environment warmer than it has ever been.

Another reason is the plentiful supply of food that the birds love: urban forests of fruit trees and flowering shrubs. Municipal councils have also planted species of eucalypts that provide more food for parrots, as well as other nectar-sipping birds. And then there are the people who feed the parrots, such as the elderly woman who lives not far from me and must spend a small fortune on the trays of birdseed she puts out on shed roofs and posts every day throughout the year. The lorikeets, along with spotted turtle-doves, flock there to line up on her fence and take turns in having their breakfast early in the morning, with return trips to stock up again during the day if they feel the urge. Of course, feeding birds is all very well while the person is alive and continues to supplement their diet, but what happens when she dies or moves elsewhere? If the birds rely on one main supply of food, removing that source can be catastrophic for their feathered dependants.

People's lorikeet-feeding habit has also led to the discovery, despite it being considered highly improbable, that rainbow lorikeets may also be omnivorous. The birds mostly feed on nectar and pollen from eucalypts and other flowering natives, or they follow seasonal blossoms and fruits in home gardens – and they also eat invertebrates. But when one group near Brisbane was spotted feeding on mincemeat a householder had put out, the news shocked Professor Darryl Jones, a Griffith University bird expert. Jones, who has been investigating the impact of backyard feeding on bird populations, knew that lorikeets usually feed on nectar and pollen they obtain from native plants and shrubs, but never mincemeat. As he told the ABC:

> I have researched what birds feed on all around the world. I'm up to date with the kinds of crazy things that birds are eating around Australia – but to see a lorikeet eating meat astonishes me.

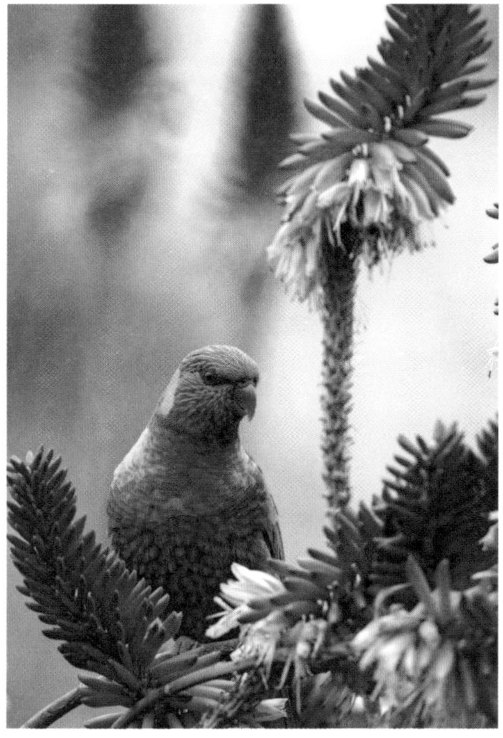

The rainbow lorikeet has invaded home gardens and public parks.

The person providing the lorikeets with minced chicken meat was Bill Watson of Elimbah, a small town north of Brisbane. Watson told reporters he had been feeding chicken mince to wild birds for more than a decade and had only recently discovered the rainbow lorikeets had also joined in. Then in 2015, scaly-breasted lorikeets started taking the food as well, and they were followed by cockatoos – at which point Jones declared he was even more astonished that three species of birds considered herbivores should have changed their diets:

> The move for a bird that normally eats pollen and nectar to eating primarily meat is absolutely extraordinary. In fact, it is of international significance and this has become a truly large and major project we've got here, that could also have all kinds of implications for the birds' health and physiology.

MOST BIRD SPECIES, of course, are unable to cope with urbanisation. Yet a notable few do take advantage of the opportunities provided by anthropogenic, or human-affected, environments. Among them, of course, are the rainbow lorikeets, which now rank among the most abundant birds found in many cities throughout Australia: 'During the evening, the species forms massive communal roosts [in Brisbane], often in remarkably disturbed locations,' Darryl Jones and Savannah Daoud-Pit write in a study they conducted into the lorikeet, investigating 'a series of fourteen roosts ranging in size from a few thousand to 60,000 birds …'[1]

The lorikeets used a wide variety of trees as roosts, although the level of light appeared to be the most important variable, probably because the darker it was, the less chance they would be detected by predators. The biologists' report notes that the growth in the populations of lorikeets has been fuelled largely by the popularity of nectar-bearing trees among home gardeners. This plus the birds' varied diet and the fact they are able to produce up to three broods in a season could be the reasons for the population explosion.

Despite what occurs in the northern sanctuaries and in many home backyards in the east coast capitals, however, BirdLife Australia warns people not to feed the lorikeets. The little creatures can be aggressive and, although they are not yet considered a threat to native birds in Australia's south-east, humans feeding them can only help increase their numbers and boost the danger to their rivals. Certainly the lorikeets' rapid population increases are already a serious problem in many cities, notably to human gardeners and orchard owners.

I discovered this when I found in my own garden in Melbourne, as many fruit orchardists had already, that the cheery rainbow-coloured bird could suddenly become greedy and destructive. Although they had been frequent visitors for years while the banksia trees were in flower, one year for the first time they began nibbling on my ripening figs, apples and nectarines – taking a peck here or there, or consuming half the

A rainbow lorikeet feeding on banksia flowers

fruit before knocking it to the ground. With the fruit now under attack from lorikeets, noisy miners, possums and fruit bats, I had to resort to covering the trees with nets to keep all those unwelcome characters away. My resident little wattlebirds (*Anthochaera chrysoptera)*, the local avian cops, also objected strongly to the presence of these interlopers but could do little when a squadron of the rainbow lorikeets arrived. Any stray lorikeet that wandered away from the flock to try getting nectar from a banksia flower, however, was immediately driven back by a dive-bombing wattlebird.

ANOTHER STUDY INTO the rapid population expansion of lorikeets in Melbourne and its surrounds investigated the influence of road density, tree cover and the season of the year.[2] Through this research it became clear the lorikeets prefer places where roads are not too closely spaced and tree cover is not too sparse. They like bushy surrounds and they also need hollow trees to breed; yet the suburbs of Melbourne have too few of these – only one for every 12 hectares across the entire metropolis. This suggests the birds might be breeding outside the metropolitan area while spending their leisure time in the city. Or, as one wag put it, that 'the city's for hanging out with mates and grabbing something to eat – and the country's for having kids'.

Rainbow lorikeets mature around nine months of age, but most females do not start nesting and laying eggs until they have eighteen months to two years on the clock. In their courtship display, the male approaches the hen stretched to his full height, which is not very high – unless you're another lorikeet. With his neck arched, he bobs his head and hops along the branch while emitting a low whistle. Surprisingly, the bird's pupils constantly dilate and contract during this procedure – although how intrigued the female is by this flirting depends on how near to nesting she is and, no doubt, how attractive she finds the display and the pupil dilation.

The lorikeet's breeding season may last from August to January the following year, with nesting occurring once or twice or even three times over the season. The late Gordon Beruldsen's description of the rainbow lorikeet in *Australian Birds Their Nests and Eggs* states that the birds prefer an unlined hollow for their nest, a knot hole or broken-off dead spout in a large tree 25 metres or more above the ground. While both sexes prepare the nest cavity and feed the young, only the female incubates the two round white eggs she lays on wood-dust. But this, of course, is dependent on the lorikeets finding an appropriate home – a crucial issue given the continuing decline in the number of trees with hollows in urban habitats as Australia's cities expand ever outwards.

To determine the distribution and type of tree-hollows in Sydney, a team of three biologists surveyed 264 sites. As they expected, the number of hollows and hollow-bearing trees varied significantly, with all urban habitats having far fewer trees with hollows than did continuous forest or remnants of former forest. But visits by rainbow lorikeets, sulphur-crested cockatoos (*Cacatua galerita*) and Australian king parrots (*Alisterus scapularis*) were each significantly associated with different hollows, most importantly the shape, its orientation and the type of tree. As the researchers say in their report:

> Knowledge of the distribution of hollow-bearing trees throughout landscapes, as well as the characteristics of hollows that are associated with particular species of parrot, is crucial to conserve populations of hollow-dependent bird species in urban areas.[3]

AS WELL AS their (accidental) introduction to Perth and its surrounds, rainbow lorikeets have also been released in Auckland in New Zealand,

Amsterdam in the Netherlands and even Hong Kong. What happened with the birds in Perth, however, should serve as a cautionary tale: some lorikeets were mistakenly freed south-west of the city in the 1960s by staff at the University of Western Australia and they became well established within twenty years. Then their population exploded and, as the impact of the birds on the environment became increasingly obvious, it was not long before the authorities classed them as an avian pest. They also took deadly action to curb their numbers – as also happened in New Zealand, where the conservation department initially tried to control and then finally started to eradicate them.

A major impact of the little parrot in Western Australia is the way it competes with indigenous bird species, dominating their sources of food and fighting over increasingly scarce nesting hollows. Biologists report that other birds, such as the purple-crowned lorikeet and Carnaby's black cockatoo, have been adversely affected and even displaced from their own territories – a disaster for the endangered Carnaby's cockatoo. This displacement also occurs to victims of the noisy miner – another example of a bird that will often violently drive other species out of their usual habitats.

The lives of birds can sometimes resemble a war zone where fights occur within and between different species throughout the day. Watching from my study window, I see constant interactions and sometimes outright conflict between the different birds that inhabit the area around the house as one species defends its territory or food sources against intruders, including members of its own kind from other territories.

A report on BirdLife Australia's webpage discussing the rainbow lorikeets of Perth notes that the birds had become established in the late 1960s and by the 1980s the population was expanding beyond the city:

> The problem with these lorikeets is that they are aggressive around nesting hollows, preventing native birds from nesting. They have even been recorded dragging the nestlings of Australian Ringnecks

from hollows and dropping them onto the ground, then occupying the hollow themselves.

Researchers at Perth's Murdoch University are reconstructing the routes of invasion and exploring ways of managing rainbow lorikeets as well as another pest parrot species, the little corella (*Cacatua sanguinea*). Dr Peter Spencer, who heads the wildlife DNA laboratory in Murdoch's school of biological sciences, says the lorikeets have become an increasing issue for the general public and the horticulture industry in and around the metropolitan area:

> They are a major pest in causing damage to horticulture … and they create nuisance noise, [and] damage to backyard fruit crops, fouling goods with their droppings and competing with other species.

He adds that the birds have created strongholds in Perth's established western suburbs, often where date and cotton palms occur, as well as communal roosts in mature Norfolk Island pines in suburbs such as Cottesloe, while exotic flowering eucalypts seem to play an important role in their increasing numbers.

Biologists investigating the destructive impact of troublemaking pest birds usually have serious reservations about publicly releasing details when any culling takes place because they fear an outcry. Not in Western Australia, though, where the Department of Agriculture happily warned the public in 2011 that shooting the lorikeets would help reduce the damage and losses the birds were causing to fruitgrowers. Admittedly, the department did join with the Department of Environment and Conservation in publishing a rainbow lorikeet management strategy – a plan whose main objective was to slash the birds' numbers in rural areas via 'controlled shoots' and to try restricting them to metropolitan Perth.

When large flocks at Perth's airport were claimed to pose an 'air threat' to planes arriving and departing, seven thousand birds were killed near the site while departmental officers and grape-grower groups shot another 33,000 in the Swan Valley and outer metropolitan areas. News of a slaughter of birds on that scale would have generated public marches and outrage in Melbourne and other cities, but a departmental spokesman in Perth merely observed that 'due to our research, we now have the knowledge and methodology to manage the pest – and the cost of managing each bird has now been halved'.

The birds are now subject to an Acclimatised Fauna Notice in Western Australia's south-west land division under legislation administered by the Department of Parks and Wildlife. This means, according to the department's website, that they can be shot or live-trapped on private land 'in accordance with an open season notice, without the need to obtain a damage licence from the department'.

Given the size of the current lorikeet population in Perth, the department admits that eradication is unlikely. But it also says,

> a reduction in the numbers at key locations may be possible [while] to do nothing will lead to further damage from a spreading population, more complaints and even less chance of managing the problem in the future.

And it adds this grim comment:

> To prevent satellite populations becoming established in the wild, small groups of lorikeets originating from escaped or released birds have been retrieved or removed from many country locations. It is also essential that any lorikeets in the wild outside the existing Perth range be immediately reported so they can be safely retrieved or removed …

DESPITE THE ATTEMPTS at eliminating the species out west, the spread of rainbow lorikeets elsewhere around Australia continues. Early in 2014, a woman in Mildura spotted two of the birds snacking on seeds from a birdfeeder in her backyard. A few days later they were back, bringing another couple with them, adding to the spotter's surprise because it was the first time she had seen the colourful creatures in the Murray River city – and she had lived there all her life. Birdwatchers believe massive bushfires that had raged through Victoria's Grampians National Park in January 2006 not only had an enormous impact on the park's rich flora and fauna but had also forced some of its animals to find refuge in other places. For birds, that meant flying long distances to locate new sources of food – apparently even as far as Mildura, nearly 600 kilometres away.

On 4 January 2014, under the dramatic headline 'Ticking time bomb: Rainbow lorikeets pose threat to fruit industries', the *Sunraysia Daily*, Mildura's local newspaper, reported that until the first lorikeets were seen in the city, the nearest population of the species was a colony nearly 200 kilometres away in Hopetoun, 'probably established by aviary escapees'. Writes the paper's Mildura reporter, Graeme O'Neil:

> The 2006 conflagration in the Grampians raged for more than a week, devastating the entire eastern half of the park, including more than 50 per cent of the park's eucalypt woodlands. With their preferred food trees decimated, the park's several lorikeet species went looking for nectar further afield.

Musk lorikeets left the Grampians in huge flocks and descended on orchards around Harcourt, south-east of Bendigo, causing millions of dollars' worth of damage to the ripening fuji and pink lady apple crops. Rainbow lorikeets appear to have also dispersed and some seem to have found their way to Mildura, where their numbers are on the rise.

VARIOUS COLOURED FORMS of the rainbow lorikeet occur naturally in south and east Indonesia, New Guinea, the Solomon Islands, Vanuatu, New Caledonia and, originally, in the north and east of Australia, where they roost and then take off at dawn. They form foraging flocks of up to fifty birds that can travel more than 50 kilometres to feeding sites, flying high, rarely going to ground, and spending most of their time in the outer foliage of trees. Some thirty species of lorikeet are found around the southern Pacific Ocean spread across the various islands and in Papua New Guinea and Indonesia while seven species or subspecies live in this country – the rainbow lorikeet, red-collared lorikeet, scaly-breasted lorikeet, musk lorikeet, purple-crowned lorikeet, little lorikeet and varied lorikeet.

Most of these species are not troublesome to humans except the rainbow lorikeet, which has become a major agricultural pest in the Northern Territory, Queensland, the fruit-growing regions of the Adelaide Hills in South Australia and, more recently, the south of Western Australia.

In other words, one of Australia's most startlingly beautiful small birds has become a distinctly unpopular invader out west and up north. Not so much a multi-coloured mob of angels as a kaleidoscopic bunch of little devils: 'Rainbow lorikeets think the world is theirs for the taking,' writes Ann Lanagan, describing her own feelings about the birds and Australian politicians in a sharp commentary published in *The Age*'s letter pages: 'They sit up in the gum trees, shrieking their heads off, ripping blossoms from the branches and chucking them on the ground. Rather like parliament really …'

9

The East Coast Mafia: Masked and Dangerous

More than a million square kilometres of eastern Australia have been invaded by criminals. The bandits wear black masks over their eyes, foreheads and chins, and they operate in gangs that are having a devastating impact on other species – and on the environment. The criminals are so destructive that calls have been made for drastic action, including shooting the evildoers before they cause even more damage ...

THEY SOUND LIKE human thugs but these are violent birds: noisy miners, easily identified by their bright-yellow bills and legs, and pale-grey back and white belly. This fierce fighter, classified under the mild description of 'honeyeater', is one of the few native birds to have become serious pests across the entire eastern half of Australia, worse than even those pesky rainbow lorikeets in Western Australia. These avian blackguards are not called noisy miners for nothing: their raucous cries of '*week*, *week*, *week*' and scolding can go on for much of the day, especially when a group is driving off other birds from its territory, as has been happening across the woodlands of southern and eastern Australia.

In a study outlined in more detail later in this chapter, biologists describe how some regions have become controlled by 'this single hyper-aggressive native bird … which have excluded at least 80 per cent of small bird species from otherwise suitable habitats'.[1] The biologists refer to the miner as a 'reverse keystone' species, aggressively excluding almost all small-bodied birds from its territories, with a serious impact on the composition and diversity of entire groups of birds. This forced evacuation results in a shift from a wide range of birds with varying foraging strategies to a homogenised one dominated by large-bodied and ground-feeding species with a high proportion of avian predators.

The noisy miner's widening distribution and destructive effect on other birds is a product of what the biologists call their 'positive response to anthropogenic landscape change'. That is, human changes to the landscape have enabled the birds to occupy increasing areas of what used to be the well-treed Australian bush with diverse plant and animal life. The aggressive birds' expanding takeover of the bush, plus their impact on other bird species, is a potent combination, 'potentially leading to widespread and pervasive ecological effects', say the scientists. The options for managing noisy miners, however, differ between regions and vegetation types: in some areas, restoring the original 'structural complexity' of the landscape may make the habitat less suitable for noisy miners and, over time, force them away while allowing small birds to re-colonise their former homes. Then again, shooting the noisy miners has been rated as 'relatively low-cost, quickly effective, and long-lasting' – a deadly solution adopted by Western Australian authorities to control that other avian pest, rainbow lorikeets.

On my own bush block, with its large banksias, tea trees and a range of flowering plants, I am similarly facing ongoing battles with intruding noisy miners. The dominant avian species on my land on Melbourne's Port Phillip Bay are wattlebirds, notably the little wattlebird (*Anthochaera chrysoptera*), which is actually a medium to large honey-eater and itself an aggressor with smaller species. I knew noisy miners were about because I could see and hear a colony that congregated near a local primary school where there are open sportsgrounds surrounded by bush. But the birds rarely appeared in my backyard, until one day a small number arrived and began to make themselves comfortable. I did my best to drive them off but it seemed an invasion had begun. I was shocked one morning to discover the wretched birds were breeding on my block: there were parents and cheeping offspring demanding to be fed.

My efforts to make the place unpleasant for the birds by throwing sticks at them and shooing them away were not having much success when it seemed the wattlebirds had also tired of the intruders' bossy ways. They began to retaliate – attacking individuals or pairs of miners – and forcing them to flee. My local avian police seem to have stopped a wholesale invasion, and although the miners still return to wash and drink at the birdbath and feed off the banksias, they rarely escape the attention of the aggressive wattlebirds.

Unfortunately, as Professor Michael Clarke says, what happened at my place is exactly what noisy miners are doing in the suburbs across Australia and out in the bush, where they attack resident birds with intimidating numbers of up to two hundred. With large-scale clearing for farming having eliminated up to 90 per cent of Australia's original temperate woodlands, the disappearance of the bush has led to a population explosion of noisy miners. The birds now occupy huge tracts of rural land along the eastern seaboard – as well, of course, as in the gardens of increasing numbers of suburban homes. As Clarke says:

> We've basically created tens of thousands of hectares of ideal miner habitats. We've delivered it to them on a platter and they just do what they've always done – and that is take over. They have become the mafia of the east-coast bird world by relentlessly attacking intruders in their territory and they even tackle much larger birds such as kookaburras and herons which can't ward off their massed attacks.

> Australians must now wrestle with the philosophical challenge of accepting that a native species could be a pest and that something has to be done. To do nothing is to drive other native species to extinction.

Clarke is a professor of zoology and head of the school of life sciences at La Trobe University in Melbourne, where he has an ongoing research interest in threatened species. With fellow La Trobe researchers, Clarke spent more than a decade observing noisy miners and counting their numbers across eastern Australia. He says the miner is one of the few native species to have had a serious impact on large areas of bushland, while their effects on other birds are so severe that controlling their numbers through habitat modification and culling have to be considered. It is not just that noisy miners drive other native birds away from leafy suburban areas and eucalypt woodlands, but that they also upset the balance between the plants, insects and other fauna. After replacing their insect-eating competitors, the invading miners do not eat the same range or numbers of the little invertebrates, which can ultimately cause trees to die from insect damage. In turn, this can lead to the loss of whole woodland communities – and ultimately the end of the miners themselves in the areas they helped to destroy.

Some species of birds have already become rare or endangered because of the noisy miners' actions, with insect-eaters such as the hooded robin and jacky winter disappearing from forests while others, including the grey-crowned babbler and regent honeyeater, are in serious decline. Even on La Trobe's expansive Bundoora campus in the north of Melbourne, noisy miner birds have taken over car parks and wooded areas – resulting in the forced exodus of other local native birds.

Typically between twenty and 200 miners will colonise a territory of up to 10 hectares, where they operate as 'team-based collectives' based on families with breeding pairs helped by non-breeding, closely related males. The noisy miner is one of four species of native Australian miner, which are different again from the exotic common myna that was brought to Australia from India and southern China. Sometimes called 'flying rats', the common mynas are also increasing their range and they have likewise become serious pests in many urban and some rural areas. Before the noisy miners arrived around my home, common mynas were everywhere; since the noisy miners turned up and their numbers increased, the mynas have mostly disappeared.

Clarke's research into the noisy miner followed an investigation in the mid 1990s by one of his PhD students, Merilyn Grey, on the effects of removing noisy miners from habitats near Benalla and Violet Town in central Victoria. Many of the birds were captured in nets and killed painlessly by gas – an issue the researchers preferred not to discuss publicly because of the outcry whenever there is talk of culling native animals or birds. Clarke's private response, however, was this:

> Our reluctance to acknowledge that native species can become pests shows how easily we confuse concern for the welfare of an individual animal with conservation. They are not necessarily the same thing; conservation has broader goals of preserving whole populations, species, communities and ecosystems. And sometimes this involves making hard choices that have serious implications for individual animals. We need to appreciate that to do nothing could potentially affect the survival of entire species and ecological communities.

As Grey's study revealed, eliminating most of the miners from an area allowed other species to move back almost immediately. Because the noisy miners that were left did not have large numbers on their side, they were forced to cohabit with the other species. Like most bullies, they stopped their attacks when they found themselves in a minority. The influx of different bird species led to a reduction in tree damage as the newcomers resumed their consumption of leaf-eating insects. At the time of our first interview in 2008, Clarke and his team of researchers had spent the previous three years identifying the habitat characteristics of twenty-eight sites in Victoria where noisy miner colonies lived on the edges of large forest or woodland remnants. With a $180,000 Australian Research Council grant, he set out to discover how far into the bush the birds penetrated – it typically ranged from 150 to more than 300 metres – and how the miner populations varied according to soil fertility.

Not surprisingly, the more fertile the soil (thus the more reliable the eucalypts' nectar production), the greater the number of miners; access to a constant supply of food is important for a sedentary species like the miner. The trouble is that the miners occupy the most fertile parts of a landscape, which are also the areas other birds would have liked to exploit. So they end up monopolising 'the best bits of real estate', as Clarke puts it. The research has implications for revegetation methods and the way bush corridors are being created across Australia to link woodland areas that have become separate islands in an open landscape. The corridors are critically important for animals less mobile than birds, such as reptiles, amphibians and marsupials, to move from one area of bush to another without being attacked by predators. But corridors that are too narrow can lead to the miners dominating them entirely, so the emphasis needs to be on enlarging corridor plantings and extending them so they are wide enough to create miner-free habitats.

Clarke also investigated what other environmental aspects were attractive or unattractive to noisy miners. What could be used to drive them off an overcrowded territory? Part of his research involved studying relatively rare sites for miners, such as the Barmah Forest on the Murray River near Echuca and other areas in northern Victoria, as well as in Gippsland, where noisy miners live but are rarely the dominant species. Another hypothesis he confirmed was that it was only by arriving in loose flocks that other species such as musk lorikeets could infiltrate the noisy miners' defences and gain access to the resources in their territories. Any incoming species has to have sufficient numbers itself to gain a foothold in miner territory – yet many would-be intruders lack numbers because the loss of their previous habitats has led to population declines.

While Clarke's research was focused more on Australia's south-east region, another group of Queensland biologists were studying the effect of noisy miners on the savanna woodlands of north-eastern Australia.[2] The researchers knew that an overabundant native species could have a significant cascading effect on other wildlife, resulting in a sharp drop in numbers of other bird species. The tropical savannas of northern Australia consist of largely unmodified woodlands, and two species of *Manorina* occur naturally in this region – the noisy miner and the yellow-throated miner (*Manorina flavigula*).

To find out the effect of these species on bird numbers and variety, the biologists used data collected from bird surveys at 511 sites across northern Queensland involving 179 noisy miner sites and 332 yellow-throated miner sites between 1998 and 2010. They found that 'Forty-five [bird] species varied significantly in abundance with increasing miner numbers, while the overall effect of yellow-throated miners on other birds seemed even more pronounced.'

As Clarke and his colleagues had found, the Queensland team also discovered that the actions of people on the landscape were an equal or even more important predictor of the range and numbers of the nuisance birds. The researchers concluded that despite the superficially intact nature of northern Australian woodlands, the spread of open pastures and poor land management was creating conditions for increasing numbers of noisy miners, compounding their negative impact.

THEN AGAIN, NOISY and yellow-throated miners aren't the only birds to exert a harmful impact on their own environment. The Gondwana Rainforests World Heritage Area in northern New South Wales is also suffering from the dominance of another miner – a species of honeyeater commonly called the bellbird or, more correctly, the bell miner (*Manorina melanophrys*). When fuelled by sugar, this little songster behaves so aggressively in defending its food source that it could be said to love the forest to death. The tinkling sound of the bell miner might be attractive to the ears of human visitors, but if the birds are calling constantly from dawn to dusk every hour of every day throughout the year, as they do, this creates a wall of sound that drives other birds away. In contrast with the mass attacks by noisy miners, this small melodious creature uses its voice, multiplied numerous times by others, to warn any intruders: 'Stay out! This forest is already occupied!'

The problem the bell miners cause is that they covet a sugary substance called lerp, which is created by a minute sap-sucking insect called a psyllid. The bell miners effectively farm the insects by removing just the lerp, thereby stimulating the psyllid to make more. When all the smaller birds that eat the sap-sucking insects are kept away, however,

The bell miner uses a 'wall of sound' to drive off intruders but could end up destroying its own habitat.

the psyllid numbers build up, weakening the trees' defences, and the trees start to die from the top in a process called dieback.

In a seven-year project to study the effect of bell miners on their environment, four researchers from the UNE explored the role that lantana, an invasive neotropical shrub, played in the rise in bell miner numbers. Once established, the lantana provides a dense understorey that the miners use for nesting. The birds rely on it to breed and aggressively exclude all smaller and similar-sized birds from their colonies, thereby reducing avian diversity. The researchers monitored the impact of removing the lantana on miner numbers in several sites.[3] The lantana was kept under control for seven years at the test sites, with regeneration of other native plants at the understorey, midstorey and canopy levels replacing the loss of the lantana. The bell miners eventually vacated one of the treated plots but persisted in the control plots and the other treated plots.

The researchers found that the miners' response was correlated with the differing structure of the forest: the birds left the forested area at the first site where a sparse understorey of shrubs less than 5 metres high had been created while retaining a dense midstorey of up to 15 metres and a canopy even higher. The bell miners stayed on, however, at the sites with a dense understorey but a sparse midstorey and canopy. The UNE researchers conclude:

> We therefore predict that forest restoration that simultaneously reduces lantana under-storey and increases mid-storey density will be most successful in reducing the abundance of the despotic bell miner and increasing avian diversity in rehabilitated sites.

Commenting on these outcomes, lead author Kathryn Lambert, a UNE research associate whose work on grey-crowned babblers moving into the city of Dubbo is described in chapter 7, notes that noisy miners and bell miners both live naturally in forested ecosystems.[4] They do not take over habitats in undisturbed wild areas and instead exist in balance with the plants and other birds. Human disturbance of forests has tipped the scales in the favour of both species of miner.

> The bell miner and the noisy miner are becoming 'winners' in this case, while specialist species like the Regent honeyeaters which rely on nectar-producing eucalypts, are becoming 'losers'. All of these changes have actually been caused by people. We have removed and changed the habitat to a huge extent, and some bird species have benefited greatly while others have suffered,

Lambert says.

> So, if we are the culprits, what can we do? By planting more native plants in our gardens we can encourage other bird species and make it less likely they will be chased away by dominating species. If everyone did this, it would create entire landscapes where bird communities were much more healthy and diverse.

MEANWHILE, HOMEOWNERS AND gardeners in the towns and cities are unwittingly contributing to the rowdy bird's population explosion. By planting native trees and nectar-producing shrubs with eucalypts surrounded by lawns, we have created perfect places for the noisy miner to set up house. Clarke says we might have to change our gardens so they no longer have lawns abutted by eucalypts, so as to make them less reliable sources of food attractive to miners: 'If we moved away from nectar-rich plants and to more dense and prickly native shrubs, we might also be able to create some refuges for the smaller native birds.'

Or, as Lambert says, home gardeners should create a multilayered habitat of ground covers, small and medium shrubs, and trees that

The hyper-aggressive noisy miner uses massed attacks to drive off competitors.

Home gardeners are creating ideal conditions for the bossy noisy miner.

provide food and shelter locations all year round for a variety of species. The plants should be diverse, be close together to form dense, protective thickets, and include climbers within medium-to-tall shrubs and trees, along with nectar-bearing and seed-bearing plants: 'Even in gardens where noisy miners dominate, smaller birds can survive in a dense understorey,' she says. 'Lawns can also be replaced with native grasses that produce seed to attract finches and other seed-eaters such as crimson rosellas.'

For his part, Clarke admits that Victoria and New South Wales are facing major challenges – although it is hardly the noisy miner's fault that they are taking advantage of the changes caused by the humans:

> At the same time, we can't stand aside and allow a whole range of bushland birds to disappear that were abundant in this state before Europeans arrived. I don't think that's an option.

The results of Clarke's investigations into the noisy miner were recorded as the first outcome of a project that was an unusually complex and time-consuming collaboration between fifteen researchers.[5] Headed by Martine Maron, an ecologist and associate professor at the University of Queensland, the team considered the factors affecting noisy miner sites and their effects at the ecosystem level.

This involved compiling a massive amount of data that had been collected about the birds by various research groups across a vast area of eastern Australia. In fact, the number of sites studied by different groups totalled an astonishing 50,000 in thirty-seven bioregions. Maron's team then used these findings to develop and test theoretical models of noisy miner occupancy, hoping this would lead to new management tools. They tested the models using data from the multiple studies across eastern Australia to determine whether and where noisy miner numbers were increasing. They devised recommendations on where action to control the impacts of the birds was necessary, and, finally, decided which approaches were likely to be most cost effective. The review and analyses confirmed that the noisy miner had been given a mighty boost as a result of humans demolishing and fragmenting natural habitats across the country, along with other changes that made it easier for the birds to detect and intercept potential competitors.

The biologists identified a strong link between the noisy miner and the 'depressed richness and abundance of smaller birds', particularly those that fed on nectar and ate insects. There was also evidence of a decline in the condition of trees because small birds were no longer there to reduce the populations of attacking insects, while the spread of different plants was affected by altered pollination and seed dispersal. The analysis revealed that the birds had become increasingly prevalent in nine bioregions, although they tended to keep to sites close to the edges of forest and woodland. The biologists outline options for managing noisy miner numbers, although these differ between regions and vegetation types.[6] In some areas, restoring plant complexity could make the habitats less attractive to noisy miners and, over time, allow recolonisation by small birds, as research on bell miners had shown. But, there was also evidence that direct control by simply shooting the miners could be relatively low-cost, quickly effective, and long-lasting – as the Western Australians had discovered in their battles with the lorikeets. The biologists add, however, that such action should only be taken where miners are causing severe ecological problems and there is a reasonable chance of the small birds that had been driven out returning to their former homes.

The miners now face a dire threat: the scientists called for the species to be nominated for 'aggressive action' under the *NSW Threatened Species Conservation Act*, and for 'aggressive exclusion of birds from potential woodland and forest habitat' under federal legislation. Government committees at the state and federal level have supported the proposals and, as these are accepted, the noisy miners are likely to be in for a lethal shock.

10

Magpies: Mozarts of the Bush

One

Along the road the magpies walk
with hands in pockets, left and right.
They tilt their heads, and stroll and talk.
In their well-fitted black and white.

They look like certain gentlemen
who seem most nonchalant and wise
until their meal is served – and then
what clashing beaks, what greedy eyes!

Excerpt from 'Magpies' in *Collected Poems* by Judith Wright

One of Australia's most loved native birds is still commonly seen in cities and towns across the nation. Yet BirdLife Australia's major report, The State of Australia's Birds, *shows magpie numbers have been falling sharply along the east coast since 1998. This chapter, however, focuses on a particular area in country Victoria where the magpie population appears to be remaining steady or even increasing. That's according to dedicated researchers who have been monitoring them for more than twenty years – with surprising results …*

THE FIGHTING IS as bad as anything seen in Afghanistan or the Middle East. Along the 14 kilometres of bush track, spectacular aerial battles and fierce confrontations on the ground occur between the warring factions. Lives are lost, many of the participants suffer severe injuries, but still the conflict continues. And, unlike some battles, here it seems destined to go on forever.

Watching the struggle in the sky, Jane Hughes lowers her high-powered telescope. 'These are some of the most territorial creatures on Earth,' she says.

> They use cooperative defence strategies to carve out and maintain a permanent, year-round territory that is essential to them for breeding. Every member of the group – male or female, young or old – takes part in attacking intruders and that can include singing, aggressive posturing – or fighting battles.

Young Australian magpies at play, learning to fight their future enemies

The way Hughes describes the bird, it sounds more like a fighter pilot – a kind of Biggles of the bush. At dawn and at dusk, flocks of the birds swoop and dive on each other. In a dive they resemble V-2 rockets and, with beaks that make a dagger seem blunt, they are just about as dangerous. Sometimes, a group will fight it out on the ground – wrestling and trying to peck their enemies' eyes out or choke them to death. But hang on – we are talking about magpies here, those melodious creatures whose gurgling call sounds as if Mozart had heard water running down a plughole and set it to music. To many Australians, the magpie is the country's most charming bird – intelligent, as anyone who has looked into their bright brown eyes can tell, and long-lived. Strutting about on the grass, the magpie could be a model for a frock-coated maître d'. But a belligerent, battle-scarred warrior?

Sitting in the car that acts as a hide for Hughes and her research assistants, watching a family of magpies in a setting as tranquil as a painting of a sleeping possum, the idea that any one of these birds could be a Mad Max warrior seems surreal. In front of us, a small stream meanders across the paddock and around it are majestic examples of

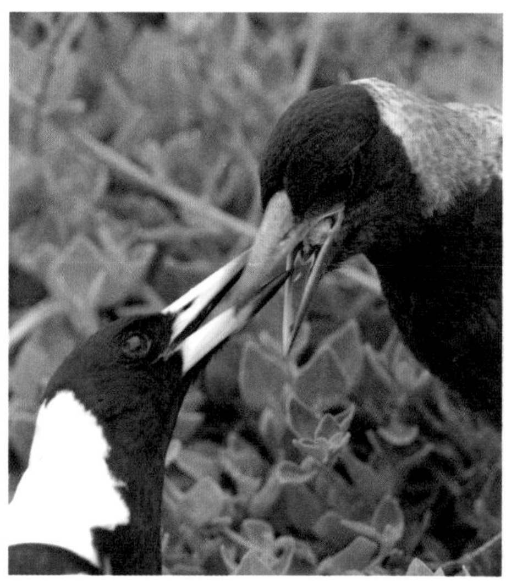

A magpie dad disgorges dinner for junior.

river red gums – old man trees with mighty trunks and great spreading branches. Five or six magpies are on the ground or in the air; most appear to be taking turns feeding babies in a couple of nests high in the trees. These branch-based bassinets are untidy affairs, a bundle of sticks shoved together as if someone had planned to start a fire aloft. Hughes has the eyes of a hawk and seems able to tell, even without telescope or binoculars, the colours of each bird's leg band: 'That's a male we must have caught in 1992 but he's lost the green band,' she murmurs to Nick Cilento, one of the research assistants. 'Did you see him feed the chick? Oh look: orange-yellow-white went all submissive when the big male flew in ...'

I FIRST SPENT some time with Professor Jane Hughes in 1996 while she was studying magpies outside Seymour in central Victoria. She was working with three postgraduate assistants from Griffith University in Brisbane. Over the previous four years, they had been capturing, taking blood samples from and banding almost all the magpies living in the seventy or so territories that by then had been carefully mapped along 10 kilometres of a rough bush track. As Hughes explains:

> To band them, the young are caught about a month after they fledge in a trap that their parents are familiar with because we put in grated cheese which they love. We leave the traps open most of the time so the birds can go in and out freely, and only close both ends when we want to catch a fledgling.

The young birds are banded with numbered stainless steel bands supplied by the Australian Bird and Bat Banding Authority and each has its own individual number. But, as Hughes points out, this isn't much use to researchers looking through a telescope, so the team also puts on

The back colour of a magpie varies according to its subspecies. In southern Victoria, the male of one subspecies has a white back and the female pale grey. Elsewhere, males and females have a black saddle on the back.

powder-coated coloured bands to enable each bird to be identified from a distance. The colour on the left leg tells the year the bird was banded, and the combination on the right leg identifies the individual bird. Each has three coloured bands on the right leg, and no two birds have the same combination in the same order from top to bottom. At the time I made my first journey to the site, some 600 magpies had been identified and banded, making the study area not only unique but also an ornithologist's dream. After occasional email contacts over the following years, I made another visit in early 2011 to see the magpie enthusiasts at work again on the Seymour site.

Hughes has a chortling laugh and an infectious enthusiasm that no doubt explain why her graduate students down the years were happy to join her and spend weeks watching magpies for hours on end. By 2011 the researcher was still making regular trips to the area, but had cut them back to twice yearly. By then she and her team had also accumulated records of 2100 magpies. With one of the two teams at a starting point along the track and the second at the other end, the watchers spent twenty minutes at each territory, trying to identify all the birds, before moving on to the next, where the observations are repeated. Over the ten days, they observe each of the territories at least three times and, while it might seem a pleasant way to do research, it is not the most exciting, even with Hughes' ever-present enthusiasm. It is also laborious: the researchers must be up before dawn to watch for territorial displays and, later in the year, to set out the traps to catch young birds that have not been banded. They take a break for morning tea and at lunchtime, but are back later in the afternoon and keep working until nightfall. Every three days, in the evening, all the results must be fed into a computer.

As a result of what had become one of the longest scientific investigations of its kind in Australasia, the team uncovered startling new information about the magpie's life cycle, its territorial behaviour, its wonderful carolling songs and the significance of the colour of the feathers on its back. The latter was an important aspect of the Victorian research because the area is in a 'hybrid zone' where birds of different back colours live side by side. Magpies in the north and south-eastern regions, and in the western parts of Australia, have different back colours and were once thought to be separate species, but each is now known to be a subspecies. In southern Victoria, males of one subspecies have pure white backs and the females' are pale grey. Along the remaining eastern mainland, the sexes of the two other subspecies differ from each other only in minor ways: both sexes have a black saddle across the back, the only difference between them being that males have white napes and females pale-grey napes.

ONE UNEXPECTED DISCOVERY of the Hughes research concerns a previously unknown fact about sex among the magpies: despite being lifelong partners in rearing their young and defending their territory, adults of both genders are liable to sneak off and copulate with other magpies when the partner is away or not watching. 'Genetic analysis, *CSI*-style, shows magpies are extremely promiscuous,' Hughes says.

> Although they live in highly territorial groups which they fiercely defend, many of the young birds born in a territory are fathered by males from outside. The extent of this promiscuity seems to differ between magpies in different parts of their distribution – West Australian magpies being the worst so far! But there are also variations within a population with some females always mating with their social partner and others never doing so.

In the Western Australia study,[1] Hughes found that more than 80 per cent of the fledgling magpies born in a territory one year were sired by males from outside the home base. It seems that despite living in a long-term partnership with her male mate, the female was taking off before dawn or at night to have a fling with someone else's mate. The finding meant that few of the chicks within a territory were sired by the social partner of the female, but there was also startling evidence that about one in every ten juveniles was not the genetic offspring of any female within a particular territory. The implication here is that some females take a leaf from the cuckoo's book and sneak in and lay their eggs in the nest of a bird from another territory! As Hughes notes:

> Taken together, these findings are remarkable considering the highly territorial nature of the species and the extent of territorial defence practised by all members of a group towards birds from outside during daylight hours … In long-lived sedentary species, a very low rate of territory turnover may reduce the chance of independent breeding for young birds and promote the existence of family groups.

> In such species, mating outside the group is a way of avoiding high levels of mating among close relatives.

Promiscuity on this scale serves as a way of avoiding inbreeding and the attendant rise in birth defects. Magpies are not alone in this. Many other birds are also promiscuous – notably, red-backed fairy-wrens, which have been called 'the least faithful birds in the world'. The discovery of such promiscuity among magpies, however, would not have come as a surprise to David P. Barash, an American professor of psychology at the University of Washington. He published a book in 2001called *The Myth of Monogamy*, in which he notes that biologists had long accepted monogamy as being rare in mammals whereas birds were mistakenly taken as 'the poster children for monogamous fidelity'.[2] In fact, a renowned British evolutionary biologist called David Lack had even declared in the 1960s that 92 per cent of the nearly 10,000 bird species then known were monogamous.

Later studies by other biologists, however, proved how wrong Lack was. With the advent of DNA testing, an avalanche of research findings revealed that the proportion of nestlings not fathered by their social male parent was sometimes as high as 40 per cent. By the 1990s such revelations had reached a point where, as Barash says, cases in which a 'monogamous species' proved to be truly monogamous were the notable ones. This led to the occasional appearance of reassuring accounts in scientific journals with titles such as 'DNA fingerprinting reveals low incidence of extra-pair fertilisations in the Lesser Kestrel ...'

In investigating why so many species of permanently partnered birds are highly promiscuous, Barash has concluded that the pay-off appears to be indirect, via genetic benefits accruing to the 'out-of-wedlock' offspring:

> By mating with males who are especially fit or who possess secondary sexual traits that are particularly appealing to other females,

would-be mothers can apparently increase the fitness as well as the eventual sexual attractiveness of their offspring.

JANE HUGHES AND her team began exploring this issue in depth during their studies along the hybrid zone, a narrow region about 100 kilometres wide stretching from central Victoria across into South Australia. Here, white-backed and black-backed magpies have produced intermediate forms of black-and-white backed offspring, with the intermediates having varying widths of the black saddle on their backs. The magpies inhabiting the zone live in permanent territorial groups that range in size from three to fifteen birds, with a group usually consisting of a dominant male and female and subordinate adults and juveniles that have fledged in previous years within the territory. New birds also occasionally join a territory as helpers.

From one to five female birds will then build separate nests within a territory, although the dominant female is the first to nest each year. The top male will feed his nesting partner (the top female) while other members of the group feed the nestlings and fledglings. Nestlings are sometimes fed by multiple adult males and females. The Hughes team discovered that magpies in the hybrid zone breed regularly outside their 'pair-bond', with more than a third of nestlings the product of a female copulating with a male outside her territory. There was wide variation in the occurrence of this 'partner swapping', however: some territories had very few or no 'illegitimate' offspring, while at least one had all the newborn birds fertilised by a male outsider!

One possible reason for the birds' exceptional promiscuity is that the female magpie goes looking for a stronger mate, as Barash suggested. It could be an instinctive attempt to prevent inbreeding within the close-knit territorial group – hence the females copulate with an outsider whose genes differ, regardless of his size or colouring.

The initial goal of the study was to test hypotheses concerning the effect of colouring on mate choice by females in the hybrid zone: first, would the brightest coloured males be less likely to have straying partners? Or would males that did not match the plumage of their partner be more likely? Yet when the data were analysed, the researchers found no significant relationship between back colour and the probability of a male's partner copulating outside the relationship.

They also tested a hypothesis that females would be more likely to mate with males outside their territory if the dominant male was a close relative. Because Hughes had been following the territorial groups since 1992, she knew that some were composed of very closely related birds. But, contrary to expectations, there was no evidence for any relationship between relatedness and probability of extra-pair fertilisation. Females were not more or less likely to cuckold the dominant male if they were closely related to him. They did, however, find clear differences between the territories, with some females consistently mating with the dominant male and others consistently mating with outside males, regardless of his plumage pattern or relatedness to the female breeder.[3] Other factors associated with male fitness may be important, although a study of a pure white-backed population that attempted to estimate other components of fitness, such as male weight and their internal and external parasite load, also found no relationship with the proportion of external affairs between the birds. Hughes says:

> If natural selection indeed favours black-backed magpies in the north, the question still remains why all magpies are not black-backed. One possible explanation is that black and white feathers provide different levels of resistance to disease or parasites. However, the work that has been done in this area suggests that black feathers are more resistant to bacteria so while this provides an additional selective advantage for black-backed birds in the north, it does not explain the apparent advantage of white-backed birds in the south.

Then there is the issue of whether white-backed birds sitting on a nest are more vulnerable to attack by raptors such as hawks. The eyes of birds can see a greater range of colours than those of humans, and many have excellent eyesight in the ultraviolet part of the spectrum. This means a white-backed bird on a nest will stand out, and Hughes believes that land-clearing for farming and housing has contributed to a decline in their numbers: with fewer trees in their habitat, the white-backed birds became more vulnerable.

> Our hypothesis with regard to back colour was that although white-back males may be more vulnerable to predators, they may also be more attractive to females because they are brighter coloured, especially under UV light which magpies can see.

SO HOW DID this unusually long and detailed study come about? Hughes began the research into magpie behaviour in 1975 at La Trobe University in Melbourne. There she met her future husband, Peter Mather, who earned his PhD also at that university and has taken part in many of the magpie investigations. She then won a lecturing position at Griffith and moved north to finish her doctoral thesis in 1978 while Mather took up a post at the Queensland University of Technology. They were married in 1979, had two children, and it was not until 1987 that they resumed the study into magpies. Not surprisingly perhaps, the family members are devoted fans of the Collingwood Football Club, otherwise known as the Magpies.

To undertake research on forty or more different sites across Australia over nearly three decades shows a special kind of dedication, especially given the lack of government support for the project: 'Funding was always a problem. A lot of my own money went into the project but some also comes from consultancies our department takes on,' Hughes says. 'No-one seems prepared to back really long-term research like ours.'

Research by Hughes and her team, however, has uncovered many secrets about magpie lives that might never have been known. For example, their research has shown that once a family of magpies establishes a territory it tends to stay put from one year to the next. Typically a magpie may not travel much more than a kilometre in its entire life – which can last for twenty years and beyond.

Hughes' lengthy studies of magpies has revealed the long lives of the birds: up until 2014, she could still identify birds in the Seymour study area that she had banded as adults twenty-two years earlier. Not any longer, though – the last of the birds she first handled had died by 2015. Still, the fact that some magpies can live well beyond their twenty-first birthday means anyone undertaking a study of them has to be prepared to devote many years to the research. And that's a question often put to biologists who have spent years or even decades studying the one animal: Why do they do it?

'I think magpies are wonderful,' Hughes says.

> I guess biologists do tend to think that about each of the animals they work with but magpies have much more personality than most birds ... After you've watched a territory for a while you know which one will be dive-bombing the galahs or which one is going to try feeding sticks to the baby! They are very intelligent and seem to have a sense of humour, a sense of fun.

No doubt another reason for pursuing research for years into just the one animal is the joy of discovery, of being on the spot when the evidence backs the researcher's original hypothesis. The investigations by Hughes and her co-workers have shown, for instance, not only that magpies are promiscuous but that they are also cooperative breeders, with each member of the Seymour group helping feed the young.

Does studying magpies contribute in any way to improving the lot of humankind then? Well no, Hughes admits, most of it has little direct application to humans – although research undertaken by graduate student Nick Cilento into magpie attacks on people in Brisbane could help some avoid being struck. No, she says, the basic argument is the same as for all pure research – it is the drive to uncover knowledge simply for its own sake.

In April 2017, however, Hughes and her students returned to the Seymour region for the last time, 25 years after the project had begun. Looking back, she says:

> I never thought when I began this project that I would continue it for twenty-five years. We hoped to have all the answers in the first three years when we had lots of funding. However, the more we learned about these extraordinary birds, the more we realised how much we did not know. Our major question was to compare reproductive success between the birds' different plumage forms but, once we discovered how very long-lived they are, it became clear three years would not tell us much at all.

So Hughes and 'a bunch of very dedicated volunteers', as she calls her invaluable helpers, spent between four and six weeks at the study site every year from 1992 on, enjoying, she says, every minute of it! As she notes drily, 'Now that we have ceased fieldwork, we have the long and exciting task of pulling all the twenty-five years' worth of data together.'

11

Magpies: Mozarts of the Bush

Two

Perth writer Peter Hancock says a legend among the Noongar people in Western Australia was that the sky was once so close to the ground that trees could not grow, people had to crawl and all the birds were forced to walk everywhere. Working together, the birds managed to prop up the sky with sticks, but the sky was so heavy it threatened to break the sticks and collapse to Earth again – with potentially disastrous consequences. Clever magpies, however, took a long stick in their beaks and pushed it up and up until the sky sprang into its proper place, revealing the sun and, with it, the first dawn. 'The magpies' boastful singing each morning is to remind everybody of their important role in creation and its unique song is reflected in its Noongar name, "coolbardie",' Hancock says.

IT WAS NOT until 1802, though, that the magpie was first described by an English ornithologist, John Latham, who used Latin to dub the bird *Coracias tibicen*, from *tibicen* or 'flute-player', because of its melodious call. The magpie, of course, is one of Australia's most highly admired songbirds, with its wide variety of calls – many of which are remarkably complex, as we will see later. Meanwhile, the common name we know the magpie by today came about because the first nostalgic English settlers thought it resembled the long-tailed European magpie, although it has nothing in common with that corvid species except the black-and-white plumage.

Although the Australian magpie's scientific or taxonomic title was *Gymnorhina tibicen*, a genetic study published in 2013 revealed the magpie was closely related to the black butcherbird. So its name was changed to *Cracticus tibicen* – after the butcherbird family name of *Cracticidae*. The ancestor of the magpie is thought to have split from the butcherbirds between 8 million and 4 million years ago, long before the first humans wandered the planet.

Biologists believe the magpie's ancestor probably had its home in a rainforest. But the move long ago from forest to Australia's open plains made the magpie fiercer and probably a lot smarter. (The issue of how avian intelligence differs between species of birds and why the corvids, the crow group that magpies belong to, are rated as the most intelligent is the subject of another chapter.) Although they are related to and resemble butcherbirds and currawongs, magpies move around on the ground by walking rather than hopping as the other species do. But it is in the air that the magpie displays its aerial skills as a fighter – and as a bomber, a talent that many unhappy humans discover during the bird's breeding season.

IT'S SEPTEMBER AND hostilities have broken out up and down the east coast of Australia. The enemy strikes from above, and always attacks from behind. Casualties have been reported and the dive-bombings that began with the onset of spring have become more frequent. Zoologists have been called in to devise some means of defence, but they have also suffered from the swift and silent enemy. Yes, from September to November each year in eastern Australia it is magpie madness time and few people, even children, are safe. During nesting, you barely see the black-and-white flash as the magpie turns into a flying missile, swooping down on unsuspecting humans and delivering painful and often dangerous pecks.

A Brisbane newspaper once reported that at one school a fierce magpie had cut the faces of more than a hundred children. Throngs of screaming parents at the school gate were trying to get their terrified children to run quickly across the open spaces to the main building, where a doctor was waiting to provide first aid. Nick Cilento is familiar with the Brisbane situation and has often been victimised by magpies himself. He decided to investigate their attacks for his honours thesis at Griffith University and, leaving aside his work with Hughes for the study, Cilento spent six months before, during and after an entire magpie breeding season observing their attacks on other humans. He also assisted a team undertaking a survey about magpie attacks that involved 5000 respondents – the results showed that 96 per cent of men and 75 per cent of women had been victims at some time in their lives.

Walking adults were rarely attacked but children were, with boys, the usual chuckers of rocks and sticks, in particular becoming prime targets, as were bicycle riders, joggers and posties. Some birds seemed to pick their victims with great care: a woman pushing a pram could be attacked even while the magpie ignored boys pelting it with sticks. But Cilento discovered that only about one in twenty mating pairs of birds attacked humans and, of these, only a small number were fiercely aggressive, as if something they had experienced 'had turned them into madmen'.

He then set out to draw a magpie's attention to himself by riding his pushbike through the territory. The attacking bird was typically a male (the testes of which expand tenfold during the breeding season, meaning their bodies must be pulsating with testosterone). The bird usually glides silently down from an elevated position so as to approach the intruder from the rear. Sometimes the attack consists of a single swoop, but Cilento was once hit a dozen times on his helmet by the same bird as he pedalled through its territory.

Magpie attacks are always directed at the head. Their weapons of choice are a closed beak or open claws, or they bite and leave two fine cuts where the skin has been pinched and sliced. They also dive-bomb, with the bird flying fast and using its full body weigh to buffet the back of the intruder's neck or head. This sort of attack can stun and may cause serious bruising.

The magpies' behaviour follows predictable patterns, and individual birds respond to humans according to their own past experience and learning. They are obviously capable of recognising and attacking particular people, which adds credence to the belief in their cognitive abilities. Unfortunately, aggressive magpies represent a serious human–wildlife conflict that is not easily reconciled: 'Males get a good response attacking people. They generally don't hurt themselves and it looks good to the females when they chase this big predator away.' In the thesis Cilento wrote on his research, he says:

> Females seem to understand that humans are a threat only when their fledglings are spending a lot of time on the ground and are vulnerable, which is when the female may become aggressive.

Also, Cilento says the lack of any references to magpie attacks on humans in Aboriginal mythology suggests the problem is now linked to large numbers of people living in close proximity to each other – and to the magpies. The attacks appear to be simply a response to repetitious stimuli: someone may be bombed on a particular footpath and ignored if they are off it, even if they move closer to the nest. Worse still, some birds cannot be persuaded to change their ways: one man told Cilento he was attacked as a boy and the same bird was still dive-bombing him twenty-five years later ...

IN A SECOND study of magpie attacks that also took place in Brisbane, Griffith University biologist Professor Darryl Jones and two other researchers compared ten pairs of aggressive magpies with ten non-aggressive pairs. Jones, whose work with rainbow lorikeets was discussed in chapter 8, says the research involved banding the magpies so they could be identified, as well as taking blood samples to measure the testosterone levels in the males at various stages during the breeding season. Their findings strongly supported the contention that attacks on humans were a result of the male birds defending their nestlings – and were not linked to their territoriality.[1]

Surprisingly, the study found that heightened testosterone levels in the male magpies during the breeding season were not related to their aggressiveness towards humans. In fact, the testosterone level peaked immediately before the female laid her eggs and was significantly lower during the period of maximum attacks on passers-by. Odder still, there were no differences in the testosterone levels of aggressive and non-aggressive male magpies. So much for higher testosterone generating violence in males.

For his part, Nick Cilento doubts that the traditional method of removing – that is, shooting – a troublesome bird is the best way of dealing with the problem. He suggests further research be undertaken and for experiments to be done where humans supplement the magpies' diet by giving them food. Make friends, not war, seems to be the philosophy. That may be so, and could be worth a try, although some people would argue that the Australian magpie remains the most serious avian menace in the world. In advice to people worried about being attacked by magpies, BirdLife Australia says it is important to remember that magpies are native wildlife, so it is illegal to harm them. It is also important to remember that they only swoop at people for a few weeks during the nesting season – mainly during the period when young birds have just left the nest and are being protected by their parents.

The simplest and best solution is to avoid the area for a few weeks but, if this isn't practical, another suggestion is to wave a stick above your head, while cyclists sometimes attach stiff plastic strips to their helmets so they project about 10 to 15 centimetres above the head. If victims have tried these suggestions and they have not worked, BirdLife Australia says local state conservation officers may be able to assist, 'though this is at their discretion – and remember, it is illegal to harm magpies …'

THE CHORUS OF a family of magpies is a very organised thing, says Dr Susan Farabaugh.

> They sing together in a group and the song is like a madrigal: there is an order to it with everyone having his or her own part. First there is an introductory warble that is solitary and which anyone can sing and they can share that across the sexes. But the carolling they do as a chorus is sex specific in the over-all structure: with female-type carols and male-type carols, but it's also organised so that everyone has a part by singing a different note.

They also have impressive individual repertoires:

> A magpie might have a repertoire of thirty different songs and each bird has its own individual song that it works out for itself. Each group may share a few of its songs with a neighbour and they answer that neighbour's song with the one they share.

But, far from a glorious hymn of praise to the morning, the magpie's carolling is in reality a war cry – a challenge to any enemy who happens to be listening to just try invading:

> When you sing a shared song with your neighbour it is very significant – and usually very aggressive. You are telling him exactly where you are: 'Hey, Joe – we're here so don't even think about it!' The song, in fact, is a territorial advertisement; it's intended to let everyone else know that our place still belongs to US – the ones you fought yesterday.

Farabaugh and a fellow American biologist, Dr Eleanor Brown, collaborated with Jane Hughes in her earlier studies of magpies. They subsequently conducted investigations into magpie territorial defences. Using tape recorders and spectrograms, they recorded hundreds of magpie songs and analysed the sound spectrum of each, then went into the field and experimented by playing different songs back to the birds to test their reactions.

Magpies have acute hearing and, because of the way sound degrades over a distance, can accurately tell where another group is in the area. Farabaugh says they can also identify who is doing the singing:

> Everyone knows when a bird dies because they recognise all those voices. I was watching one territory and saw a male from two territories away arrive and realised he was intending to carve out his own little patch. Females kept coming in and coming in because they knew – everyone knew from the noise he was making – that this was a moment when a new territory was being formed. It was amazing.

Not only can the magpie change the pitch of its song over four octaves, but the bird has also been known to mimic more than thirty-five species of native and introduced bird species, as well as dogs and horses, as discussed below – which places it in the same class as lyrebirds, whose own amazing capacities are outlined in chapters 13 and 14. Ornithologists say that magpies are also capable of mimicking human speech when living close to people, although after a lifetime of listening to them I've not heard one, nor have I seen a bird that has been caged for years that can speak. But the evidence from studies is clear – they are excellent mimics.

Professor Gisela Kaplan has a chapter on mimicry and imitation in her book *Bird Minds*, where she discusses magpies as mimics and relates their capacity to mimic other birds to 'cognitive complexity'.[2] After spending ten years searching for and analysing magpie mimicry, Kaplan identified twenty-eight types of 'unambiguous mimicry' – not just confined to the songs of other birds, but the sounds mammals make as well, notably dogs barking and horses neighing. She says magpies also produce imitations of the human voice and can whistle 'in an almost human fashion':

> My recordings include phrases such as 'Go away' and 'I've got dinner for you' … [but] mimicry in magpies is a small subset of sounds within an extraordinarily large repertoire …

Kaplan, an adjunct professor in the Centre for Neuroscience and Animal Behaviour at the University of New England, is renowned for her work on the mental abilities of birds. She dismisses earlier scientific claims that bird mimicry was simply 'a reflex action and thus may be among the most rudimentary of imitation behaviour'. Instead, she says acquiring 'new mimicked snippets' requires a receptive brain and memory:

> It requires a brain that is 'plastic' enough and has the capacity to acquire new sounds not part of its species-specific repertoire, with

> special auditory feedback mechanisms, and the possibility of storing sound as memory, plus a vocal apparatus that can produce the mimicked sound.

Kaplan also focuses on lyrebirds as Australia's most accomplished mimics. But, unlike male lyrebirds, magpies are not mimicking other birds as part of a breeding ritual to attract a mate. As she notes, so strong is the mimicking of the male lyrebird in trying to lure a mate that his 'breeding song is not even his own'. To be able to achieve his mastery of the songs of other birds, Kaplan says the lyrebird must have a plastic brain capable of copying increasing numbers of the calls that it adds to its repertoire from season to season – and solely with the aim of attracting a female to its mound.

That is not the case with the magpie's complex, musical warbling call – one of the most familiar and delightful birdsongs to be heard in Australian suburbs and out in the bush. Even when it is alone and not under threat, a magpie may set up a quiet warbling as if talking to itself; these personal chats have been recorded lasting up to seventy minutes.

12

Selfish Genes and Cooperative Breeders

Humans have been said to possess a 'selfish gene' that encourages us to help others as a way of ensuring the survival of our species. British evolutionary biologist Richard Dawkins introduced the term with his 1976 book of the same title, where he wrote:

> [Natural] selection has favoured genes that cooperate with others. In the fierce competition for scarce resources … there must have been a premium on central coordination rather than anarchy within the communal body.

But do birds have a selfish gene too, and is that why the young of so many species stay on to help their parents when a new generation arrives? If so, could this be the reason why certain species are surviving when others are disappearing from our world?

COOPERATIVE BREEDING AMONG birds has been described as an example of altruism in nature. Famous Australian expert on antipodean wildlife Dr Tim Flannery wrote about this in his book *The Future Eaters*, referring to the many Australian birds that have a social structure in which one or more young stay with their parents into adulthood.[1] These individuals forgo the chance to raise young for themselves, choosing instead to help their parents feed their younger brothers and sisters. 'Kookaburras, noisy miners and blue wrens all exhibit this behaviour,' Flannery says.

> Indeed, it is extremely widespread, almost characteristic of many Australian birds of Gondwanan origin. Elsewhere, it is an extremely rare strategy and about 85 per cent of all species worldwide that exhibit it are Australian. The strategy is clearly beneficial, for breeding pairs with such helpers at the nest raise more young than those who lack them.

Magpies in south-eastern Australia are among many birds that could be described as cooperative breeders. Yet in other parts of Australia, as Professor Jane Hughes points out, the situation can vary markedly. Hughes has been studying magpies for more than twenty-five years and she notes that in Queensland, almost all magpie territories consist of a single pair of birds – with both adults feeding the young:

> But then each year the young are kicked out before the adults start breeding again. In the southeast, on the other hand, the magpie groups are much bigger and several birds will care for the young.

Researchers at the Percy FitzPatrick Institute of African Ornithology at the University of Cape Town in South Africa question claims that birds are unselfish cooperative breeders to help ensure the survival of a species.[2] Lengthy studies by researchers at the institute focused on cooperative breeding in five African bird species over several years. The researchers point out that cooperative breeding creates an 'apparent conundrum' because it runs counter to Darwin's theory of natural selection whereby individuals invest only in their own reproduction so as to guarantee the survival of their genes. This makes an explanation for cooperative breeding

> one of the most tantalising holy grails of behavioural ecology. Globally, this is a rare social system – only about 3 per cent of the world's birds are thought to breed cooperatively although most of these species are capable, at least under some conditions, of breeding successfully without helpers.

Other authorities put the cooperative breeder figure at 8 per cent, and some, even higher. Many species of cooperative breeding birds have been the focus of intense study, with researchers often concentrating on the extent to which helpers contribute to a group successfully producing and rearing baby birds. Still, they have not yet uncovered a unifying theory to explain the behaviour. In some species, helpers do contribute to rearing offspring while in others they seemingly confer no benefit or may even be harmful.

The idea that there may be elements of altruism at play has also been disputed by Australian and German biologists. They demonstrated that among purple-crowned fairy-wrens, the helpers were in reality 'cunningly planning for their own future when they helped with raising the young of others'.[3] The helpers even seemed to be balancing the amount of assistance they gave with the benefits they themselves expected to receive in the future.

This study is also another example of the remarkable efforts that researchers of avian behaviour around the world are prepared to make to uncover the secret lives of our feathered friends. Dr Anne Peters, from Monash University in Melbourne, spent four years working with two other biologists to conduct a demanding investigation into the cooperative breeding behaviour of the purple-crowned fairy-wren in northern Australia.

Purple-crowned fairy-wrens live as socially monogamous breeders.

Bestowed with their scientific name of *Malurus coronatus* because adult males develop spectacular bright-purple feathers on their crown during the breeding season, these delightful tiny birds weigh in at 10 to 12 grams each. During the non-breeding season, however, the colourful crown of the males is replaced with grey-brown feathers and their black masks are reduced to black cheek patches.

Dominant pairs of the wrens live as socially monogamous breeders – unlike their promiscuous cousins, the superb fairy-wrens – although, as Peters says, this could be more because of a lack of opportunity than conjugal loyalty:

> The territories of Purple-crowned Fairy-wrens are usually spread out like beads on a string [along a creek] with neighbours on each side; so it's hard for any of them to be sneaky and have an affair with a favoured male or female in another territory.

The biologists first caught the wrens in mist nets and attached different-coloured bands to their tiny legs so they could be easily distinguished. In the course of the four years of research, they undertook nearly 200 separate studies, recording the individual feeding rate for each member of a group that included fifty-four helpers, called subordinates. The nests themselves were made from strips of soft bark and dry grasses, well concealed in cane grass or among the leaves of low pandanus palms. Seventeen of the helpers were also observed attending more than one nest, so each subordinate was involved with an average of 1.4 nests. This was out of a total of 286 times that the observers watched individual feeding taking place.

These 'feeding watches' usually took place on consecutive days between four and ten days after hatching, with the team alternating the times by starting between 6 and 10.45 am and between 2.30 and 6 pm. Peters says the various groups and the territory boundaries of the purple-crowned fairy-wrens are stable year round. During weekly population censuses, the biologists recorded the size of each group and the social status of each of the uniquely colour-banded group members. The birds were identified as breeders or subordinates based on behavioural cues – the most obvious being that only the dominant pair of wrens would sing duets.

Fairy-wrens are habitual cooperative breeders and the helpers are generally older siblings or half-siblings of the current nestlings. Their behaviour has sometimes been explained by ornithologists as an instinctive desire to see more of their shared genes entering the gene pool, yet the three researchers found that these apparently altruistic assistants were actually playing a selfish game: they provided more assistance when their chances of inheriting the current breeding territory were greater – so they were, in fact, hoping to raise their own future assistants.

> Ours is the first study to show that helpers at the nest adjust their behaviour precisely according to multiple potential rewards: They provide food to kin and to unrelated nestlings to produce their own

future helpers. However, we suspect that once other researchers look at their study species in this dual light, more cases will be found of helpers that can do their sums.

The biologists tested whether assumptions behind the different hypotheses regarding helping behaviour were correct, as well as whether and to what extent any potential benefits applied. They studied the relationships between the helper birds and the male and female breeders and the likelihood of a helper inheriting a breeding position in their own territory. One of the findings was that 'queues for inheritance' were stable: the order in the queue didn't change, and younger subordinates never inherited a breeding position if an older same-sex subordinate was present.

In fifteen of twenty-nine cases when a resident breeder disappeared, the most senior subordinate of the same sex took over the breeding position. At the same time, and consistent with 'expectations of inbreeding avoidance', fewer subordinates inherited breeding positions if they were related to a breeder of the opposite sex.

Peters says:

> We first worked out which assumptions of the current hypotheses were met with *Malurus coronatus*. The pay-to-stay hypothesis that says subordinates must help in order to be allowed to stay in the group; and the passive group 'augmentation hypothesis' that says when helpers increase group size, they gain associated survival benefits – the more birds in a group the less chance of one being seized by a predator. Neither appears applicable because these require all subordinates to contribute to raising the offspring which is not the case for these wrens.

While those two hypotheses were borne out, she says:

> Kin selection provides one adaptive explanation for costly helping behaviour in that the subordinates adjusted their efforts according to

how closely or not they were related to the chicks; that is, they tended to feed their own siblings more than those they were less-related to. Also, by feeding nestlings, the helpers boosted the production of fledglings and their survival, and therefore gained potential benefits by producing their own helpers.

Anne Peters 'fell in love with fairy-wrens' during her studies and has been investigating them ever since. Holding one of the tiny birds, she explains that because of her work over the years she knows who its parents are, its grandparents, who its siblings are, and 'its cousins twice removed':

> And, because the birds tend to stay around, this allows me to answer questions for example about environmental issues, their life success ... After ten years, some of the birds I've banded are still alive so if I want to be able to make statements about their life-chances of success, I need to go on for much longer.

Peters has soldiered on in the extremely demanding work because she admires the fairy-wrens greatly:

> I really want to continue [this research] because they are just as clever and devious as we are! That's what gives people the passion to spend the long hours, to keep going in the face of a quadrillion insect bites and getting scratched by grass and bitten by flies, because of the insights you learn into why animals do what they do, to find out how extremely clever birds are – and how complicated.[4]

ABOUT THE SAME time that Anne Peters and her colleagues were studying cooperative breeding among the purple-crowned fairy-wrens,

Dr Lucy Browning and a team of biologists were seeking similar answers with a bird called the chestnut-crowned babbler. Their study took place with a population of babblers in the red desert country around Broken Hill at the University of New South Wales (UNSW) Arid Zone Research Station. Their results, however, were contrary to those the Peters team had found.[5] The chestnut-crowned babbler, whose scientific name is *Pomatostomus ruficeps*, is a medium-sized bird with a white throat, white-tipped tail and a down-curved bill. Endemic to the arid and semi-arid areas of south-eastern Australia, the bird is a member of the *Pomatostomidae* family, which is comprised of five species of Australo-Papuan babblers. Amazingly, the chestnut-crowned is also the first bird to have been discovered using its calling sounds as 'words' that make sense to other birds of the species, like human speech! More on that shortly.

Browning, at the time a postdoctoral research associate at UNSW, was also conducting the study into the chestnut-crowned babbler to

Chestnut-crowned babbler: the first bird known to use its calling sounds as 'words'

test various theories about cooperative breeding. She and the other researchers thought the babblers offered a perfect opportunity to assess the two theories about why birds engage in cooperative breeding: group augmentation and kin selection. As mentioned, the theory of group augmentation suggests that the birds cooperate to raise young so their group is as large as possible: a selfish motive, because there is safety in numbers.

'The alternative theory, kin selection, proposes that because we share DNA with our relatives, helping family members to succeed might help pass these "unselfish genes" on to the next generation,' Browning says.

> In other words, promoting the welfare of your brothers and sisters, who share approximately half of your genes, helps to propagate a line of future helpers. Chestnut-crowned babblers provided us with a chance to test the two theories because babblers can choose who to help in their group.

The desert environment in outback Australia where the birds live is harsh, and extra help rearing chicks can mean the difference between life and death for many nestlings. Most members in a babbler group help look after the chicks, despite not being the parents themselves. The researchers note, though, that, like any team activity, some individuals 'do the lion's share of all the work, while others do nothing at all'. Still, they found that babblers seem primarily driven by an 'altruistic urge' to help their family and, even though they might be better off living in a larger, non-breeding group, they invariably choose to help their breeding relatives instead. At the same time, the helper birds seem to work much harder when they are looking after their brothers and sisters than with more distant kin.

The Browning team fitted the babblers with tiny transponders so it was possible for the researchers to see which nests they visited and how many times they fed the chicks as a way of figuring out who was helping which ones. Babblers breed in domed nests and must pass through an entrance hole to access the nest, so by fitting an electromagnetic coil around the nest entrance, the researchers ensured all tagged birds entering the nest were recorded automatically, along with the date and time. This meant that the feeding rate of nestlings by particular birds could be accurately measured.

Blood samples were also taken of each bird to obtain sex and DNA information that could be used to identify the birds that were breeding, as well as the helpers' relationships to the nestlings.

> The findings arising from our research are relevant for understanding how human societies evolved because much of human society is underpinned by cooperation. Kinship is clearly important for babblers and we can speculate that it may have been important for the evolution of cooperation in people too,

Browning says.

> Kin selection theory has been the central model for understanding the evolution of cooperative breeding, where non-breeders help bear the cost of rearing younger birds. We found that 98 per cent of the babblers helped with feeding the nestlings they were related to – and every one of them cared for those they were most closely related to. In fact, babblers that helped feed their half and full siblings worked three times harder than those rearing less or non-related chicks. So we conclude that kin selection plays a central role in the maintenance of cooperative breeding in this species …

Jane Hughes suggests the differing conclusions drawn from the Peters and Browning studies is probably because the two teams were investigating different species of birds. She says there are clear differences in the nature of cooperative breeding for different species and so the wrens and the babblers could have evolved in different ways. 'Obligate cooperative breeders' means that a species would be unable to survive unless it had helpers that cooperated in caring for the young.

> Magpies are different again from fairy-wrens and the babblers: they are not obligate cooperative breeders and there are variations between populations in the extent of helping behaviour. I know one researcher who worked on a white backed–only magpie population and they had only a few territories with helpers. At Seymour, where our study is located, most territories have helpers that feed the young and make major contributions to territorial defence. But they are also not the typical cooperative breeder with a single breeding pair being helped by a bunch of youngsters: more than one female among the Seymour magpies may breed in the group …

IN AN UNUSUAL coincidence, another remarkable investigation of chestnut-crowned babblers was conducted at the UNSW outback station site by a group of British and Swiss researchers after Lucy Browning and her colleagues had completed their study. This team discovered what is believed to be the first evidence of a bird using meaningless sounds in different arrangements to generate a composite sound that has meaning to the birds that hear it. (As I argue in chapter 16, anyone who has ever reared chooks has no doubt that they can communicate effectively by using different sounds that convey distinct meanings.)

The babblers in this study, however, may have been the first wild birds to show that by combining two sounds, dubbed A and B by the researchers, they were generating calls associated with specific behaviours: in flight, they used an 'A-B' (like 'ooh ahh', for example) call to make their whereabouts known, whereas when alerting their chicks that food was on the way, they combined the sounds differently to make a 'B-A-B' (or 'ooh ahh ooh') call.[6]

> The birds seemed to understand the meaning of the calls. When we played the feeding call back to them, they looked at their nests, but when they heard a flight call they looked at the sky,

says Dr Simon Townsend, from the University of Zurich.

> Although the two babbler bird calls are structurally very similar, they are produced in totally different behavioural contexts and listening birds are capable of picking up on this. The findings could aid understanding of how language evolved in the ancestors of humans.

The researchers note that the ability to generate new meaning by rearranging combinations of meaningless sounds is a fundamental component of human language. Although animal vocalisations often do comprise combinations of meaningless sounds, they say evidence that rearranging such combinations to generate 'functionally distinct meaning' has not been observed before.

During the research, the scientists used acoustic analyses, natural observations and a series of controlled playback experiments to see how the babblers used the same two sounds in different combinations to convey different meanings to the birds that were listening.

The researchers say this shows that a bird can combine two otherwise meaningless sounds to create a new sound that does convey meaning to listeners:

> One explanation is that for vocally constrained, highly social species such as chestnut-crowned babblers, evolving new meaning by rearranging existing sounds offers a faster route to increasing communicative output than evolving new sounds. The capacity to

recognise vocalisations as sound constructs composed of smaller, meaningless elements, instead of a holistic unit, may have been the first step in the emergence of the elaborate phonemic systems seen in human languages.

But the researchers say further experiments are needed to determine exactly how babblers compute and perceive the elements from the two calls. Nevertheless, news of their findings attracted media attention around the world and the BBC in Britain broadcast a report on the discovery with details and images of the babblers making the calls.[7]

13

Lyrebirds: A Scratch and Scramble Life

One

At night, he roosts in the forest canopy. In the morning, he glides down in search of a high-protein diet. His powerful legs and claws rake the soil and leaf litter for worms, grubs and beetles. A winter songster, he vocalises for hours in June and July. This 'glorified pheasant' with long, elaborate tail feathers is the Australian superb lyrebird. His spectacular courtship displays see him bringing his lyre-shaped tail 180 degrees over his body, vibrating his spread tail, stepping from side to side, strutting and jumping around on a cleared mound, and beating his wings against his sides while singing. His enemies include land clearing, feral predators, cars, sportsmen's guns and milliners. Although a poor flier, he runs well. He leads a scratch and scramble life.[1]

'IF LYREBIRDS AND scrub-birds are half-faithful facsimiles of the first songbirds, their coming heralded a new dawn for planetary acoustics,' writes Tim Low in his book *Where Song Began*. 'Never before had the world heard notes so liquid, pure and powerful: A lyrebird's song can reportedly reach a hillside three kilometres away.'

Among all of Australia's feathered songsters, the lyrebird with its descriptive scientific name of *Menura novaehollandiae* ('New Holland moon-tail'), has the most ancient past. Indeed, the Australian Museum in Sydney has fossils of ancestors of today's lyrebird that date back 15 million years, although even those antique birds were relative newcomers to the planet compared with the first birds, whose origins date back to the Jurassic period between 200 and 145 million years ago. In any case, not only is the lyrebird's lineage antediluvian but, as anyone knows who has heard its capacity for mimicry, the male of the species can also reproduce a vast range of sounds – from the plaintive cries of young magpies, koalas grunting and a kookaburra laughing to the click of a camera taking a photo and the sound of a chainsaw cutting a tree down, including the crash as it falls. A lyrebird chased up a tree by a dog is said to have barked for three weeks afterwards.

To hear some of the amazing imitations coming from a lyrebird's mouth as it tries to capture the attention of the female it lusts after, just search 'lyrebird' and click on 'Amazing bird sounds from the lyrebird'.

A male lyrebird on its mound displaying to a female by spreading its tail over its head. Photo courtesy Bernd Amesreiter

This is a clip from the brilliant David Attenborough's BBC series *The Life of Birds*, which shows the lyrebird's extraordinary vocal abilities, including an eerily exact rendition of a chainsaw in operation. A book of the series has the famed British naturalist describing how the male lyrebird creates a mound in the forest where he can display his singing and dancing routines, competing with other males to grab the attention of the rather less decorative females. With a tail in the shape of a lyre – hence the bird's name – the male begins his performance by bending his tail forward and over his back, fanning it out in a spectacular display while at the same time giving voice to the 'longest, most melodious and complex of all bird songs'.[2]

> This must mean that the females not only admire visual beauty but have, in addition, a predilection for vocal brilliance and coloratura. The males, in their need to increase the length and variety of their song and outdo their rivals, have become superlative mimics,

Attenborough says.

> They include in their cascade of trills, warbles and liquid notes, the songs of almost every bird in the surrounding forest. Even the most inexpert birdwatcher can identify and admire the accuracy of a lyre-bird's kookaburra imitation while a skilled ornithologist may be able to recognise the songs of over a dozen other birds embedded in the lyrebird's incomparable recitals.

He goes on to describe the judgemental female listening to this music as an aesthetic glutton:

> Like an over-demanding opera-goer who is only satisfied if her tenor has a slim athletic figure as well as a dazzling voice, she tries to find a mate who is as beautiful to look at as he is to listen to.

Attenborough then extends the lyrebirds' mimicry to man-made sounds – although in the book he makes it clear it is only the birds with territories close to those occupied by human beings that incorporate the new sounds they hear from across their frontiers: imitations of spot welding machines, burglar alarms and camera motor drives.

However, Dr Hollis Taylor, an American-born Australian ornithologist and musician, disputes claims that the lyrebird in the wild mimics man-made noises. Instead, Taylor argues that Attenborough is responsible for the widespread belief in a lyrebird's capacity to mimic the noise of machines because of a clever deception in how he presented this ability on film. The broadcast shows Attenborough peering from behind a tree at a male bird on his mound, 'whispering to us about the bird mimicking sounds that he hears from the forest as if it was a bird in the wild':[3]

> We see compelling footage of the bird imitating a camera's motor drive, a car alarm, and a chainsaw. But hold on! Attenborough fails to mention that two of the three lyrebirds he shows in the program were captives, one from the Healesville Wildlife Sanctuary outside Melbourne and the other from the Adelaide Zoo. This latter individual, Chook, was famed for his hammers, drills, and saws, sounds he reputedly acquired when the zoo's panda enclosure was being built. Hand-raised from a chick, he was also known to do a car alarm, as well as a human voice intoning 'Hello, Chook!' He died in 2011, aged thirty-two.

Taylor dismisses suggestions that lyrebirds in the wild mimic the noises that humans make, although other people have claimed they had heard the birds make sounds of machines in the bush where they lived or had worked. She says, however, that among recordings of so-called mechanical lyrebird sounds that people claimed to have heard and taped, none were made by machines. Instead they contained the lyrebirds' own 'typical vocalisations that can resemble man-made machines to

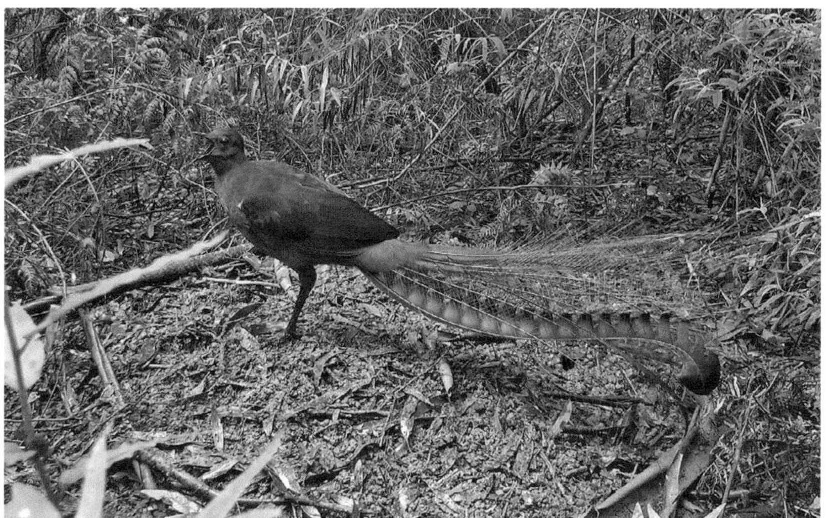

A male lyrebird on his mound calls to attract females. Photo courtesy Bernd Amesreiter

the untutored ear'. Still, Taylor admits that even if lyrebirds in captivity are the only ones able to mimic the human voice and their machines with such fidelity, 'that should be a substantial enough achievement to warrant our awe'.

TWO SPECIES OF lyrebird inhabit different parts of the bush in Australia: one is the superb lyrebird, which lives in dense forests in Victoria, across into New South Wales and the Australian Capital Territory, and as far north as the south-east of Queensland. Once seriously threatened by habitat destruction, the species is now classified as common; however, superb lyrebirds remain vulnerable to alien predators, such as cats and foxes, and ornithologists wonder if habitat protection schemes for the bird will be able to resist increased human population pressures. The other species is the lesser-known Albert's lyrebird (*Menura alberti*), a chestnut-coloured, pheasant-like bird with a slightly upswept tail.

In the past, Albert's lyrebirds were shot by hunters to be eaten in pies, or to supply tail feathers to globe-trotting curio-seekers, or simply for the fun of it. It is listed as near threatened but, with greater protection, and confined as it is to a relatively small area of rainforest between Blackwall Range in New South Wales and Mistake Range in Queensland, the lyrebird's population is believed to have stabilised.

AMONG ITS MANY unusual if not unique features, the superb lyrebird starts breeding later in life than most other passerines (perching birds), with the female beginning to lay eggs at five or six years and males beginning to copulate with them from ages of six to eight. (Compare this with the tiny welcome swallow, which begins laying eggs at only eight to fourteen months.) The male lyrebird defends a territory where he has established several display mounds and the territory also includes the breeding areas of up to eight females. After mating, the female builds a dome-shaped nest that is often low on the ground within a moist gully. She uses sticks, twigs and leaves, and has also been known to set the nest in trees, on stumps of trees, or even on the edges of cliffs.

In these latter instances, the female is seeking to escape the predation of foxes that, along with land clearing, once decimated lyrebird populations across eastern Australia. The female lays a brown-coloured egg and incubates it for forty-five to fifty days; when the newly born chick appears it is downy white in colour and will stay with its mother for up to ten weeks. During this time, the mother cares for the chick while the male shows no interest. He appears to regard his role as purely copulatory, playing no part in nest-building or rearing his offspring.

Using their powerful legs and claws as tools, lyrebirds rake leaf litter looking for worms, grubs and insects, and, for males, to build the platforms they stand on to give voice to their songs. Scientists have also discovered that in the process of building these platforms and searching for food among the leaf litter, the lyrebird is also acting as a firefighter, helping to counter the scourge of all wildlife in the Australian bush – bushfire. Just as an ecosystem engineer might, lyrebirds turn over significant quantities of litter and fuel and, in their way, not only restrict the germination of plants but also affect the whole structure of a forest. As fire ecologist Dr Steve Leonard of La Trobe University's school of zoology explains, through their raking of the leaf litter

> they prevent the establishment of a mid-layer in the vegetation. So you end up with a very open forest floor and then a tall layer of small trees and large shrubs. What's missing is a mid-shrub layer, the head-high stuff, and that's really important for fire behaviour because this is the fuel ladder that leads a fire from the floor up into the canopy where it can develop into a high-intensity fire.

In the process, the birds' actions also help preserve their preferred habitat of an open forest floor where they can scratch around to catch their food.[4]

While undertaking research in Victoria's central highlands following the devastating Black Saturday fires in February 2009, Leonard and his colleagues noticed that areas heavily worked over by lyrebirds were less likely to have been burnt. They kept seeing how the fire had stopped at the margins of gullies where it was obvious there had been considerable lyrebird activity, so they wondered whether the birds were affecting fire behaviour. With two of his colleagues, Leonard confirmed the hypothesis: lyrebirds were more common in the unburnt areas where the birds clearly preferred an open forest floor with a layer of shrubs at 2 metres high, making it easier for them to get around and forage. By contrast, severely burnt forest areas had very thick undergrowth with thousands of eucalypt seedlings that would have made it much harder for the birds to find food.[5]

'When you have a high intensity fire, lyrebirds get killed and then you have this mass regeneration of vegetation,' Leonard says.

> The lyrebirds that survive can't forage as effectively, which means you end up with more fuel and the area is more prone to burning. So there's this feedback loop between high severity fire and a low abundance of lyrebirds.

The La Trobe biologists fenced off areas in the forest to exclude the lyrebirds for a period of nine months. They then measured the fuel load in these areas and compared it with the load in areas nearby where lyrebirds were active. They found the areas with lyrebirds had on average 25 per cent lower fuel loads, equating to 1.6 tonnes per hectare less fuel, with a maximum difference of an astonishing 7.5 tonnes per hectare over the nine months.

Inserting the fuel load figures into a Forest Fire Danger Index model to predict the intensity of fire that could occur under different weather conditions, the researchers found that in the lyrebird habitats there was a significant reduction in predicted flame height. That is, the lyrebirds were essentially reducing fuel loads to such an extent that it was unlikely a fire could even start. Or, as Leonard noted: 'Even under extreme conditions, when we plugged in to the model a 35-degree day with very low humidity and strong winds, the lyrebird effect was still measurable.'

RETURNING TO THE song of the lyrebird: they sing most in the winter during the breeding season when, like many other birds, they call to declare their territory and to attract females. As Hollis Taylor says, their songs are not innate; instead, as with Australian magpies and all other songbirds, they are 'vocal learners'. In the case of male lyrebirds it seems they learn their songs, and even their mimicry of other sounds, from older males rather than directly from the cries of the different birds they hear or the mechanical noises they copy with such accuracy. Many Australian songbirds mimic other species, although ornithologists are uncertain about the function of avian mimicry. It seems likely lyrebirds mastered the art for more than just to attract females.

The voice box in birds is the syrinx, located at the base of a bird's trachea. It generates sounds without the vocal cords of mammals. Most songbirds have multiple pairs of syringeal muscles, while lyrebirds have only three pairs. Whether this simplification makes them more adept at mimicry is not known, but they are certainly far better mimics than many other birds. Taylor argues there is no evidence to suggest that lyrebirds attempt to fool other species. 'While mimicry forms most of their vocal repertoire, lyrebirds also have their own songs and calls,' Taylor says.

> Although the 'territorial' song can be melodious, the 'invitation-display' [or mating call] sounds mechanical to human ears. Twanging, clicking, scissors-grinding, thudding, whirring, galloping – these noisy or metallic sounds are the lyrebirds' own and not mimicry. Nevertheless, they are often mistaken for that.

Eric Vanderduys, a terrestrial field biologist with the CSIRO, emailed Taylor about a spotted bowerbird he saw and heard while working around Mount Isa in north Queensland. Vanderduys was so amazed at what he was hearing that he wrote down the sounds made by the bowerbird. These show that at least one other bird species is almost a mimic match for the lyrebird:

> Observed at close quarters imitating perfectly: [a] truck unloading gravel with [the] sound of individual rocks falling; cats fighting; Australian magpie; black kite; sulphur-crested cockatoo; pied butcherbird; grey-fronted honeyeater alarm/distress call; various garbled CB radio noises; reversing beeper; mine explosions;

> laughing man; truck doors closing; dog shaking itself dry – including the collar and tags rattling back and forth; Australian raven; human footsteps on gravel; a wallaroo hopping over rocks; car turning on gravel; large diesel loader starting up; many other sounds like clicks, bangs and murmurs I could identify.

Taylor says she knows of only one possible true example of the imitation of a man-made sound in a superb lyrebird's territorial song, wild or captive. This is the so-called 'flute lyrebird' of the New England Tablelands in New South Wales, whose extraordinarily complex song consists of 'flute-like tone colours'.

Taylor is conducting research that involves mapping the flute lyrebird territory in the tablelands and investigating the origins of their song. She has still to uncover a convincing explanation why these birds make sounds a flute-player would be proud to own. Nevertheless, every winter the rugged, misty rainforests of the tablelands resound with

> flute-like timbres, contrapuntal overlapping scales, and melodic contours – often with a musical competence exceeding that of a human flautist – songs that are poles apart from the territorial songs of the rest of the species in other places.

Taylor and two colleagues, Vicki Powys and Carol Probets, describe the tablelands as a rugged area, high in altitude and rainfall. It was there that one of the region's residents told the researchers he learned about the flute lyrebirds from a woman called Martha Manns, who said she first heard the lyrebird mimicking a flute in 1936:

> It gave wonderful flute imitations of the Mosquito Dance, the Keel Row [two popular 1930s tunes], and the scales. I made enquiries and was informed that some years before, one of the neighbours had a lyrebird in captivity,

Martha reportedly told him.

> The man played the flute, and the lyrebird learnt to mimic the sounds. Later, he released the bird, and then the other lyrebirds also picked up the sounds. The present generation of lyrebirds still make the flute-like sounds but not nearly as good as the original bird. It was a wonderful experience to listen to the original bird during the days and some nights as well.

Taylor goes on to comment:

> We count ourselves among those who are in admiration and awe of these singers and allow for the possibility of the story being true or partially true. We have debated among ourselves whether lyrebirds are capable of and prone to this magnitude of cultural transmission and change … [However], some of us interpret the lyrebird literature as indicating that had a captive bird been released, this lone individual would be more likely to take up the calls of the majority of singers, rather than the other singers dropping their songs to take up the song of the new arrival.

Taylor says mimicry of the calls, songs, beak snaps and wing beats of other avian species typically form 70 per cent of a lyrebird's vocal displays, with the remainder being territorial songs and other signals. Young birds do not directly mimic the sounds of other birds; rather the mimicry is 'culturally transmitted' from adult males. Territorial songs and 'suites of mimicry' are regionally distinct and generally change little over time, partly because the birds tend to be remarkably sedentary and maintain their territories for years.

This was revealed after a seven-year study in the New South Wales Central Tablelands by Vicki Powys in the 1980s and early 1990s.[6] Powys has been recording wildlife sounds and writing about birdsongs for decades and is sound editor for the Australian Wildlife Sound Recording Group. She found that a dozen distinct territorial songs were shared by the male lyrebirds within a particular group, and that these songs remained constant within the various groups across the tablelands even after many years. Powys says the songs she recorded in different parts of the region were each confined to a particular locality and did not vary in structure in seven years of monitoring:

> Twelve different dialect groups were found within a 35 kilometre radius, each comprising from five to fifty or more singing males in native forest habitats. Groups were reliably identified according to their songs and no evidence of migration was found. Regional variation in song was greatest in geographically separated habitats but song variation was still apparent at locations only 5 kilometres apart in acoustically isolated gullies. Some groups used only one territorial song but others consistently used up to three different songs and sometimes combined them. Mimicry was incorporated into some songs.

The researchers, faced with conflicting narratives from those they interviewed on the tablelands, had to find a better explanation for the flute lyrebird song than the story told by Martha Manns. At the time of my interviews, nothing they had uncovered offered a clear-cut explanation for the flute-like sounds, leaving them to conclude:

> Ultimately, this flute lyrebird tale of wonder exceeds containment, dispersed as it is across several fields of inquiry and a number of individual memories that go in and out of sync. In our search for fact or fiction, we found fact and fiction in a tangled embrace, accompanied by A Little Flute Music.[7]

14

Lyrebirds: A Scratch and Scramble Life

Two

Images of the male superb lyrebird have been used so often by various groups around Australia that it could almost, as John Gould first suggested, have become the national emblem. In his mammoth seven-volume series The Birds of Australia, *published over eight years in London during the 1840s, Gould illustrated the lyrebird, adding these words: 'Were I requested to suggest an emblem for Australia among its birds, I should without the slightest hesitation select the* Menura *or lyrebird as the most appropriate.'*

NO AUSTRALIAN GOVERNMENT has ever accepted Gould's suggestion, but other organisations have: a superb lyrebird was featured on the Australian one shilling postage stamp, first issued in 1932, and later the image was placed on the reverse of the 10 cent coin, while a stylised version can be seen in the transparent window of the 100 dollar note – as you can see if you're fortunate enough to have one. Similarly, a silhouette of the bird is the logo of the Australian Film Commission, while the

New South Wales National Parks and Wildlife Service uses a lyrebird illustration in courtship display as its logo.

It is a mark of the bird's shyness and ability to escape detection that it was not until 26 January 1798 when the first one was caught and officially recorded by a European – exactly a decade after Captain Arthur Phillip had landed in Botany Bay. Phillip's successor by that time was Governor John Hunter, who had sent a party south on that date to investigate a rumour about a colony of free white settlers hundreds of kilometres away. Three of the team returned in mid February, exhausted, but bringing with them a dead lyrebird and a diary of the arduous journey written by a youth called Barracks.

After Hunter had read the diary he sent it on to the great British naturalist Sir Joseph Banks, who had accompanied Captain Cook on his exploration of the Australian coast in 1770, and it is now among the Banks papers in Sydney's Mitchell Library. As Barracks wrote:

> On 26 January, I shot a bird about the size of a pheasant but the tail of it very much resembles a peacock, with two large long feathers which are white, orange and lead colour, and black at the ends; its body is betwixt a brown and green, brown under his neck and black upon his head. He has black legs and very long claws …

This was also among the first written accounts describing how the new human invaders, along with their introduced animals, were to wreak havoc not only on lyrebirds but most other Australian wildlife. When specimens of the superb lyrebird were later brought to England, their classification generated much debate among biologists. They were thought to belong to the *Galliformes* order – the heavy-bodied, ground-feeding birds such as turkeys, grouse, chickens, pheasants and jungle-fowl that the Europeans were familiar with – as reflected in the early names given to the superb lyrebird, including 'native pheasant'. But the idea they were related to pheasants was abandoned when the first chicks were described, although the lyrebird was not listed as a passerine (perching bird) until a paper was published in 1840, twelve years after they were first placed in their own family: *Menuridae*. Within that family they are in a single genus, *Menura* – 'moon-tail', from the Greek *meme* (moon) and *oura* (tail).

In their *Australian Bird Names: A Complete Guide*, Jeannie Gray and Ian Fraser say the name *Menura superba* was first proposed by part-time British ornithologist Thomas Davies in 1801, but that John Latham 'pinched the genus name *Menura* and added the species name, *superba*, we now use'.[1] They add that it is pretty clear Latham 'back-dated to obtain precedence'; that is, so as to be able to claim he was the first to name the bird.

LYREBIRDS ALSO FEATURE in first-hand accounts by pioneers who had begun opening up the 'great forest of South Gippsland' in Victoria during the late nineteenth century. A book of these recollections appeared as *The Land of the Lyrebird* in 1920.[2] The pioneers must have been getting on in years by the time their tales were published, but they vividly describe what it was like to clear the bush and try to make a life for themselves and their families in a vast rugged region. The book has many illustrations and photographs, including ones of lyrebirds and, inevitably, giant gumtrees. One shows the butt of a huge mountain ash with a burnt-out interior, so large it was used as a church school and a public hall that could accommodate fifty people 'with room to spare'. An early chapter was written by a 'Miss Gillan', who had obviously studied lyrebirds closely from childhood and was able to report that 'besides being famed for its glorious notes, our lyrebird is even better known for its tail'. This remarkable attachment, Miss Gillan wrote, had sixteen long, distinct feathers, twelve of them having fine and widely separated barbs,

A male lyrebird displays its wonderful tail. Photo courtesy Bernd Amesreiter

then two long middle feathers like the sides of an ancient lyre, 'or shaped like the letter S very much elongated'.

> This wonderful tail is not attained till the bird is four years old and is about two feet [60 centimetres] or more in length. The bird has the power of extending and contracting it laterally, spreading it widely when dancing. In colour, the whole bird is brown but the tail is of a lighter shade than the body and the two lyre-shaped feathers are striped bright brown and almost a lavender shade alternately. All this gorgeousness both in note and colour belongs to the male who is about the size of an English pheasant and is easily the largest songbird in the world.

Compared to this handsome dandy, the female was described as 'a quiet little drab bird with a plain little tail hardly worth mentioning'. Miss Gillan goes on to say:

> She also has a note of her own but it is merely an echo of that of her brilliant mate. In habit they are very shy and if you look for one you rarely see it. If you do it is only for an instant, being in sight one moment and away the next. It is useless to try and follow it as they run through the scrub with incredible swiftness …

For a long time the young Miss Gillan tried to locate a lyrebird's nest with no success, finally discovering one by accident. One afternoon, as she was coming home from school, she noticed a drop of water among some undergrowth near the path and went to see where the water was coming from. There she discovered that what she thought to be a drop of water was really the glint of the sun on the beautiful, big bright eye of a lyrebird sitting on her nest. As the girl approached the bird flew away, so she peeped in the nest hoping to find several eggs but there was only one. (She later learned that the hen never lays more than one in a season.) It was shaped like a magpie's egg, only much larger, and dark-grey in colour, mottled with a darker shade of grey.

This female lyrebird is about to feed her chick. Photo courtesy Bernd Amesreiter

The nest was 'fine and roomy', built in among the roots of a fallen tree and covered completely, the opening being at the side. It consisted of small sticks, bark and dried grass and the soft brown, mossy substance taken from tree ferns. The young girl visited the nest twice a day and the mother bird became so tame she hopped off the nest on to a neighbouring twig as the girl arrived, but returned to the nest as soon as the girl's back was turned. In due course the egg hatched, and what a curious-looking creature the young bird was: to the girl there seemed to be nothing visible but one huge mouth, which opened and closed automatically. She then saw, however, that the chick was covered with a light grey down, although its bones seemed far too big and strong for its skin. In a few days, it seemed to have found its feet because every time it was disturbed it would stand up in the nest and stretch itself again and again till it seemed to be growing 'bigger and bigger before my very eyes'.

Miss Gillan records that the favourite places for lyrebird nests were among the roots of a fallen tree, on broken tree stumps and among tree ferns, although never very far off the ground. But this habit of building near the ground proved disastrous for the lyrebirds after foxes made their appearance in Gippsland. Even at that time lyrebirds had become scarce in this part of Gippsland, although an attempt was made to establish them in the National Park at Wilsons Promontory.

In a later chapter another local, Mr L.C. Cook, also contributes a story about his experiences with lyrebirds and the difficulty of catching sight of one:

> You hear him whistling away merrily and can generally approach almost within sight of him; he continues whistling and just as you think you cannot fail to see him this time there is silence and he is gone. And this is repeated until you cry enough and you return home wondering what he is like.

Despite this secrecy, and as happened with Miss Gillan, Cook became a keen observer of the lyrebird and its powers of mimicry. He may also have been the first to deduce a fact about the lyrebird's song that ornithologists only began to accept decades later:

> This inimitable mimic still reproduces the notes of birds that have long since left his locality, leading to the supposition that the young male imitates his parent's repertoire, which is natural and pleasant and reminds us of the old days when we heard our beautiful mimic imitating calls that have not been heard anywhere near this vicinity for many years.

Cook then takes this conclusion a remarkable stage further with a second astonishing deduction:

> It justifies us in seriously considering the possibility that the notes we call the lyrebird's own may, after all, not be his own but instead be the notes of birds of an extinct species.

As Cook notes, the lyrebird has no difficulty producing any notes, whether sweet, harsh, guttural or melodious, with wonderful power and an 'exquisite taste in modulation'. Like Miss Gillan, Cook also warns that the lyrebird was becoming rare for another reason than being hunted for its tail. He implores his readers:

> Because it is endeared to the hearts of Gippslanders, I would like to entreat landholders to spare them a little shelter for since the advent of the rabbit very little cover is being left for this most interesting and gifted bird.

FIFTY YEARS AFTER *Land of the Lyrebird* was published, a mild-mannered sociologist from Monash University set out on a quixotic journey in South Gippsland to celebrate the ideals of conservation – or reclamation in this case. On the site of an abandoned dairy farm, Professor Bob Birrell's aim was to re-establish an area akin to the primeval wilderness that once covered the broken tangle of hills and razor-backed spurs that make up the Strzelecki Ranges. In this re-established wilderness he hoped the lyrebird and other wildlife that had long disappeared would return, and in significant numbers.

Today, Birrell wanders across a once-treeless landscape surrounded by friends who talk in whispers, towering friends, many of them, rising 20 and 30 metres to the sky. Birrell calls them by their Latin and common names, and he knows them well, because he planted them as seedlings – all 15,000 of them. He cared for them and built wire frames to protect them from the wallabies that also came back, along with rabbits and later deer, and watched them grow. To take on a task Hercules might have baulked at seems amazing – especially as Birrell has stuck at it for more than forty years and plans to keep going for as long as he is able. Yet in the process of this huge undertaking, requiring years of often back-breaking work, Bob Birrell has created a new land for the lyrebird; so much so that today their mounds are dotted across his property and their songs can be heard throughout the day, especially in the wintry months of June and July.

Although now retired as head of Monash's Centre for Population and Urban Research, Birrell remains one of Australia's better known and often controversial academics, a tireless researcher whose sometimes startling findings have been a constant source of news stories for decades. Yet few but his closest friends are aware of his extraordinary project. From the early 1970s on, Birrell has struggled up (and often slid down) the mountainous slopes, planting his trees month after month, year after year, losing many to voracious animals but never giving up. The once-grassed farmland is now almost covered in a wide variety of eucalypts – although his favourite are mountain grey gums. On the side of a steep slope he stops to admire the giant trees: 'Look at those trunks, isn't that a wonderful sight?' he murmurs. In one gully he planted myrtle beech and sassafras, re-creating a temperate rainforest that looks like a scene from the Silurian past, with tree ferns 4 metres high. What was once a monoculture of grass, an ecological desert, now thrives with animal and bird life whose melodious songs include those of the lyrebird.

One day, to Birrell's astonishment, he discovered a lyrebird mound constructed beside the farm's large concrete water tank less than 20 metres from the old farmhouse and hidden by vegetation. Its location, and others' in similarly enclosed spaces, suggests the lyrebird may not always be seeking to attract a female when he sings on his mound … after all, that requires space around the mound to dance and show his abilities. Perhaps at times these lyrebirds sing for the sheer joy of it. 'At the time I started in the early 1970s, there was little control over land clearing,' he says, gazing out from the verandah of the farmhouse he has also restored. 'All you could see almost from here to the coast were bare hills, so the notion of preserving a bit was pretty attractive and now look what it's like.'

RISING UP FROM Gippsland's undulating landscape, the Strzelecki Ranges run roughly west to east, gaining altitude as they go. A Polish adventurer, Paul Edmund de Strzelecki, gave his name to the region after pushing his way through the forests in 1840. It was in this unforgiving land that the pioneers who followed endured some of the grimmest struggles of any Australian settlers: struggles that, for the most part, ended in tragic failure. By the late 1930s, much of the land had been turned over to farming. Yet in only a few years the farms became deserted as families gave up the battle against nature and rabbits, and abandoned their homes. One man's 145-hectare farm once carried 130 head of cattle but, after the rabbits arrived and the weeds spread over the property, its carrying capacity was reduced to two ponies …

Birrell became involved in activism in the 1970s. 'I had been inspired by what was happening in America and became active in the conservation movement … The Whitlam era ushered in a new period of hope and I looked around for a project that I could undertake.'

Birrell's grandfather had been a farmer near Foster, a township in the foothills of the Strzeleckis. A friend told Birrell about an abandoned property in the ranges that by then had been reduced to barren hills, so he bought the land and began planting. The farmhouse was derelict, with parrots living inside, and there were sheds everywhere, including pigsties and a milkshed with four bails where the cows used to be hand-milked. It had been a marginal dairy farm and Birrell thought at first that reforestation of the whole region could be done on a large scale, although that did not eventuate until much later.

Every weekend or so for the first few years, Birrell headed east to the farm and began planting hundreds of trees. When he wasn't planting he was making chicken-wire guards to protect the seedlings from the wallabies and rabbits. With his wispy beard, glasses and a voice that sometimes breaks like a teenager's when he gets excited, Birrell does not look like a passionate man of the bush but rather what he was paid to be – a somewhat eccentric academic who was much admired by the students he lectured. On a cold night in the Strzeleckis, sitting before a log fire in his farmhouse, he speaks about the project to reclaim the land and what it had entailed. Would he have started had he known what he was letting himself in for? 'My effort was purely symbolic,' he says.

> I [was] fired by idealism but I never had any illusion that this was anything more than a gesture. Then again, a lot of what I've done at university is ephemeral – books, articles and so on – whereas this is a kind of memorial … Once it's there, it takes on a life of its own, the wildlife returns, it's self-sustaining, which was the whole idea really.

Then, early one morning, Birrell was looking out the lounge room window and there was a male lyrebird on a concrete block, a remnant from an old garage, about 10 metres away. Standing dramatically erect, the large bird was showing off his full plumage with his lyre-shaped tail spread out behind him:

> I was just watching in a stunned kind of way at seeing this big, big bird with its feathers streamed out like a giant peacock. It was a majestic sight – almost prehistoric,

Birrell tells me, still excited by the unexpected vision.

> That was clear evidence the birds are flourishing despite cats, foxes, deer and even human beings. Perhaps it was the bird cultivating the mound near the tank. And I concluded then that this was one vindication of a forty-five-year project: we have created an environment where at least some of the creatures of the bush have returned and flourished …

The land Birrell restored, with its lyrebirds and temperate rainforest, has become a flourishing island in an expanding sea of clear-felled forest and man-made plantations of blue gum and *Eucalyptus nitens*, commonly known as shining gum. A visitor leaving his farm is now confronted by another monoculture: not grassed hills this time, but forests of trees all of the same size and shape, lacking the native birds and animals and the wild disorder of the Birrell farm: 'Fortunately, under the contract the state government signed with the tree plantation company, they were obliged to maintain remnants of native bush so some wildlife survives there,' he says. 'Outside my property, though, this is still a highly modified landscape but at least the efforts by environmentalists did force the government and the company to make some concessions.'

ALEC H. CHISHOLM, a renowned journalist, ornithologist and encyclopaedist, wrote a chapter on the superb lyrebird in one of his most popular books, *Bird Wonders of Australia.*[3] In it Chisholm tells of being present in the early 1930s when a team of ABC Radio technicians managed to record a male lyrebird giving an extraordinary performance. He describes how the

> artist bird poured out a cascade of charming melody, mingling his natural shouts and gurgles with a fantasia of stolen notes. The talented creature merely took whichever voices occurred to his consciousness in whatever order and flung them forth in perfect harmony …

Describing the movements of the bird, Chisholm recounts:

> Slowly, majestically, as though responding to the pressure of a secret spring, the great tail began to rise and spread. The two large outer feathers extended to each side, displaying a beautiful silver-white background and chestnut bars on the under-surface, together with a dainty black curl at the tip of each. Two long central feathers, grey, slim, gracefully curved, rose and were held at an angle above the back.

His delight evident, Chisolm continues:

> A wealth of fern-like plumes, appearing in an upright position from between the two large outer feathers, formed a silvery fan for a moment, and then descended like an elfin parasol over the back and the head. What an astonishing transformation was this! A plain brown bird, through the simple act of raising and spreading a tail so as to display the under-surface had become beautiful beyond words.

Then, to the amazement of the bird's audience, the performer began to skip from side to side. Pausing briefly again, he began a series of rhythmic notes, followed by a quaint little jumping dance:

> 'Ca-luck, ca-luck!' said the revelling bird and made two quaint jumps. 'Ca-luck, ca-luck!' he said again, and again the two jumps followed in perfect time. 'Ooooh!' whispered a small girl who was among the fascinated audience, 'he's skipping pepper!' The bird was indeed skipping to his own song, singing and chortling and dancing, and manifestly enjoying the performance as much as were the spellbound onlookers …

Chisholm also sets about correcting popular errors that had arisen about the lyrebird, including the fact that it had been misnamed as a 'lyre' bird, giving the false impression that its tail always looked like a lyre. This was probably because those who had given it the title had only ever seen a dead bird, arranged with its tail taken off and placed upright against a wall to resemble a Greek lyre – as Gould himself had done using a stuffed lyrebird for the illustration in his book on Australian birds.

MEET THE LYREBIRD whisperers: Tessy and Bernd Amesreiter, photographers who live in the foothills of the Strzelecki Ranges, are a couple with an uncanny ability to attract lyrebirds. It took them more than five years, but they have recorded scenes of lyrebird life that have never been captured before in their splendid video *The Dance of the Lyrebird*.[4] The Amesreiters came to Australia for the first time from Germany in 1982 after an Australian friend invited them to visit. 'From then on, we came every two years for up to three months,' Tessy says. 'The more time we spent in this beautiful country, the more grew our desire to live here for good and eventually we built a house in the Strzelecki foothills.'

As many others have discovered, birds can have a powerful impact on people – not just because of their beauty or their songs, but because of something that strikes a chord in human hearts. A lyrebird had this effect on the Amesreiters and it changed their lives. It started when friends in the small country community wanted photographs of a male lyrebird for a documentary that was being filmed in the area. They asked Bernd to help and that was why, in August 2009, the couple set off into the forest to find a lyrebird. They were not hopeful because they had heard how secretive the bird was but, far from being as shy as they had been told, they came across a lyrebird that behaved as if it were tame, almost like a pet.

'I think it was love at first sight on both sides,' says Tessy.

> Whenever we approached its territory, the female appeared happily singing a tuneful song. Then it began foraging in our close vicinity; it followed us around, even made eye contact. For a long time, we couldn't believe what we were experiencing from this strange little creature: friendship, love and trust – with a wild bird known to be elusive and shy!

On many early morning expeditions into the forest the little female bird would appear – but there was no sight of a male. Then one cold June morning, not far from their home, the awestruck couple witnessed a male superb lyrebird performing his magnificent courtship dance on his mound right in front of them. Tessy describes it as 'a magical experience'. That was also the time when Bernd was diagnosed with cancer, and he says the fascinating image of the lyrebird dancing and singing for them was in his mind as he was pushed into the operating theatre.

'During his convalescence,' Tessy says,

> Bernd had the urge to see more of these unique birds, to elicit their secrets. The male bird's performances, even from a distance, gave [Bernd] strength, hope and faith to overcome the fear and the

depression caused by his illness. Bernd can't deny that the lyrebirds had a curative effect on his recovery.

The Amesreiters spent countless hours in the Strzeleckis, capturing extraordinary video footage of the birds. After what they call their 'many close encounters with this icon of the bush' they decided to share the story of their love affair with the lyrebird with the world. From the hundreds of hours of images of lyrebirds they had caught on video, they produced a wonderful forty-minute compilation full of scenes of lyrebirds wandering through the bush, scratching for food, rearing baby chicks, dancing and singing.

15

Corvids: The Smartest Birds of All

In a time long ago, Australia sent crows and ravens, its own avian geniuses, to populate other countries around the world. And yes, the corvid family includes the cleverest birds on the planet, with some neuroscientists arguing they are more intelligent than chimpanzees, humans' nearest evolutionary relatives. Crows are also among the few native bird species that have learned to survive with humans by quietly invading the places where we live. Apart from their raucous calls, they are rarely noticed and this unobtrusiveness means they can live among the humans, often feeding on what we throw away, with no threat of becoming extinct – in Australia at least.

CROWS AND RAVENS – the smartest birds on the planet – belong to the family of corvids, called *Corvidae*, and their distant ancestors are believed to have evolved on the Australian fragment of Gondwana millions of years ago. Later descendants of these early birds migrated to continents across the globe. South America and the icy polar regions are the only places today where there are no crows or ravens. In the northern hemisphere, the family of *Corvidae* includes crows, ravens, rooks, jackdaws, jays, European magpies, choughs and nutcrackers.

It is out of this large group that crows and ravens in particular have won the World's Most Intelligent Bird award, and not only because they have the biggest brains for their body size – the best indication of intelligence. In fact, the ratio of total brain to body mass among corvids is equal to that of the great apes, whales and dolphins – and is only slightly lower than in humans! Broadly speaking, the *Corvidae* family in Australia includes crows and ravens, plus an extended family of mostly crow-like birds called the *Cracticinae*, with twelve species that include the Australian magpie, currawong and butcherbirds – all highly intelligent and capable of learning their songs from adult birds.

Of the five native Australian corvid species, three are called ravens and two are called crows. Ravens are the larger birds but the distinction is slight and, because they are all closely related and descended from a common ancestor, as well as being similar in size and colour, it is often difficult to tell crows from ravens. Sometimes that may only be possible by listening to their cries or, if you had a bird in the hand, then check the feathers: the bases of the feathers of crows are white, while those of the raven are grey.

Ravens are black, and their eyes are white in adulthood. They are usually seen in pairs. The feathers on the throat, called hackles, are longer than in other species; a raven tends to extend the hackles when calling, while holding its head and body in a horizontal position and keeping its wings still. Young birds resemble the adults, but have dark eyes, shorter throat hackles and often a pink, fleshy gape.

The three ravens – the Australian raven, little raven and forest raven – inhabit Australia's temperate zone, including the sheep and wheat belt, while the two native crows, the Torresian crow and the little crow, are found in the tropics and the arid zone respectively. The Torresian crow is the urban corvid usually seen north of Newcastle in New South Wales and across the border into Queensland, where Brisbane researcher

Matt Brown is investigating their intelligence, as we will see later in this chapter. Elsewhere, the Australian raven is the most common 'crow' seen in Canberra, Sydney and Perth; the little raven is an inhabitant of Melbourne and Adelaide; the forest raven can be found in Hobart; and the little crow is the one mostly seen in outback towns.

Experiments by neurologists in recent years have revealed just how bright many corvids are. Crows and ravens are really more like primates than birds, says Dr Stephen Debus, a postdoctoral researcher in environmental sciences at the University of New England.[1]

> It's thought that the mental abilities of the early corvids developed as a response to the challenges of adapting to a drying continent …
>
> Corvids are highly social, curious and opportunistic, with an exceptional long-term memory. They have become renowned for their problem-solving ability in laboratory experiments and also in the way they behave in the wild.

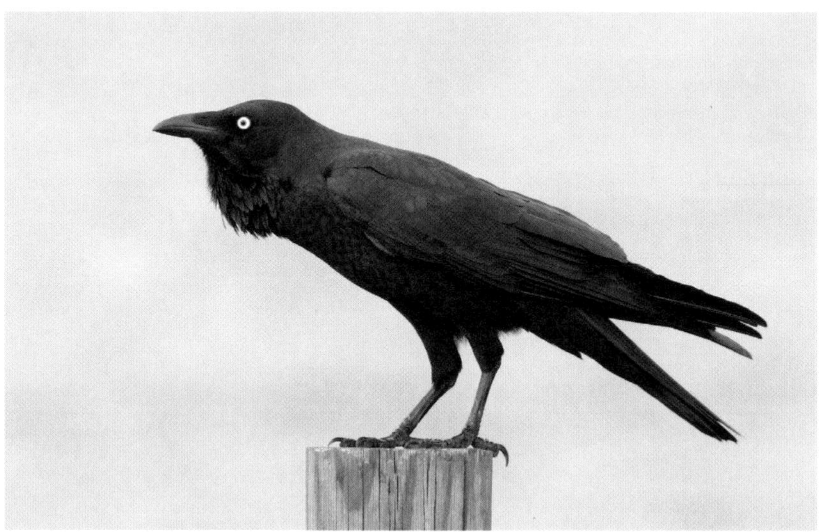

The Australian raven is one of the cleverest birds on Earth.

Little raven: the 'crow' mostly seen around Melbourne and Adelaide

Torresian crows are found north of Newcastle. In Brisbane, their numbers have increased markedly.

A wealth of information compiled by investigators in Britain, Europe and the United States has revealed that the mental abilities of corvids are related to the search for food and, as discussed in chapter 16 on chickens, to a complex social life that requires a capacity to recognise friends and enemies, and to understand the rules of hierarchy. Corvids have an exceptionally well-developed inner forebrain, which includes the hippocampus – the part of the brain involved with spatial orientation, memory and problem-solving. Hence, crows and ravens are said to be the animals, apart from us humans, with the highest capacity for memory and learning.

One of the best known American researchers into the behaviour of crows is John Marzluff, a professor of wildlife science at the University of Washington in Seattle. Among the books Marzluff has co-authored are *In the Company of Crows and Ravens*, and *Gifts of the Crow: How perception, emotion and thought allow smart birds to behave like humans*. In a study to investigate how American crows (*Corvus brachyrhynchos*) learn from their own experiences as well as transmitting that learning to other crows, Marzluff and two colleagues conducted experiments with wild crows.[2] Their aim was to explore the way crows learned from direct experience of a particular event or through social interactions with other members of a flock that had participated or watched what happened. The researchers wanted to find out how crows used both sources of information when learning to recognise the facial features of a 'dangerous human'.

At each of the various study sites, one of the experimenters would put on a unique mask to represent a 'dangerous face' before the team trapped up to fifteen crows, fitted them with identification bands on their legs, and then released them. Crows that had been trapped would later give an immediate scolding response if they saw a person wearing the 'dangerous' mask, a clear warning to unsuspecting crows to keep clear of this character, just as they would react on seeing a hawk or other raptor. Crows from the same flock that were present when some of the birds were trapped also responded angrily on seeing someone wearing the mask.

Yet crows that had never been captured or witnessed a trapping also scolded a mask-wearing researcher: from observing the reactions of other birds on seeing the mask, they had apparently realised that the mask-wearer was dangerous. Similarly, young crows, whose parents had taught them to react to someone wearing the mask, likewise made scolding cries. Further experiments with a different array of masks revealed the crows that had been trapped could later discriminate between 'dangerous' and 'neutral' masks more accurately than those that had learned to be wary through social interactions. Marzluff and his colleagues also found that the spread of learning extended to crows more than a kilometre away from where the trapping had occurred. Moreover, the birds' angry reactions continued if they saw someone wearing the dangerous mask even after five years.

ANOTHER AMERICAN FAMOUS for his investigations into avian intelligence is Erich Jarvis, a professor of neurobiology at Duke University in North Carolina. Jarvis hit world headlines in February 2005 when he called for people to start taking 'birdbrain … as a compliment'. As Jarvis and his colleagues explain, bird behaviour is actually surprisingly complex and demonstrates high intelligence: birds use tools, they sing songs, can imitate human language to communicate, they can count – and they can also lie. The widespread publicity was probably because it was prepared by an international consortium of twenty-eight experts on avian brains who collectively called for a new understanding of vertebrate brain evolution.[3] The scientists argue that birds are not stupid, their brains are not primitive, and it's time they were given full credit for their intelligence.

Earlier, Jarvis had initiated a study of the neurobiology of vocal learning, a critical behavioural basis for spoken language, using songbirds, parrots and hummingbirds as animal models. Unlike most other birds, these species have the ability to learn new sounds and pass on their vocal repertoires from one generation to the next, as is exactly the case, of course, with lyrebirds and magpies.

His call for recognition of avian intelligence did attract global media attention and, as the ideas that Jarvis and colleagues had presented began to spread, they slowly changed scientific and public attitudes. Jarvis says the so-called 'primitive' regions of avian brains are actually sophisticated processing areas that are similar to those in mammals. In fact, some birds have evolved cognitive abilities that are far more complex than those of many mammals. Learning songs or calls is rare among animals and most, including many birds, rely on innate or inborn information for their vocal communications.

Only three groups of birds – parrots, hummingbirds and songbirds – and three groups of mammals – humans, bats, and cetaceans such as whales and dolphins – are capable of vocal learning. This is regarded as the essential first step in the evolution of human language.

Even though hummingbirds have some of the smallest brains of all vertebrates, they are still capable of learning and remembering extraordinarily complex songs. 'The primary reason for hummingbirds' vocal specialisations is to defend territories and attract mates,' Jarvis says.

> And the more complex the syntax, the 'sexier the song'. Although it might seem far-fetched, I would not be surprised if these ancient receptors could someday help us identify the entire system of brain regions used for vocal learning.

That 'birdbrain' announcement in 2005 was the culmination of seven years of research by neurobiologists across the globe and led to an acceptance among scientists that evolution had created more than one way to generate complex behaviour – 'the mammal way and the bird way'. Not only were the two methods comparable to one another, but some birds have evolved cognitive abilities far more complex than many mammals. As Jarvis says:

> It's no wonder birds can do all these complex behaviours, which include pigeons memorising 725 different visual patterns and distinguishing between cubist and impressionistic paintings; scrub jays changing their food-storing behaviour to thwart thieves; or New Caledonian crows fashioning tools out of leaves and human-made materials. The vocal learning exhibited by parrots, hummingbirds and songbirds is the height of bird achievement: It's the substrate for human language. Without it, you just don't have language while some parrots can actually communicate with humans using words.

TWO MONTHS BEFORE Jarvis and his colleagues in the consortium had published their findings, two British scientists at Cambridge University compared the intelligence of crows with that of apes.[4] Nathan Emery and his wife, Nicola Clayton, note that discussions about the evolution of intelligence have focused on monkeys and apes because of their close evolutionary relationship to humans. Yet other large-brained social animals, such as corvids, also understand their physical and social worlds. In their report, Emery and Clayton review recent research that shows the way corvids use tools, how they are capable of mental 'time travel', and how they have developed keen intelligence because of their social settings. Complex cognition depended on a 'tool kit' consisting of causal reasoning, flexibility, imagination and prospection, the researchers assert.

Because corvids and apes share these cognitive tools, the Cambridge scientists argue that complex cognitive abilities have evolved multiple times, in distantly related species with vastly different brain structures, in order to solve similar socio-ecological problems, a process biologists call convergent evolution. Emery and Clayton say that, despite having very different brain structures, crows and primates use a combination of mental tools, including imagination and the anticipation of possible future events, to solve similar problems:

> These studies have found that some corvids are not only superior in intelligence to birds of other avian species (perhaps with the exception of some parrots), but also rival many non-human primates.

A similar remarkable finding, however, had been published even earlier – in Australia in 2004. Lesley Rogers and Gisela Kaplan, of the University of New England, noted that animal cognition research 'challenges the concept that primates are special and even the view that the cognitive abilities of apes [are] more advanced than that of non-primate mammals and birds'. Kaplan's latest book, *Bird Minds*, draws on her decades of research into the intelligence of birds, with scientists today mostly agreeing that it isn't physical need that makes animals smart, so much as social necessity.[5] Group living tends to be a complicated business and, for individuals to prosper, they need to understand exactly what is going on.

So, highly social creatures such as dolphins, chimps, corvids and humans tend to be large-brained and intelligent – as was emphasised further by research Clayton and Emery undertook on the social life of corvids.[6] They say that among corvids generally, the core unit is the pair bond: these partnerships have important implications for corvid social behaviour. Typically, monogamous birds form pairs in order to raise offspring together and defend their nest; but at the end of the breeding season, the pairs will often split and form new pairs the next year. But in the case of some corvids, notably rooks and jackdaws (and Australian magpies), the pairs remain together throughout the year and return to the same nesting site year after year.

'It is thought that these long-term partnerships resemble the long-term alliances of many primates and dolphins,' say Emery and Clayton.

> For example, the relationship between pair mates is established and reinforced through mutual preening and food sharing, and they enhance their dominant status by aiding one another in fights against third parties. In this way, pairs may increase their access to resources that would generally be unavailable to them as singletons.

Various studies by these two researchers, along with investigations by Jarvis and other biologists, were the beginning of a strong focus on corvid behaviour and general acceptance of the undoubted intelligence displayed by many of the different corvid species. For example, scientists have pointed to the lengthy period that young crows and other corvids spend with their parents, and how this provides many opportunities for young birds to learn various skills that help them survive for the remainder of their twenty or even thirty years. Because many corvids are cooperative breeders, as are some groups of magpies and other members of the genus *Cracticus*, the young birds also learn more from the wider group than if they were just being cared for by one or two parents.

POSSIBLY THE SMARTEST of all the corvids, at least in terms of their manipulative abilities, are the New Caledonian crows (*Corvus moneduloides*). Of all the more than 120 corvid species worldwide, these are the most famous among biologists because of the birds' highly developed toolmaking skills.

These crows have been observed trimming twigs and leaves into hooks, which they then use to fish for insect larvae in tree holes. A crow will insert the twig into the hole and when the larvae bite on the leaf, the crow yanks them out and eats them. Researchers say the New Caledonian crow is the only non-primate species where 'cumulative cultural evolution' has occurred in the crows' tool manufacture. That is, they appear to have invented new tools by modifying existing ones, then passing these innovations on to other birds in their group and then to subsequent generations.

At the University of Auckland, Gavin Hunt and colleagues studied tools the New Caledonian crows made out of pandanus leaves and inspected 5500 leaf 'stencils' left by the birds as a result of their cutting technique.[7] These indicated that later narrow and stepped tools were more advanced versions of an earlier, wider tool type. The researchers say the geographical distribution of each tool type on the island suggested a single origin, rather than multiple independent inventions. This implied that the inventions, involving delicate changes in the manufacturing process, were being passed from one individual to another. The New Caledonian crows appear also to spontaneously make tools from materials they have never encountered in the wild, as was observed in 2002 when Oxford University researcher Alex Kacelnik and colleagues were studying two New Caledonian crows called Betty and Abel.

Betty's toolmaking abilities came to light by accident during an experiment in which she and Abel had to choose between a hooked and a straight wire for retrieving pieces of pig heart, their favourite food. The piece had been placed inside a small bucket within a vertical pipe and the crows were tested to see if they could retrieve it. As the researchers discovered, when Abel made off with the hooked wire, Betty bent the straight wire into a hook and used the tool to lift the bucket from the pipe. This experiment was the first time the crows had been presented with wire, yet out of ten successful retrievals, Betty bent the wire into a hook nine times while Abel retrieved the food once, without bending the wire. The process would usually start with Betty trying to get the food bucket with the straight wire, but then she would make a hook by bending it in different ways, usually by snagging one end of the wire under something, and then using the bent hook to pick up the bucket.

Although Gavin Hunt had already observed New Caledonian crows in the wild also making hooks, the way that Betty and Abel had adapted the new material of the wire to achieve their purpose was definitely novel, and appeared deliberate and thoughtful. Scientists say that intentional tool manufacture, even if it is generalising a previous experience to a novel context, is rare in the animal world. Stephen Debus summarises the many talents of corvids when he draws on the northern hemisphere studies to argue that crows – and it seems most other members of the corvid family – learn, remember, and use insight to solve challenges:

> They drop shellfish and nuts on hard surfaces to crack them. They hide and recover stored food months later in winter when food is otherwise scarce. And they use objects as tools and even form their own tools, such as spikes and hooks, to winkle out food from crevices.
>
> Corvids recognise people carrying guns, they avoid traps, and they follow and harass large predators for food, or follow trappers and steal bait from traps. In Australia, they have learnt to turn road-killed cane toads over and eat them from the belly, thus avoiding the dorsal poison glands. Corvids have complex and sophisticated play behaviour. Most play is training for later life, and to show off their prowess to peers or potential mates.

Crows in particular seem to do things that people do, such as 'talk' to each other, steal and hide things, tease other species and also play, Debus says.

> So it's possible we're all learning from one another. The natural adaptability and intelligence of corvids has allowed them to exploit

the many opportunities our wasteful urban life has created for them, such as in cities where, because they are no longer shot, they have almost lost their fear of people, and brazenly raid rubbish bins and garbage dumps, spreading rubbish from bins that are not crow-proof.

UP UNTIL NOW, almost all the research on corvid intelligence has been carried out in the northern hemisphere. But Brisbane-based researcher Matt Brown decided to counter this by investigating the local Torresian crows to see how they measured up in the IQ stakes compared with their clever cousins on the other side of the equator. The research was for his PhD at Griffith University, and Brown opted to work with birds in the wild rather than capture them and subject them to various tests in the laboratory, as has been mostly the case in the northern hemisphere. Researchers there would argue that the test birds can then be subject to standard conditions, where what happens is carefully controlled, and the testing can be precisely varied for each bird, whether or not they have been captured and brought in from the wild or reared in captivity.

Brown, however, says of his research, conducted with free adult birds:

> Most of my studies take place on the university campus or in a forest or in someone's backyard. And that is very unusual for cognition studies. It takes a lot of time and energy to do this with wild birds – which is the main reason why most people do their studies in the lab. That's the case even with captured wild birds where they can be starved and then given a food reward to make them participate. In my case, the crows can simply fly away if they're not interested in getting a worm or a wrapper from McDonald's.

Although the effort required to gain at least some trust with wild crows is considerable, as are the difficulties of subjecting them to various tests, Brown believes he gained important data based on the natural responses of his subjects:

> You remove natural variations by undertaking research in a lab and while you might get 'cleaner' data, at what point does the animal you are experimenting with no longer represent the species you are studying?

One project he conducted was with his PhD supervisor, Professor Darryl Jones, whose work with rainbow lorikeets and magpies has been covered elsewhere in this book. With the Torresian crows, Brown and Jones set out to discover the extent to which the birds suffered from neophobia: a fear of new things.

Brown, who conducted the experiments, began putting out objects the crows could not have seen before and found that they were particularly neophobic: anything new that was introduced into their environment was clearly regarded with deep suspicion. Yet when he ran the same tests with currawongs, butcherbirds and magpies – relatives of crows and ravens called corvoids – he discovered these were not neophobic and seemed unconcerned when something new appeared. That, says Brown, raises an interesting question: If crows are so neophobic, why are they the second most numerous bird in Brisbane (after rainbow lorikeets)?

By becoming known to the crows in the territories where he carried out his experiments, Brown gained a degree of trust and was able to give the birds various tests of their cognitive abilities. One was shape discrimination: could the crows tell the difference between objects with two different shapes by relating that to a food source? Other researchers have done this with different bird species, including farmyard fowl, and found, for example, that some species could learn to tell the difference between circles and triangles. In Brown's case,

> I used wooden bowls with different shapes … I put the bowls out in a hidden spot – the crows are territorial so if you put the bowls in the same place each time, you get the same bird over and over again. This way, a bird or pair of birds can be trained and, over the course of many weeks, they will get used to the bowls and then to turning over a bowl with a particular shape to get a reward. But it takes a long time …

As he explains, the first stage of this experiment is called 'associated learning', where the crows associate the shape of a particular bowl with a reward. The second stage is determining if the crows are able to discriminate one shape from another, again using the promise of a reward for choosing the right one. Brown then began expanding the test to include counting by marking different numbers (in the style of dice) on bowls of the same shape to see if the birds could learn to tell the difference between larger and smaller numbers. He argues that while there is no real need for the birds to possess an ability to count in the wild, if they can solve a problem that is completely alien to them, it suggests they have the capacity to learn new things: 'My study is really more about how Australian crows measure up compared with all these foreign crows that have been shown to have these abilities.'

Brown says his test crows certainly seem to have many of the intelligence traits of the Old World and New World crows:

> For instance, I know they can recognise human faces: I've had crows that have learned to follow me because they know if they do I may have some food for them. I don't wear the same clothes each day, so what are they recognising? I know for at least a short term that they can recognise a human face.

In another study, he tested his crows on self-recognition, a test that researchers often use as a proxy for self-consciousness. Known as the mirror self-recognition test (or MSR), this was a technique developed in 1970 by American psychologist Gordon Gallup to determine whether a non-human animal possessed the ability to recognise itself; that is, that it has the sense it is an individual, separate from the environment. Typically, a researcher will mark the animal with a red dot or some other colour and then see if it notices the mark and tries to remove it, indicating that it recognises itself in the mirror.

Few species, however, have passed the test – in fact, up until recent times, of all the animals tested only the Eurasian magpie, the great apes (excluding gorillas), a single Asiatic elephant, dolphins and possibly other cetaceans, and some ants (!) appear to have shown self-recognition. Gorillas, several monkey species, giant pandas, sea lions, pigeons and dogs have all failed. Some researchers, however, dispute the validity of the test on the grounds that animals such as dogs rely mostly on other senses than vision, while species such as gorillas respond angrily to seeing what appears to be a strange member of their group without taking the time to consider the image more carefully.

When Brown tested his crows, he leaned a mirror against a wall in their territory and noted that the reaction of the crows to seeing their reflection was quite different to that of other birds:

> I'm not sure if I can call it self-recognition, but a pigeon or a peewee will attack its image in a mirror and treat it like another member of their species whereas crows seem to be more inquisitive. They move their head from side to side and move slightly one way or the other and watch what the reflection does. Then they will investigate what is behind the mirror. What is interesting is that 'corvoids', non-crow members of the corvid family such as butcherbirds, also do quite well on these tasks.

Not just a pretty voice – grey butcherbirds also do well on intelligence tests.

Another experiment he undertook was intended to see if the Torresian crows had an understanding of cause and effect. He had discovered almost at the start of his research that crows fly off if they think they are being observed. So he would always have to hide while watching how the crows performed on his tests but, for this one, he set up movement-sensitive cameras to capture the action.

Brown devised two transparent perspex boxes, each with a piece of string going through a hole on one side. He tied a piece of meat to one of the strings and a bit of wood to the other string. If a crow pulled on the correct string, the lid would open and the crow could pull the meat out of the box as a reward; but if it pulled on the wrong string, the lid on the box would stay closed and there was no reward.

> It took four tries to get a box that would work but, with the fourth version I made, I finally had one where the box would stay closed

when the bird pulled the wrong string. The problem each time this happened was that the box had to be manually reset and quite often it would take about an hour between trials. The results on the video recorder, however, were clear: the crows did learn to see the connection between pulling on the string with a piece of meat attached and getting that as a reward.

Brown finds crows endlessly fascinating, and describes their presence in Brisbane as almost a parallel world functioning alongside the humans:

> Walking down the street in the West End of Brisbane one day, I went past a newsagent as a crow wandered inside. I watched and it grabbed a packet of crisps, opened it on the floor and started eating the crisps. Sometimes they can be non-fearful but if you pay attention to them they freak out. They seem to be quite happy going about their daily lives yet they just don't want to be noticed – which is really strange because they're as loud as hell, especially early in the morning!

As for the role they play in our environment, Brown says that without them there would be many more carcasses of dead animals, a lot more roadkill, yet many people blame them for ripping things out of rubbish bins. The bins can be made bird-proof, he says, yet many people would prefer to get rid of the crows than take preventative action.

> The Brisbane crows are very much an 'edge' species: they live on the fringe of an urban environment yet Brisbane has become a 200-kilometre wide habitat for crows and they are now here in huge numbers. They were rare in the city's early days and they used to be quite shy but today they've adapted to our environment and become common everywhere.

AUSTRALIAN CROWS ARE also under investigation by Dr Thom van Dooren, who in 2013 began an intriguing long-term research project into crows in Australia and in five other localities around the world. A senior lecturer in the school of humanities and languages at the University of New South Wales, van Dooren is exploring 'the dynamic interface between people and wildlife in this period of incredible social and environmental transformation'.

Van Dooren's project, 'Encountering Crows: living with wildlife in a changing world',[8] isn't lacking in ambition or challenges. He intends to explore the experiences of crows from the forests of Guam and Hawaii to the industrial landscape of the Port of Rotterdam and the crowded streets of Tokyo. He says the project will 'take crows as guides' into a range of complex questions about how humans ought to live with wildlife in a changing world:

> As a virtually ubiquitous presence around the world … crows offer us a diverse range of instructive sites for exploring the challenges and possibilities of living well with non-human others.

The crows most of us are familiar with are those that survive or thrive on what humans throw away, that have taken up residence in cities and on farms in a way that few other animals have done, while also thriving off their contact with humans. But there are also endangered crows – predominantly forest and fruit specialists – pushed to the edge of extinction by human activity, such as the Hawaiian and Mariana crows: 'Consequently, crows today find themselves tangled up in many of the key contestations over how we ought to live in and manage environments.'

On the webpage he created to provide ongoing updates as his research progresses, van Dooren says crows that are relatively similar biologically are engaged in a diverse set of relationships with humans: Some are 'deeply loved and passionately conserved'; others are predominantly viewed as pests, scavengers on the detritus of human life, and perhaps even agents of extinction through their predation of endangered species. In the case of the Torresian crow in Brisbane, van Dooren has already done some work on the birds there and has been collaborating with Darryl Jones, the Griffith University biologist. In an outline of his project, van Dooren briefly describes each case study, starting with the Brisbane birds:

> At around 3:30 am in summer in Brisbane, when most of the human inhabitants of the city are still sleeping, large groups of Torresian crows (*Corvus orru*) begin to stir. Having roosted together overnight in groups, ranging from dozens to many hundreds of birds, their raucous morning calls can certainly disturb some people. This noise is one of the primary complaints made against crows by some locals whose responses range from resignation to murderous rage. Others are upset about the mess they make and their (possible) impact on other local bird populations. In this work I'm looking at contestations between people who love and hate crows, and the difficulty of forging inclusive multi-species communities.

He notes that nowhere else in Australia do crows, including Torresian crows living elsewhere, gather in such large groups as they do in Brisbane. It seems that the ready availability of resources in the city, perhaps alongside other as yet unidentified factors, has given rise to a new way of life …

CLEVER AS THEY are though, intelligence alone is not enough to save the world's smartest birds from human predation or the effects of climate change. What then of domestically bred birds such as chickens – do they have relatively large brains or are they just 'silly as a wet hen'? The answers might surprise.

16

The Clever Birds People Like to Eat

Chickens are neither wild nor threatened with extinction; on the contrary, the world's total chicken numbers are variously estimated to range from 20 to 50 billion. Yet their wild heritage, coupled with the way they have been bred down the centuries, has created one of the smartest birds on Earth. Scientists who have studied chickens (Gallus gallus domesticus), *describe how the birds possess communication skills equal to those of some primates, and that they also use sophisticated signals to convey their meaning. According to a report in* Scientific American *'Mounting evidence indicates that the common chicken is much smarter than it has been given credit for. The birds are cunning, devious and capable of empathy. That chickens are so brainy hints that such intelligence is more common in the animal kingdom than once thought. This emerging picture of the chicken mind also has ethical implications for how society treats farmed birds.'*[1] *And, one might add, all other birds as well.*

CHARLES DARWIN WAS convinced the domesticated chicken was the result of many generations of breeding from the wild red jungle fowl. But Swedish researchers have found that the origins of the world's most common bird are a little more complicated. Working at Uppsala University, the researchers mapped the genes that give most domesticated chickens yellow legs and discovered their genetic heredity derived from another closely related species – the grey jungle fowl. The researchers say the grey jungle fowl was probably crossed with an early form of the domesticated chicken back in the mists of time.[2]

If you search 'Are chickens intelligent?', 679,000 results pop up in 0.50 seconds and many relate to research showing that yes, they are. Most people, however, would probably expect such a search to generate very few links since chickens are supposedly dopey. In recent years, though, this has become a widely explored topic and researchers around the globe describe the manifold ways that 'chooks', as Australians know them, do display high intelligence.

In a similar vein, in the *All Animals* magazine, Ruthanne Johnson starts with a tongue-in-cheek opening line: 'Scientists have just begun

A proud rooster: his hens may be smarter but he is clever as well

to scratch the surface when it comes to understanding bird brains.'[3] She continues:

> But already, studies have shown remarkable cognitive abilities in the world's most intensively farmed animal. Like humans, chickens recognise one another; they take cues from one another; they look to their mothers for guidance and they have a sense of time. And they communicate with more than 24 vocalisations, each with a different meaning.

Johnson, a staff writer with the Humane Society of the United States, notes that even before hatching, chicks talk to their mother:

> Stress peeps tell her they're cold, prompting her to turn or move the egg in the nest. A purring-like sound lets her know they're comfortable. By the time they hatch, they know Mum's voice.

Chickens also use different calls for aerial and land-based predators. 'It's like they have a word for it,' says Sara Shields of Humane Society International. Shields did her PhD on the behaviour and welfare of broiler chickens and is now an advocate for banning factory farming of animals.

> Chickens are also selective in sounding alarms, making fewer calls when they're alone and none in the presence of, say, a quail. So they have to be thinking about who's around them.

In one study where hens had learned that red-coloured food was good, their chicks in an adjacent, glass-walled enclosure were given blue-coloured food. When the hens saw their chicks eating the wrong-coloured seeds, they began scratching, pecking and vocalising to convey the perceived error. 'That is one of the true teaching examples that we have data for in the animal kingdom.'

'Albert Chickenstein,' writes Ruthanne Johnson in her article, noting, as had the *Scientific American* researchers, that chickens were far from being 'birdbrains':

> Chickens are capable of solving complex problems, counting, and using geometry. And they start young: In one test, five-day-old chicks showed their ability to identify a target based on its numerical place in a series of ten. The young birds were presented with a row of identical holes, one of which contained food. When the apparatus was rotated, they were still able to return to the designated hole.

In another training test, chickens were taught to consistently peck at one of four unique geometric shapes, even as the order of shapes changed. When the target shape, a rectangle say, was removed, they waited until it returned to peck to get a reward.

Other researchers have similarly discovered how quickly young chickens learn: it can take the average human child a couple of years to grasp some early principles of numeracy, while a chick can do this within a couple of hours of hatching. Despite not being able to count, the chick knows how many there are in a group of objects and can distinguish between each one – up to five of them. Likewise, offered food in different sizes, it grasps the significance and always goes for the biggest.

Human babies can take a year for their brains to realise that objects and people still exist when they move out of sight. Experiments have shown, however, that birds' brains have a much better understanding of object permanence, as this concept is called: a young chick knows an object still exists even when it is removed, and it will go looking for it.

Hens also have the capacity for self-control where food is involved. In one experiment, scientists devised a situation where they fed a group of chickens from a tray that limited how many birds could eat there at any one time. But those first to the food had much less time to eat because the chooks waiting behind them were forcing the pace. After a while more than 90 per cent of the chickens eventually realised that if they waited, they could all eat for longer, totally reversing the pecking order. 'A case of, "You first, dear, I insist!" This puts chicken intelligence on a par with a four-year-old child. Quite a feat,' Johnson writes.

> Perhaps even more astonishing is that chickens can use the height and position of the sun to navigate, where most of us can't do it without a mobile phone, Google Maps and GPS. But the birds can, from being only a fortnight old, exhibit the same skills that ancient sailors used to cross the oceans.

When a friend brought around four young birds to our house, I, like anyone who owns three or more chooks soon discovers, noticed with interest how the pecking order developed among them almost immediately. I was unaware initially that the scrawniest chicken was actually a rooster and he was relegated to the bottom but, as he grew larger, Zeus, as we called him, soon made it clear where he stood. But the three hens had already sorted out the subsequent line of authority, and the order never varied until the chooks began to die of old age. That the birds communicated with each other all the time in the yard was obvious, and the different sounds each made were clearly understood by the others.

In a neighbour's yard one day I was watching a mother hen and her squad of fluffy new chicks scattered about. The hen looked up at the sky and made a distinctive cluck. Instantly, the chicks rushed to where she crouched beneath a shrub and hid under her feathers. They were no more than a few days old, yet when the mother seemed to call out, 'Come here at once you lot, that's a hungry hawk circling above us', their response was immediate.

Similarly, before I was forced to take Zeus away – a result of his propensity for early morning crowing – I watched how he communicated with his small flock, making a particular clicking noise when he had discovered something in the dirt that seemed particularly delectable.

A hen would rush over to receive this morsel from the master himself and, no doubt, she returned the kindness later in other natural ways. In larger flocks with two or more roosters, chickens have complex mating rituals where the females evaluate the males on their ability to provide food before choosing which to mate with. That was why Zeus was keen to let his hens know when he had a particular delicacy that he wanted to share: he was a mere male currying favour with his discerning females.

One day, I bought two more chickens from a farmer and took them home to add to our small brood. One of the young birds had clearly been dominant in her previous flock but when she attempted to prove her place at the top to my birds, two of them suddenly mounted a feather-filled attack. This startling group assault promptly sorted the newcomer out, placing her at number four while the other new chicken, of course, became lowest on the pecking order – although she already knew her ranking. Most people are probably aware of this social hierarchy in a flock of birds, yet it struck me then that to be a part of the social group and know one's place, especially in a large flock, a chicken needs the ability to reason, to have a long-term memory as to who is where on the ladder, and be able to develop relationships over time with other members of the flock.

IN HIS BOOK *The Magic and Mystery of Birds*, American writer Noah Strycker devotes a chapter to chicken pecking orders.[4] Strycker notes that the order breaks down completely in chicken coops when the total number of birds exceeds about thirty, probably because chickens have trouble recognising more than that many familiar faces: 'At that point, the birds can't keep track of one another closely enough to enforce dominance, and the group becomes egalitarian,' Strycker says. Scientists who have studied chickens also describe how the birds possess communication skills equal to those of some primates, and that they also use sophisticated signals to convey their meaning.

Andy Lamey, whose research is described in more detail later in this chapter, describes research that showed how chickens respond to tests where they must learn the details of the tests first, hold them in memory for varying periods of time, and react using their memory of these learned behaviours by choosing an 'optimal' reward. He says this requires practising self-control – that is, the ability to resist immediate gratification for a later benefit.

> It is relatively uncontroversial to ascribe greater cognitive abilities to chickens than to [human] newborns. For example, the ability to retain recognition of partly hidden shapes, an ability possessed by two-day-old chicks, does not emerge in humans until four to seven months,

Lamey writes.

> Tests of two-day-old chicks' abilities to recover fully occluded objects have also found that they mastered some aspects of stage four of the so-called Piaget scale of object permanence, a level human infants do not begin to reach before three and a half months of age.

TWO AUSTRALIAN RESEARCHERS at Sydney's Macquarie University, Professor Chris Evans and Dr K-Lynn Smith, spent more than twenty years investigating the intelligence of chickens. After one study, they concluded that because chickens mostly lived in a complex society, they had to 'get along and out-compete their friends and neighbours, which is probably what is driving their intelligence or cognition'.[5] Before Chris Evans died, and even after he became wheelchair-bound, paralysed and rendered speechless by motor neurone disease, he continued working in his Macquarie laboratory, unravelling the secrets of communication between chickens. With Smith he created a virtual reality world for the chickens they were studying, allowing him to introduce virtual companions and virtual predators to the chickens and then record the birds' responses.

In this way Evans and Smith learned to decipher the language of the henhouse. They discovered, as those who keep chickens have known for years, that chickens do communicate with one another, and will even change messages based on which other birds are around. Their research confirmed that chickens are intelligent and that they should certainly not be kept in the grotesque conditions of battery farms.

On the ABC science show *Catalyst* in June 2010, three years after he was diagnosed with motor neurone disease, Evans was interviewed about his work with chickens:

> [Chickens] can signal with remarkable precision about critical events in their world, such as the appearance of a particular type of predator, or the discovery of food. And they are not always truthful. Males attempt to lure hens with deceptive food calling, but females remember each male's track record and quickly become sceptical of those that are unreliable. In nature, hens can sort the wheat from the chaff, either by memorising a male's appearance – they all have distinctive faces – or by learning his vocal idiosyncrasies.[6]

Evans's work changed many people's attitudes to chickens. His colleague K-Lin Smith says:

> We need to stop seeing chickens as egg-laying machines and change the conditions they live in. Chickens are the most underestimated animals on the planet. People think they are stupid and automatically respond to things; if there's food, they eat, if they're scared, they make a sound. This is not true. Their communications are sophisticated.

For their research, the two scientists were awarded an Australian Museum Eureka Prize in August 2010, in the category of 'scientific research that contributes to animal protection'. Awarding the prize, Australian Museum director Frank Howarth said they had won because 'changing people's perceptions about the intelligence of chickens is important to building a consensus for ending factory farming':

> They have highlighted how the social environment is critical to chickens, and that intensive farming places chickens in an unnatural environment where they cannot display their natural social behaviour. This is known to lead to social stress and is one way in which cages compromise the welfare of chickens.

BUT CAN PEOPLE'S perceptions of chickens as just 'egg-laying machines' be changed? Researchers at the University of Adelaide decided to see whether veterinary science students' general feelings about chooks would change if they were taught to train chickens. The study involved 100 first-year vet students whose attitudes to chickens were investigated before and after they had undertaken practical classes involving 'clicker-training' of chickens.[7] The students paired clickers with food, so the chickens learned a click meant they had done what was wanted and would be rewarded. Their first task was to get the chickens to peck on a red target. This behaviour was 'shaped', meaning initially the chicken was clicked and rewarded immediately with food when it looked at the target. Progressively, rewards were only given when the chicken got closer and closer, until it actually pecked the target. Chickens soon learned colour discrimination and they learned to peck on the red target, rather than a green or a yellow one.

'We showed that attitudes to animals are linked to how clever we think that they are,' says Dr Susan Hazel, a senior lecturer in animal behaviour at the university.

> When students learnt to clicker train the chickens – who do pick up colour discrimination incredibly quickly – they were more likely to think that chickens are more intelligent than they had before the class. The students were also more likely to think that chickens can experience boredom, frustration and happiness.

Hazel says the experiment was also highly effective in teaching students the basics of animal training, and several told her later how they had used that information in training their own animals.

> Animals learn all of the time, even when we are not deliberately training them. Understanding how they learn is integral to being able to manage or train animals effectively. Chickens are descendants of wild jungle fowl and, to survive, they had to learn quickly what food was good to peck at and what they should ignore. The students not only learnt about how to train an animal, they also learnt that chickens were much smarter than they had realised, and that changed their views of chickens forever.

Female students in the class tended to rate the intelligence and emotional sensitivity of chickens more highly than the male students did, although both genders showed shifts in attitude to the birds: students agreed more with statements saying that chickens are easy to teach tricks to, are intelligent, and have individual personalities. They disagreed more that chickens are difficult to train and are slow learners. This all leads to the question: Are chickens seen by many people as no more than a source of food simply because most people have never had any close contact with an actual live bird? Would their attitudes be any different if they knew that, around the world today, most of the estimated *20 billion* domestic chickens kept in factory farms lead unhappy, crowded lives that are often nasty, brutal and short – usually not lasting more than six weeks?

ACCORDING TO THE Australian Chicken Meat Federation more than 550 million chickens are killed for their flesh each year in Australia, with the average Australian consuming nearly 50 kilograms of chicken meat annually, far more than the red meat and pork that the average person gobbles down. In a discussion on the ethics of whether chickens should be reared solely to feed humans, Dr Andy Lamey raises the notion of the birds possessing a 'primitive self-consciousness' and what this means in terms of breeding them for food.[8] Given the likelihood that chickens are self-conscious, Lamey concludes that chickens 'warrant a degree of moral standing that falls short of that enjoyed by persons, but still exceeds the minimal standing of being merely conscious entities'.

Lamey was formerly a philosopher at Monash University in Melbourne and is now in the philosophy department at the University of California, San Diego. He begins his discussion on ethics by describing how research into the structure of the avian brain has 'triggered a major shift in understanding avian cognition'. As he says, for the past century scientists had thought the neocortex of the human brain was a prerequisite for higher intelligence so, because the neocortex is found only in mammals, research into the cognitive abilities of other animals was considered pointless. Birds were assumed to lack the brain structures necessary for non-instinctive behaviour, therefore there was little reason to investigate their intelligence.

The studies mentioned earlier refer to the interaction between mother hens and their chicks as important in understanding the level of self-conscious awareness in chickens. The researchers concluded that hens modified their own behaviour in response to perceived feeding errors their chicks made, clearly wishing to instruct them in what type of food to avoid and which to eat and how to eat it. As well, the hens remembered through trial and error which of the food items they were given were edible and which weren't, and later passed that knowledge on to their chicks. Says Lamey:

> Maternal food displays facilitate this type of learning, as the hen pecks at a palatable food item while vocalising, or picks it up and drops it. For the chick to benefit from this type of behaviour it has to recognise that the hen is engaging in a behaviour, that of pecking at food, that it also can engage in. It has to be dimly aware that both it and the hen can eat the same thing.

On the other hand, for a hen to be concerned about her chicks' perceived food error, she has to recognise an affinity between a chick's action and what she was doing when she ate the unpalatable food. She has to have some awareness that the chick is doing what she did, 'which presupposes an awareness that the chick is the kind of thing that she is'.

Lamey mentions the work of Erich Jarvis and other neuroscientists whose findings about avian cognition are discussed in chapter 15. The changes in researchers' attitudes to avian intelligence that have occurred over recent decades arose from the realisation that functions performed by the neocortex in mammals are carried out by different parts of the avian brain. This new picture of avian cognition, Lamey argues, also calls into question the popular notion that primates such as humans and the great apes occupy a position of exceptional cognitive standing among animals:

> Although it is common for moral theorists to ascribe different degrees of moral standing to entities with different degrees of cognitive

> ability, to my knowledge no moral philosopher has noted the revised view of avian cognition and inquired into its ramifications for our understanding of the moral standing of birds … Given the revised view of avian cognition, it is worth asking whether any species of bird might also possess primitive self-consciousness and, if so, what degree of moral standing this entails.

Lamey focused on chickens not only because more chickens are killed by humans than any other land animal, but also because their cognitive abilities have been extensively re-examined in recent years, so their moral standing is of 'more than passing interest'. The more than 550 million chickens slain for their meat each year in Australia have been selectively bred to grow ever faster and bigger. The result is that today's six-week-old chicken is six times heavier than a six-week-old of an equivalent breed would have been sixty years ago. As a direct consequence, critics say another 20 million chickens die in their sheds from being trampled to death, or from starvation and thirst because they are unable to lift their own unnatural bodyweight to reach food and water.

Along with growing larger, this new breed of chicken is also more aggressive: Noah Strycker points out that chickens were first domesticated from the jungle fowl to be used for cockfighting, not for food. Like most other birds, chickens have well-defined colour vision that is far superior to that of humans and, for whatever reason, the colour red seems to inflame their sense of aggression. So, if a chicken is injured by being pecked by a higher status bird and she starts to bleed, other chickens in the coop become fascinated by the bright red wound and peck at it repeatedly, sometimes inflicting serious damage or even death.

Andy Lamey draws on Australian philosopher Peter Singer's widely accepted 'principle of equal consideration' in asserting the ethical implications of the findings that chickens are at least primitively self-conscious. In *Defense of Animals* Singer writes that where humans and animals have a comparable interest in, say, avoiding suffering, the animal's interests deserve as much moral weight as the human's interests: 'So equal consideration implies that the moral presumption against causing animals to suffer is about as strong as the presumption against causing humans to suffer.'[9]

When it comes to a morally relevant feature such as primitive self-consciousness, if chickens possess this but humans fail to recognise it because of 'an overly scrupulous standard of proof', we could potentially do something morally wrong, Lamey argues. For example, we might kill them – yet their cognitive abilities and corresponding moral status does not permit this. The best way to avoid this, he says, is to err on the side of recognising their primitive self-consciousness. Because the most common reason for killing chickens is so people can eat them, Lamey says this does not 'measure up' in moral terms. The chicken loses its life when it does not really need to because humans can live without chicken in their diets. For this reason, there is no justification for their killing:

> Rather, a moral wrong occurs when we kill a primitively self-conscious entity for such a purpose. The advertising that directs us to eat chickens because they are 'finger licking good', for example, would seem to reflect a morally trivial reason to kill them. That we enjoy how something tastes is not sufficient grounds to override the chickens' interest in continued existence. Indeed the mere fact that we take pleasure in eating an animal does not warrant any moral significance whatsoever.

THE CHICKENS I reared tended to live five or six years before quietly passing away. On one occasion, a large but elderly white leghorn called Betsy appeared to have decided to call it quits. She just sat in the straw in the shed I'd built, day after day, not moving or hopping up onto the rods I'd made for the chickens to roost on. I gave her water and seeds but, while she took an occasional sip, she made no effort to eat and seemed content to just sit there, like a grandma in a rocking chair with her knitting. The other hens seemed to show sympathy but left her alone and so the days passed until I found her one morning stretched out, cold and dead. A curious but peaceful death.

In describing the emotions that birds experience and how much they resemble humans, neurobiologist Gisela Kaplan tells of the empathy they posess, how they may even console other birds, may have a sense of justice, may show deep affection for their partner and grieve for their loss:

> I witnessed the mate of a fatally injured tawny frogmouth not moving from the spot next to its dead partner for three days, and then dying on the fourth … So birds are more similar to humans than had ever been thought, but with an important difference: birds are generally not aggressive without cause.[10]

Anyone who has reared or cared for chickens and watched them as they go about their busy lives would recognise the truth of Kaplan's comments about these birds – the ones that many people would prefer to eat rather than admire.

17

Songbirds: Australia's Gift to the World

The long-held view has been that the world's songbirds originated in the northern hemisphere millions of years ago and slowly spread south to Asia and, ultimately, Australia. Over recent decades Australian scientists began challenging this and, in a startling breakthrough, the evolutionary origins of at least three different groups of birds have been shown to have arisen in ancient Australia and Papua New Guinea – and then to have spread north around the rest of the globe. Today, it is widely accepted that eastern Gondwana, where the early Australian continent was stirring, was the birthplace of songbirds, parrots and pigeons. Biologists say this helps explain the birds' close relationship with Australian vegetation and their extraordinary behaviours, including why Australian birds are more likely to be intelligent, aggressive, loud, melodious, socially cooperative, environmentally influential – and more important in the pollination of plants than anywhere else. All because their ancestors originated in Gondwana all those millions of years ago.

IN HIS BOOK *Where Song Began: Australia's birds and how they changed the world,* Australian biologist and prolific author Tim Low describes how the long-held claims of European and American scientists about the northern origins of songbirds were hopelessly wrong, as proven by scientific analyses of bird DNA in the latter part of the twentieth century, which showed not only that this view was mistaken, but that the reverse was actually the case.

Charles Darwin argued for a migration of birds and other animals from the north to the south. In his *On the Origin of Species*, Darwin writes:

> I suspect that this preponderant migration from the north to the south is due to the greater extent of land in the north, and to the northern forms having existed in their homes in greater numbers, and having consequently been advanced through natural selection and competition to a higher stage of perfection, or domineering power, than the southern forms ...

How wrong the great founder of evolution was! This confident assertion, however, became the view of biologists for most of the past two centuries. Few had any reason to doubt that songbirds had their genesis in the northern hemisphere because, the biologists could argue, weren't fossils of the world's first bird, archaeopteryx, discovered in Germany? Therefore, Australia could only have received its songbirds by feathered migrants from the north heading south through Asia. In the 1960s and '70s, however, an American ornithologist and microbiologist called Charles Sibley began investigating the genetic background of birds – and that changed everything. Sibley and a collaborator, Jon Ahlquist, pioneered a technique called DNA kinetics to investigate evolutionary relationships between birds through DNA–DNA hybridisation. This was based on the fact that each DNA molecule is comprised of two intertwined strands of nucleotides – the famous double helix. If the strands are heated, they will separate but then, as they cool, mutual attraction between the nucleotide strands makes them bond back together again.

Scientists had shown that to compare the origins of two different animal species, their DNA could be cut into small segments, the strands separated by heating and then mixed: how strongly they then rejoined would indicate the degree of relationship between them. That is, the greater the genetic differences between the species, the weaker the bond between the strands that rejoined so the less heat would be needed to separate them again. Conversely, closer temporal links – that is, a more recent common ancestor – between species would require more heat to separate the strands. When this technique was applied to primate relationships, for example, it indicated that humans and chimpanzees carried DNA more similar to each other than to that of orangutans or gorillas.

Conducting their research over ten years at Yale and other American universities, Sibley and Ahlquist tested 1600 bird species from around the globe. They found that while DNA strands from Australian birds kept clinging to each other, this did not happen when they were tested with Asian birds – which were supposed to have been their most recent ancestors. The two researchers' claims to have resolved the true relationships between the modern orders of birds were highly contentious, however, and other ornithologists and biologists viewed them with great scepticism and even, according to some critics, as 'little more than snake-oil salesmanship'. As Sibley's contacts with his American colleagues became increasingly strained, he began corresponding extensively with overseas experts, including an Australian ornithologist at the CSIRO called Richard Schodde.

By the late 1980s, Sibley's ongoing studies had begun to attract increasing support. His revised phylogeny of living birds – their evolutionary family history – had been set out according to his DNA analysis and published in various journals; although initially highly controversial, his arguments were also influential and ultimately became accepted. As Low says, the work of Sibley and Ahlquist resulted in a new classification that linked Australian songbirds into a vast radiation from the southern into the northern hemisphere, showing that:

> Not only had the birds actually evolved in Australia but that the southern continent had been an exporter of songbirds on a grand scale. Many of Europe's and America's feathered finest – including their magpies, jays and shrikes – were part of that Australian radiation and were genetically closer to Australian birds than to most other northern birds.

The incubating DNA strands showed songbirds falling into two groups, the *Passerida* (songbird) and the *Corvida* (crow) families, which had poured out of Australia (or more likely an archipelago around Papua New Guinea). Sibley did not say that northern hemisphere jays and shrikes had evolved in Australia but that an Australian ancestor reaching Asia long ago had spawned these and other types of birds. In any case, the latest evidence shows that all the world's birds can be arranged into some forty orders, yet over half of all species alive today fall into just one – that of the perching birds, the *Passeriformes,* also known as passerines. As Low points out:

> They are the outstanding success story among birds. Most perching birds – eighty per cent of the total – belong in one sub-order, that of the songbirds, and they include all those renowned for their singing.

Then a young Australian scientist at Melbourne University called Les Christidis teamed up with Dick Schodde to test Sibley's findings. Rather than compare bird DNA, though, Christidis decided to compare proteins in the organs and muscles of different birds to see if they told the same story. The proteins, however, did not show a clear division of songbirds into two large groups but rather a cluster among the *Corvida*, with lyrebirds set apart. Christidis drew up his own evolutionary tree by placing closely related birds (according to his protein analysis) on adjoining twigs to show recent separation from a common ancestor. The more the proteins differed the greater the distance between branches.

On his tree, the lyrebird was the most distant, evidence of its long evolutionary past from more recently evolved species, so it was located on the lowest and longest branch, where scrub-birds also perched.

As Low writes, these are the 'sisters' of all other songbirds. The first songbird produced two daughter species, one giving rise to lyrebirds and scrub-birds and the other to everything else:

> With the *Passerida* forming one massive branch within the crown of the songbird tree, lyrebirds and scrub-birds forming the lowest branch and other Australian birds on other branches, an Australian origin is implied for every songster in an English country garden. All songbirds, in other words, have Australian roots.

INVESTIGATIONS INTO THE origins of the world's landmasses as they are today have revealed that, more than 500 million years ago, our planet looked entirely different. What has been called the 'supercontinent' of Gondwana included most of the countries in today's southern hemisphere. This took in the Australian continent, Antarctica, South America, Africa and Madagascar – and all the islands in between – but also the Arabian Peninsula and the Indian subcontinent. Movement of Earth's plate tectonics over millions of years, however, caused the latter two regions, the Arabian Peninsula and India, to shift to the northern hemisphere while New Zealand, then part of a large area called Zealandia, drifted away from Gondwana about 85 million years ago. The ancestors of today's birds in Australia, Antarctica and South America then evolved in two directions: the songbirds that thrived in Australia and the suboscines, a branch of passerines that includes most of the birds now in South America whose songs are innate or 'instinctive'.

That is, they do not learn their songs from adult birds or from others of the species, as Australian songbirds do.

In a pioneering investigation two American neuroscientists, Allison Doupe and Mark Konishi at the California Institute of Technology, the famed Caltech, tackled the question of how songbirds learn their songs if they are not innate.[1] Their findings showed that despite their small brains, birds have a complex network of neurons concerned with learning songs and storing them in their memory. This learning is assisted by 'mirror neurons' that, as happens in humans, enable young birds to commit heard sounds to memory. These special neurons are as active in the listening bird's brain as if it were singing itself; so when the bird sings the song again, it can then be checked against the stored memory. In her book *Bird Minds*, Professor Gisela Kaplan, an expert on bird brains, calls this 'a brilliant biological solution to achieve learning, as has also been found in humans'.

In a description of the neuroscience graduate program on the Caltech website, Doupe outlines the work the lab had been doing on 'the neural basis of vocal learning in songbirds'. She describes how an animal's nervous system 'mediates behavior, especially complex behaviors that must be learned' and that birdsong provides a very useful model for the study of these issues, with particular parallels to the way humans learn to speak:

> Song is an intricate motor act that is learned by young birds in two distinct phases, both of which depend on the animal's auditory experience: First, the bird memorises a tutor song and this is called sensory learning, mostly from its father. Later, the bird begins to sing by itself, and, in a manner analogous to the acquisition of speech by human infants, uses auditory feedback to refine and correct its vocalisations until it produces an approximate match of the memorised tutor song, which is called sensorimotor learning.

Doupe continues:

> There are critical periods for sensory learning of song, just as there are for some types of human learning. Moreover, a discrete set of brain areas … controls song learning and production. Both the song system and the adult song behaviour are sexually dimorphic [that is they differ according to the sex of the birds], and are regulated by sex steroids. Finally, song learning and singing are highly social behaviours, and are modulated by social cues. All of these features give birdsong the potential to shed light on the neural basis of learning, and on factors which control and limit learning.

This was also a topic explored by the ABC's *Catalyst* program, where some of the key players were introduced, including Tim Low, Professor Les Christidis and Dr Walter Boles, the two scientists who helped change the opinions of the world's biologists about the origins of songbirds: 'We didn't get the split of the Australian songbirds and the Old World songbirds, we actually got the Old World songbirds sitting within the Australian songbirds [on our evolutionary tree],' Christidis explains during the program.[2]

> We just kept looking and thinking, 'Is there an error here? Is there something we're missing?' But, no, that's where they were sitting … There may have been fossils here to prove our case, but there wasn't actually anyone actively working on them. Very few people were working on fossils and certainly no-one on songbirds, till Walter came along.

That Walter is Dr Walter Boles, head of the ornithology collection at the Australian Museum in Sydney, who spent much of his time searching for bird fossils at one of Australia's most famous sites, Riversleigh in north-west Queensland. As he says on the program: 'You don't know what you're going to look at and you start putting things under a microscope and suddenly you say, "Ah-ha".'

That 'Ah-ha' was his discovery in 1993 of a fragment of wing bone that, when dated, set a new world record for its age – a tiny object that Boles says was probably from a bird about the size of a finch:

> I'm guessing that what it lacks in size, it makes up for in significance because this was the earliest record of songbirds anywhere in the world, and by a substantial amount – like 25 million years earlier – which meant this bird was too early to have evolved in the northern hemisphere and then moved south.

Not just songbirds either – further DNA research and more fossil studies revealed Australia to be the ancestral home of parrots and pigeons as well. If all these groups of birds were combined, Low notes, it meant a majority of individual birds in the world had Australian ancestors – and he adds:

> The two groups of birds that overwhelmingly stand out for intelligence are the songbirds and the parrots and they both originated in Australia. It's just fascinating: We gave the world intelligent birds and not only that, the fossil record and the genetic record would imply we had smart parrots and songbirds in Australia at least ten or twenty or maybe more million years before there were intelligent apes. So, in Australia, you would have had the most intelligent organisms in the world!

But what a tragedy it would be if these 'most intelligent organisms', which have survived here for possibly more than 100 million years, were to be wiped off the face of Earth because of the actions of today's most intelligent beings – the human species.

18

The Origins and the Future of Birds

Birds are living dinosaurs. Or at least they are the descendants of one branch of dinosaurs, evolving from a group of theropods with many steps along the way during the Mesozoic Era (which lasted from about 252 million to 66 million years ago). The lineage of the 10,000 or so bird species on this planet today can be traced back at least 160 million years – more than forty times longer that the mere 4 million or so years since the ancestors of humans first trod this earth. A close relationship between birds and dinosaurs was first proposed in the nineteenth century after the discovery of the primitive bird-like dinosaur archaeopteryx, in what is now southern Germany.

ARCHAEOPTERYX WAS CRUISING the skies 150 million years ago and was roughly the size of a magpie, with broad wings and a long tail. It was covered with feathers similar in structure to those of modern-day birds, although it also had small teeth, which the ancestors of birds lost in the long course of evolution. Birds today still share many unique skeletal features with the theropod dinosaurs – the so-called 'predatory dinosaurs' that include the tyrannosaurus and velociraptor – such as hollow bones, breastbones and a wishbone. Discovery of fossilised soft tissue from a tyrannosaurus rex in 2005, and follow-up research in 2007, allowed scientists to compare the cells and protein sequencing of collagen tissue between the tyrannosaur and modern-day birds.[1] This proved the two species were more closely related to each other than to species of crocodiles – another reptile branch of dinosaur descendants.

DINOSAUR REMAINS HAVE been found on every continent on Earth, including Australia, and a wide array of these creatures dominated the planet's ecosystems for millions of years. At the time they were the dominant species Australia was still joined to Antarctica, forming the eastern part of Gondwana. Palaeontologists who have located and studied dinosaur fossils in Australia have found many similarities between the Gondwana dinosaurs and those that lived in the northern hemisphere, including tyrannosaurid theropods that had many bird-like features. Some species of theropods were able to survive in high latitudes, even within the Antarctic Circle, enduring at least three months of winter darkness every year, insulated by a feathery down-like covering.

Studies of the first feathered dinosaurs revealed that at least some moulted like birds do, while also replacing downy juvenile feathers with more structured adult feathers. CT scans have also shown that many dinosaurs had enlarged brains, with bird-like proportions of the various brain lobes. Different theories have been developed as to when birds evolved and began to spread around the world, but there is agreement that the ancestor of all songbirds originated in Australia at a time when the Australian landmass was separated from all other land by a vast ocean in all directions.[2] If this was the case, though, how did

10,000 species of birds evolve across the entire planet from a single ancestral species on an isolated continent?

This question was a challenge that a group of nine American biologists took on. The team used genetic and fossil data to reconstruct an evolutionary family tree for songbirds. They then linked this to information on different species' geographic locations to work out how the early songbirds were able to spread between different continents over the course of millions of years. Their research confirmed that songbirds originated in Australia a little more than 30 million years ago, but they then began to extend their range to other parts of Earth much faster than any scientists had previously thought.

This early migration appears to have begun some 24 million years ago after two of Earth's tectonic plates collided, forcing a group of islands up from the ocean floor, effectively building a bridge between the early Australian continent and Asia – thereby allowing the Australian songbirds to island-hop their way to Asia and beyond. It provided the first land link between Australasia and the south-eastern tip of Asia, the eastern boundary of which is known as the Wallace Line.

This was originally identified by the English naturalist Alfred Russel Wallace as the eastern boundary of Asian land mammals and therefore the boundary of the Indomalaya and Australasia ecozones. The islands east of the Wallace Line are known as Wallacea, and are considered part of Australasia. Wallace, of course, was the biologist who developed his own theory of evolution as Darwin was developing his (to Darwin's astonishment when Wallace sent him his own conclusions about 'survival of the fittest').

The burst of diversification that occurred when the islands were formed in Wallacea, the American biologists say, provided

> the first dispersal corridor out of Australia, and resulted in independent waves of songbird expansion through Asia to the rest of the globe. Our results reconcile songbird evolution with Earth history and link

> a major radiation of terrestrial biodiversity to early diversification within an isolated Australian continent.[3]

Complicating this discussion, however, was a paper, published nine months before the Americans released their results, by two other scientists at the American Museum of Natural History in New York.[4] They similarly combined DNA sequences of 'clock-like genes' for most avian families with 130 fossil birds to generate a new time tree for modern birds:

> We found that the most recent common ancestor of modern birds inhabited South America around 95 million years ago, but it was not until 66 million years ago [when the asteroid struck Mexico] that modern birds began to diversify rapidly around the world. Birds used two main dispersion routes: reaching the Old World through North America, and reaching Australia and Zealandia through Antarctica.

Their analysis, however, was overturned by the collective findings of an international team of researchers, as the next section shows.

FRIDAY 12 DECEMBER 2014 was a momentous day for human understanding of the evolution of birds. On this day twenty-nine scientific papers were simultaneously published in eight top academic journals, including *Science*, the premier publication of the American Association for the Advancement of Science.[5] The release of this mass of scientific commentary attracted the media's attention around the world while setting studies of the long history of birds in a new direction.

Debate among Australian scientists over the findings outlined in the papers published that day started with a commentary by two notable ornithologists, Dr Katherine Buchanan, editor of *Emu Austral Ornithology*, and Dr Leo Joseph, director of the Australian National Wildlife Collection at the CSIRO in Canberra, who described the occasion as 'a red letter day in the history of ornithology':

> The body of work [released on 12 December], representing output from more than 200 researchers in 80 laboratories in 20 countries, reaches into almost every corner of ornithology. A flagship paper stands on the shoulders of earlier and contemporary work to achieve a nearly complete understanding of relationships among the world's major bird groups and the timing of the major events in their evolution ...[6]

The contents of these papers were revolutionary, revealing a vast array of new information about the 160 million–year history of the world's birds, their relationship to dinosaurs and crocodiles, and 'the detailed molecular evolution that made birds the feathered, toothless wonders that they are today', as Buchanan and Joseph describe them.

The findings, released on the same day by members of the global Avian Phylogenomics Consortium, opened new windows into the origins and evolution of birds while also overturning many long-held beliefs about their past. Reported almost simultaneously via eight papers in a special issue of *Science*, as well as twenty-one other papers in top journals, the results continue to reshape the history of ornithology.

One of the consortium founders is Dr Erich Jarvis, a neurobiologist now at the American Duke Institute for Brain Science, whose work on the brains of birds was discussed in chapter 15. Speaking at the launch of the latest set of papers, Jarvis said their publication was 'a truly exciting moment':

> Lots of fundamental questions now can be resolved with more genomic data from a broader sampling. I got into this project because of my interest in birds as a model for vocal learning and speech production in humans, and it has opened up some amazing new vistas on brain evolution. This first round of analyses offers some remarkable new ideas about bird evolution ... based on whole-genome data.

A genome is the full complement of DNA sequences in an organism; it represents the code for the transcription and production of the proteins that build and define a bird or insect or animal. The second flagship paper describes 'the big picture of genome evolution in birds' while others cover how vocal learning may have independently evolved in a few bird groups and in the human brain's speech regions; how birds lost their teeth; how crocodile genomes evolved; as well as the ways in which singing behaviour regulates genes in the brain.

Another key consortium leader is Guojie Zhang of the Beijing Genomics Institute in China. In an extraordinarily complex undertaking, Zhang worked with Jarvis and Thomas Gilbert of Denmark's Natural History Museum to sequence, assemble and compare the full genomes of forty-eight species of birds representing all major branches of modern birds, resulting in 'the largest whole genomic study across a single vertebrate class to date', according to Zhang.

The scientists say that previous attempts to reconstruct the avian family tree using partial DNA sequencing or anatomical and behavioural traits had led to contradiction and confusion. Because modern birds had split into different species early, and in quick succession after the asteroid struck Mexico 66 million years ago and wiped out the dinosaurs, they did not evolve enough distinct genetic differences at the genomic level to clearly determine their early branching order on the family tree. To resolve the timing and relationships of modern birds, the consortium authors used whole-genome DNA sequences to infer the tree.

'In the past, people have been using ten to twenty genes to try to infer species' relationships,' Jarvis says.

> What we've learned from doing this whole-genome approach is that we can infer a somewhat different phylogeny [family tree] than what has been proposed in the past. We've figured out that protein-coding genes tell the wrong story; you need non-coding sequences, including the intergenic regions.

The new tree identifies the early branches of the neoaves, the evolving new birds, and supports conclusions about some relationships that have been long-debated. For example, the findings indicate there were three independent origins for waterbirds, while the common ancestor of land birds, including songbirds, parrots, woodpeckers, owls, eagles and falcons, was an 'apex predator' that also gave rise to the giant 'terror birds' that once roamed the Americas.

In another controversial surprise, Jarvis and Zhang's whole-genome analysis dates the evolutionary expansion of the 'new birds' to the time soon after the mass extinction. This, however, contradicts the widespread belief that birds had evolved up to 80 million years earlier, as some recent studies had proposed. Instead, the new genomic data suggests that only a few bird lines survived the crushing blow of the massive asteroid and that these gave rise to the 10,000 neoaves species that comprise 95 per cent of all bird species alive today. The worldwide extinction event that killed off all the dinosaurs bar the avian theropods – along with most other animals and plants – created a huge number of empty environmental niches that allowed the rapid evolution of new birds.

'The popular view until now has been that the extraordinary diversity of birds began during the dinosaur age but we found little support for this,' says Professor Simon Ho, an evolutionary biologist at the University of Sydney. Ho headed a major section of the research into the evolutionary timescale of birds. He applied a technique known as 'molecular clock' analysis to estimate the evolutionary timescales of birds using genome data and fossil evidence. His research helped confirm that some of the first lineages of modern birds appeared at least 100 million years ago but that almost all of the modern groups of birds diversified in a small window of less than 10 million years, just after the dinosaurs were wiped out by the asteroid.

> Our team had to develop a range of new methods to handle the largest bird data set ever assembled. These required the equivalent of more than 400 years of computing power across nine supercomputers,

Ho says.

> The team was able to work out the relationships among the major groups of modern birds, showing that our previous understanding of birds had been clouded by the appearance of similar traits and habits in distantly related groups. So while grebes and cormorants are both waterbirds with webbed feet that dive to catch their prey they are, despite these similarities, from completely distinct lineages.

Another significant finding was that the ancestor of most of the land birds known today was probably an apex predator that gave rise to raptors, eagles, owls and falcons in rapid succession before leading to land birds such as songbirds and woodpeckers: 'With the demise of the dinosaurs, birds and mammals were able to become more diverse and to occupy all of the niches that had previously been dominated by dinosaurs,' Ho says.

> This was one of the most significant episodes in the history of life on earth and it is tremendously exciting that this major scientific international effort has made these advances in our understanding.

SOME OF THE most interesting findings had to do with birds' DNA; how they learn to sing; what the different sex chromosomes of some birds can tell us; and why some birds are so susceptible to environmental changes.

Despite their biological intricacies, microbiologists found that birds are surprisingly light on DNA. A study led by Guijie Zhang found that, compared with other reptile genomes, avian genomes appear to have lost hundreds of genes in their early evolution after birds split from reptiles. 'Many of these genes have essential functions in humans, such as in reproduction, skeleton formation and lung systems,' Zhang says.

> The loss of these key genes may have had a significant effect on the evolution of many distinct phenotypes of birds. This is an exciting finding, because it is quite different from what people normally think, which is that innovation is normally created by new genetic material, not the loss of it. Sometimes, less is more.

The scientists found that the genomic structure of birds has stayed the same, remarkably so, among the different species for more than 100 million years. The biologists say this pattern of what is called convergent evolution may be the underlying mechanism that explains how distant bird species independently evolved a similar genetic make-up. Zhang says analyses on particular gene families helps to explain how birds evolved a lighter skeleton, a distinct lung system, dietary specialties, and colour.

Another interesting finding to come out of the DNA research is that analyses of whole genomes of the chicken, turkey, duck, zebra finch and budgerigar found that the chicken has the most similar overall chromosome pattern to an avian ancestor believed to have been a feathered dinosaur.

Various studies have also shed light on how songbirds learn their songs when they are young. The fact that young songbirds learn by listening to older male birds appears to have evolved at least twice over millions of years and is linked to convergent evolution occurring in many bird proteins. One of the studies in *Science* reports that songbird brains, as with those of parrots and hummingbirds, have specialised circuits that control vocal learning. This is the same in the speech regions of human brains, where similar convergent changes have occurred in more than fifty genes involved with forming neural connections. The biologists say that these are key candidate genes for the development and motor control of vocal learning.

The research also looked into how different bird species are at markedly different stages in the evolution of their sex chromosomes. The ostrich and emu belong on one of the older branches of the bird family tree and they have sex chromosomes that resemble those of their ancestors. Some modern birds, such as the chicken and zebra finch, have sex chromosomes that contain few active genes. The biologists say this opens a new set of questions about how differences in the sex chromosomes may result in differences in appearance between the sexes of various birds: peacocks and peahens look dramatically different, for example, whereas male and female crows are indistinguishable.

Birds are like the proverbial canary in the coalmine because of their sensitivity to environmental changes. In a study led by Chinese scientists and Erich Jarvis, the researchers analysed the genomes of species that have recently become almost extinct, including the crested ibis in Asia and the bald eagle in the Americas. They found genes that break down environmental toxins have a higher rate of mutations in these species and they have a lower diversity of immune system genes. In a recovering crested ibis population, genes involved in brain function and metabolism appear to be evolving more rapidly. The researchers found more genomic diversity in the recovering population than was expected, giving greater hope for saving species facing the threat of extinction.

AFTER BRIEFLY SUMMARISING the main findings from the various papers, Leo Joseph and Katherine Buchanan conclude their report with these words:

> One could be forgiven for thinking that the world's birds … have played a very long-running joke on us ornithologists. We have repeatedly been tricked into going down the road of many a wrong hypothesis … We once thought that … many of the passerines of the Australian region are closely related to their northern hemisphere namesakes when they are not; that owlet-nightjars are closely related to nightjars when they are closest relatives to swifts and hummingbirds. The new work sees us at last being very close to understanding the big picture of avian relationships …

But breakthroughs in science are subject to the scrutiny of other scientists who check the findings by conducting their own tests or experiments to confirm or reject the claims being made. In September 2015, three Australian biologists disputed the assertion that an explosion of new bird species had followed the mass extinction of dinosaurs and other animals and plants. In a comment in *Science*, Kieren Mitchell, Alan Cooper and Matthew Phillips say that the conclusions reached by Jarvis and co. are 'poorly supported by the fossil record' and that they had reached a different conclusion: that the diversity among bird species had, in fact, occurred millions of years earlier when theropod dinosaurs were evolving into true birds.[7]

That debate continues, although it seems most of the other results from the mass of research remain unchallenged – at least for the moment. So much for the past; let's turn to see what the future might hold for the birds of today.

19

Tackling the Extinction Threat

In this book we have seen too many disturbing accounts of the dire threats facing birdlife in Australia and around the world. In the 'lucky country', we live in an overpopulated, excessively urbanised nation on a scarred and fragmented land with the prospect of more severe droughts and savage storms to come: direct consequences of this warming planet. Further extinctions of birds seem inevitable, even beyond the 150 or more species that may already have been wiped out or will be dispossessed in the near future. Yet there is some hope, as the following accounts reveal, when people passionate about birds set out to reverse the path to extinction …

GOVERNMENT ACTION TO counter the disaster that many Australian birds are facing has rarely been strong or consistent; state and federal politicians seem largely indifferent to or dismissive of the dangers that climate change represents to all species on this continent, including us. What is happening to birds, however, is a pointer to our own future because they are foretellers of our demise – unless we act now to avert the catastrophe awaiting us all.

In 2016 five senior biologists from five Australian universities issued a grim warning that the nation is confronting 'an ecosystem collapse' affecting plants, animals and birds across the country.[1] The scientists note that the millennium drought of the 2000s has pushed southern Australia's bird communities 'over the edge':

> On the back of historic declines, primarily due to land clearing, two-thirds of bird species markedly declined further as the drought took hold. The assumption, or perhaps hope, was that these declines were part of a natural cycle and that the drought's end would bring a return to normal. This did not happen …

In fact, half of the bird species, including galahs, rosellas and fairy-wrens, are still far less common than they were before the drought. Southern Australian bird communities have dramatically changed in as little as two decades. With another period of drought looming, the future of Australia's birds has become even more uncertain. Although the 'battle for Australian biodiversity' can still be won,[2] biologists around

Even the ubiquitous galah is much less common after drought.

the world agree that decisive action on climate change is needed now. The likelihood of any 'decisive action' on the scale required to counter the effects already occurring, however, is doubtful – especially when Australian federal governments seem more concerned with cutting spending than saving the lives of native animals and birds.

It should come as no surprise to learn that Australia ranks among the forty most underfunded countries for biodiversity conservation – a list of names otherwise dominated by developing nations such as India, China and most of Asia, along with tropical parts of South America. Similarly, budget allocations to the federal environment department (now the Department of Environment and Energy) amount to less than 0.5 per cent of total government spending. What a contrast that is to the federal government's announcement in 2016 that it was planning to allocate nearly $50 billion to a French company to build a fleet of twelve submarines. Then came the Coalition's pre-election promise in 2016 to spend the same massive sum to slash taxes on business across the land, including multinational giants already under fire for shifting their profits offshore.

Yet the same government had earlier used its annual budget in May 2016 to cut spending on the CSIRO by a further $115 million, with the possible loss of another 300 scientific staff, many working in the field of climate change. This was the third successive budget that imposed cuts on the nation's top scientific organisation. This budget attack, however, generated outrage across Australia and around the world, attracting critical comments from former vice-president of the United States Al Gore and the World Climate Research Program. One of the most public of all staff to face redundancy was Dr John Church, a leading expert on global sea level rises – an outcome of climate change that is certain to push more species over the cliff.

CSIRO scientists have long been at the forefront of research across numerous fields in Australia, including their studies of birdlife – the many species of which will seriously suffer from climate change and rising seas. The scientists have also contributed significant information about other challenges facing birds and the actions that should be taken to ensure their survival – as the many references to CSIRO publications in this book demonstrate. But how long such investigations by its biologists can continue is uncertain given the questions over future funding.

Hearteningly, in an unexpected move in early August 2016, the government made a sudden about-turn and ordered the CSIRO executive and board to 'put the focus back on climate science'. The new strategy includes fifteen new climate science positions and research investment worth $37 million over ten years, although this would hardly make up for the cuts that had already been imposed. The strategy was to be developed in consultation with the scientific community and Australia's chief scientist, Dr Alan Finkel. When the CSIRO cuts were initially announced, the 140-strong staff of climate scientists was reduced to thirty-five. Now, the organisation's budget was to increase by about $100 million over three years and overall staffing levels would also increase by 200.[3]

This whole confused affair was another sorry tale in the long history of the Australian government bungling major challenges that have the potential to affect every citizen in some way or another. In any case, however uncertain the budget situation facing Australia's principal research organisation, the fact is that the cost of saving the nation's bird species is not high, either in monetary terms or considering the crucial role they play in helping maintain many of Australia's ecosystems.

This is laid out in the CSIRO publication *Climate Change Adaptation Plan for Australian Birds*.[4] Professor Stephen Garnett from the Northern Territory's Charles Darwin University and seven other senior environmentalists contributed to the 265-page document, focusing on ways of saving fifty-nine bird species that are highly sensitive and highly exposed to rising temperatures across Australia. They warn that increases in deadly bushfires and heat waves caused by climate change will affect a great many bird species: temperatures above 45°C sustained for several hours, for example, can cause birds to drop dead, either from hyperthermia or unsustainable rates of water loss. Smaller species are even more vulnerable, while non-lethal spells of hot weather can reduce the foraging efficiency of birds, leading to loss of body mass and even starvation.

As well as outlining the particular adaptation strategies needed to save each of the fifty-nine bird species listed in the book – which range from banded fruit doves and beach stone curlews to pied currawongs and scarlet robins – the biologists also calculate the cost of establishing sustainable populations of each species. (Expenditure would have to cover expanding protected areas, improving habitat quality, protecting and increasing refuges, establishing new habitats, preparing species management plans and assisting colonisation. Then there would be the need to create captive breeding facilities for seriously threatened species, and monitoring programs.)

The biologists calculate the total cost of maintaining just one threatened species under an appropriate management plan would be $220,000

The beach stone curlew is under threat.

As a nest predator, the pied currawong may be pushing smaller birds out of our suburbs.

a year, a figure that appears remarkably low. That means the total sum needed to cover all fifty-nine species would amount to slightly less than $13 million – or an eighth of the $100 million–plus that federal politicians claim in personal expenses each year, and a trifling sum compared with the federal government's annual budget of around $450 *billion*.

But the scientists accept that the options available to save birds under threat from climate change are limited; money alone will not be enough unless the world's major emitters of greenhouse gases take immediate action. Because that seems extremely unlikely, decisions will have to be made regarding species that may have to be 'officially abandoned to climate change'; an avian version of triage where the most important or significant species are saved and the rest left to their fate.

> In lieu of global action to cut greenhouse gas emissions and reduce the rate of climate change, rules [regarding saving or abandoning species] need to be developed soon or the attempts will be

> misdirected as the effort required is overwhelmed by the size of the extinction crisis bearing down on us,

Garnett and his colleagues declare.

Incidentally, Australian writer Sue Taylor created a splendid book based on the fifty-nine endangered birds listed in the Adaptation Plan.[5] Each of the fifty-nine birds has a beautiful image of an actual print that first appeared in John Gould's *The Birds of Australia*, along with a four-page description of the bird. Although titled *John Gould's Extinct and Endangered Birds of Australia*, none of the birds included has yet become extinct – at least as far as is known at the time of writing.

COPING WITH THE grim prospect of extinction is also an issue tackled by two environmental lawyers at the University of Tasmania: Phillipa McCormack and Jan McDonald.[6] They point out that Australia has gained the unenviable title of the first country in the world to lose a mammal species because of climate change. The Bramble Cay melomys, a native rodent found on one tiny sand island in a remote part of the Great Barrier Reef, reportedly became extinct after rising seas destroyed its habitat (as mentioned in chapter 6):

> Melomys' likely extinction is a symptom of the massive changes taking place across the natural world and that, faced with these changes, we cannot possibly save every species unless vast sums are allocated,

the lawyers write.

> We should be trying to conserve everything we can, or at least minimising the number of plants, animals and ecosystems that are lost. The problem is that ... [o]ur conservation laws were drafted

> on the assumption that if human intervention could be avoided or managed, plants and animals would survive in their natural, pristine environments. We now know that that is not the case … Climate change will rapidly accelerate environmental change [while] shifting temperature and rainfall will shift the specific conditions that species depend on to survive. Everything will be on the move.

This was also the theme of a big conference, Species on the Move, held in Hobart in February 2016. Two hundred fifty-nine specialists from more than forty countries presented a mountain of evidence about the lasting impact of climate change on the world's animals and plants. The audience was told how studies of thousands of species show most are already moving from their habitats or altering their life cycles, mainly because of climate change, how animals are moving higher up the slopes of mountains in north Queensland while subtropical fish have been caught in cold Tasmanian waters, lured there by an 'ocean hotspot' after the waters had warmed nearly four times faster than the global average. Since 1900, about half of all species studied have shifted their ranges toward the north or south poles by as much as 1600 kilometres, and to higher elevations by up to 400 metres. The future for those species unable to move, of course, is adapt or die.

American biologist Camille Parmesan, a lead author for the Intergovernmental Panel on Climate Change, told the conference that two-thirds of the world's species had begun 'breeding, migrating or blooming earlier in spring'. Every major group that had been studied – birds, trees, herbs, butterflies, mammals, amphibians, corals, invertebrates, fish, marine mammals and plankton – had been affected.

> Species are on the move, in tropical and temperate lands and seas all the way to frozen or not-so-frozen Arctic and Antarctic regions while the rising pace of change is forcing some species into a pattern of almost continuous migration.

As McCormack and McDonald argue, however, many plants and animals will not be able to move or to move fast enough to keep pace with climate change on their own:

> To conserve these species, we may need to engage in high intervention conservation strategies such as assisted colonisation. This involves moving an individual, population or species to a place where it has never been found before – except conservation laws in Australia are not designed to accommodate these kinds of dynamic and proactive approaches to conservation management. Instead they promote keeping or returning the environment to what it used to be, whether it is pristine or not.

Existing laws, that is, could actually impede conservation in a changing world. In a second essay, McCormack, McDonald and three other environmentalists refer to the ways existing laws emphasise maintaining the current status and location of ecosystems or returning them to an 'undisturbed' state.[7] The laws place high value on biodiversity 'that is rare, native and wild; and they emphasise reserves, especially on public land, as the sites for most conservation effort'. Such laws typically require government agencies to conserve national parks in their 'natural state' (usually defined by the plants and animals that are already there or that have been found there in the past). Given the current conditions, some species might need to be moved into national parks, even if they have never been found there before, or removed from national parks to somewhere more climatically suitable – except current laws do not allow this to occur.

Rather than adopt an outdated idea of what is 'natural', Australia needs new objectives that focus on diversity and ecosystem function and health, the team argues. If introducing plants or animals into a national park increases their chances of surviving under climate change without affecting the health of the park's ecosystems, they should not be excluded just because the species is not 'native' to that specific park. Such an approach would help species adapt by being able to move across boundaries. The Tasmanians say that choices based on what species should be funded are rarely transparent and the public is rarely consulted about what people value the most:

> We need to have a national conversation about how we value species and ecosystems in a changing world. If more people realised that we cannot save everything, perhaps more people would demand that appropriate funding is allocated to saving as much as possible. While funding remains limited, we need objectives … that clearly define the criteria we are using for targeting some species for protection while letting others go. We urgently need a national conversation about what reform is needed to ensure the best possible conservation results for Australia's precious wildlife, plants and ecosystems …

UNFORTUNATELY, GOVERNMENTS TOO often act in ways that are completely contrary to conservation goals. Consider the New South Wales Liberal government, which, in May 2016, proposed removing all restrictions on land clearance across the state – a move that would clearly have a disastrous impact on the state's birds, animals and plants. In language reminiscent of *Nineteen Eighty Four*, the government claimed these so-called 'reforms' were to conserve 'biodiversity and facilitate ecologically sustainable development'.[8] In reality, the changes would effectively scrap existing limits on what landholders could do and give them a free rein to clear as much of their properties as they wished. The same situation happened in Queensland when the one-term Newman government abandoned restrictions on how much private land could be cleared of its bush – with the inevitable consequence that land clearances across the state jumped by 300 per cent in a mere three years.

In New South Wales, the government's 'reforms' will also inevitably lead to large increases in land clearance, increased carbon emissions and more threats to endangered species, says University of Western Sydney research lecturer Neil Perry:

> Essentially, the government will repeal the *Native Vegetation Act*, which restricted land clearance on farms, and replace it with a market-based approach that provides flexibility for farmers to clear land. While the NVA had certain exemptions where land clearance was allowed, the new *Biodiversity Conservation Act* has many more … for example, [what the Act deems as] low-risk vegetation includes land that has been cleared at some point in the last 25 years, and grasslands assessed as being of low conservation value …[9]

In contrast to this pandering to powerful rural lobbying, the federal Labor government in 2007 established an unusual Environmental Stewardship Programme that could be a model for tackling extinction rates among some species by providing grants to farmers to conserve threatened ecosystems on their properties.[10] The aim was for species that had disappeared locally to return and recolonise the land – as happened when biologists conducted a similar experiment in Victoria, as described in chapter 7. Under the stewardship program, however, instead of researchers conducting a regeneration program, the government offered grants to farmers who signed contracts to deliver results for up to fifteen years.

Nearly 300 'land managers' across New South Wales, Queensland and South Australia agreed to take part. In return for receiving a total of $150 million, they implemented conservation management plans for landscapes covering a variety of threatened woodlands and grasslands, home to hundreds of species of native birds, including the superb and turquoise parrots, marsupials such as the squirrel glider, and thousands of native plants. As has happened in many other important regions in Australia, areas such as the box-gum grassy woodlands had been cleared of up to 95 per cent of their original habitat for wheat growing and sheep grazing – these are now, ironically and somewhat belatedly, listed nationally as 'critically endangered …'

The other unusual aspect of the scheme was that, soon after it was launched, the Australian National University (ANU) was commissioned to design and undertake an ongoing monitoring program. This meant that biologists from the university's Fenner School of Environment and Society have been keeping tabs on what the farmers have been doing for more than six years. In a preliminary report, four members of the team describe the results as 'exciting', although it is early yet: the last of the contracts will not end until 2027.

> Farmers undertake controlled grazing by livestock in woodland remnants, replant native woodland, avoid firewood harvesting, stop removing rocks from the bush, and control weeds and feral animals. So far, the data show that the farmers are doing a good job and it is money very well spent,

the ecologists write.[11]

> To find out if the program is working, we have to compare managed (conserved) areas with 'control patches' where land owners haven't done anything. This comparison shows that funded management patches have fewer environmental weeds, greater native plant species richness, more natural regeneration of native plants, smaller areas of erodible bare ground, and more species of woodland birds. In the space of six years, the Australian government, in concert with Australian farmers through modest investment, has generated

significant, positive environmental changes on farms. In fact, the box gum project can set the bar for many other conservation programs.

As the ANU biologists point out, the impacts go beyond just improving the environment and saving species, because there have also been notable social benefits: farmers are now highly motivated to deliver better environmental outcomes on their farms and 'to showcase the integration of multiple objectives of agricultural production and conservation'. The income stream they receive has helped some survive 'the almost unprecedented hardships' associated with the millennium drought in the mid to late 2000s, while anecdotal evidence suggests that farmers engaged in successful environmental programs suffer fewer mental health problems. The landholder goodwill arising from the program and the change in attitude towards land management will far outweigh the fifteen-year investment in the program, the biologists say. Also, the long-term funding model is a more sensible approach than one-off payments, and provides a realistic timeframe to achieve results: 'Landscape recovery will span multiple governmental cycles and every dollar must be spent wisely. Programs like [this one] give some guidance on how large-scale environmental programs can be more successful.'

STRONG LAWS CAN also help threatened species recover, sometimes with quite spectacular results, as a study by American biologists has revealed.[12] They report that 85 per cent of continental United States birds that are now protected under the federal *Endangered Species Act* have increased or stabilised their population numbers since being listed – with the average population increase an astonishing 624 per cent. Unlike Australia, where birds and animals can be classed as vulnerable, endangered or critically endangered while their habitats remain unprotected, in the United States the habitat of threatened species is carefully monitored. As well, 90 per cent of United States birds listed as threatened all have detailed federal recovery plans.

The report says that the numbers of threatened and endangered birds, though in great danger of extinction, increased much more than birds not listed under the Act. The researchers attribute this outcome to societal support for protection of endangered species and the intense management of threatened birds within a strong, clear, well-established regulatory context. This management is generally guided by clear federal recovery goals. Most management decisions are made under a 'best available science' standard that encourages scientific updating while 'limiting the influence of contrary economic and political interests'; and most plans and decisions made under the *Endangered Species Act* are subject to public review and enforcement. In other words, almost exactly the opposite of what currently occurs in Australia.

'Sensitive but unprotected birds, on the other hand, tend to be passively or indirectly managed through broad, mostly discretionary, inconsistently funded and often incomplete regional, ecosystem and habitat-based systems,' the biologists write.

> They provide important ecosystem protections and undoubtedly have slowed the decline of many species, but are not as effective as the highly directed, quantitative and species-specific provisions of the Endangered Species Act.

Such provisions, unfortunately, do not apply in Australia.

While the number of birds first protected under the United States Act between 1967 and 1970 has on average increased by more than 600 per cent since 1968, those of unprotected birds actually fell by up to 67 per cent in the same time. As the biologists comment:

> Our results not only demonstrate the tremendous success of the Act, [as well as] the species-specific management of public lands, they

highlight the fact that even relatively common species may need help to prevent them from becoming endangered in future. It is important to find a way to stabilise or restore those populations before they reach the point where Endangered Species Act protections are needed.

Ninety per cent of United States birds currently listed as threatened have formal recovery plans prepared under the direction of federal, state and academic scientists through the US Fish and Wildlife Service. More than half the plans specify the length of time expected to achieve full recovery goals, with the average period expected for full recovery estimated to be sixty-three years! To date, the average time birds have been listed under the act is only thirty-six years – so the expected year of full recovery for these species will not occur until 2038. That is, the Act and the management plans are expected to operate for decades to ensure the survival of threatened species, in contrast to the somewhat ad hoc arrangements that exist in Australia.

Samantha Vine, head of conservation at BirdLife Australia, says these results demonstrate the need for stronger nature laws here in Australia:

> If birds in Australia are to thrive, we need a new generation of environment laws and governance that actually protects the places and birds that Australians love ... to protect and recover threatened species we must protect critical habitat ... The survival of threatened birds such as Carnaby's black-cockatoos, Regent honeyeaters, Swift parrots and Eastern curlews all depend on strong environment laws.

ALTHOUGH THERE IS little evidence that federal or state governments will enact laws guaranteeing the survival of endangered species in the same way that the United States did fifty years ago, there is still some hope. In part this is because more and more concerned people across

Australia are taking action to try to ensure that threatened birds and their environments do survive. A splendid example of what can be achieved by a few dedicated individuals is a scheme in Victoria aimed at saving the regent honeyeater, among Australia's most threatened birds. The Regent Honeyeater Recovery Project was established in northern Victoria in the early 1990s by the then Victorian Department of Conservation and Environment but quickly became independent and managed by local farmers.[13]

The project is now run through an incorporated body with local activist and bird-lover Ray Thomas as project coordinator and 115 farmers actively involved as stakeholders. Victoria's Department of Sustainability and Environment provides office space while grants from the federal government's Natural Heritage Trust have been the main source of funding in recent years. Self-generated income is now earned from the 50,000 or so seedlings propagated and planted each year by

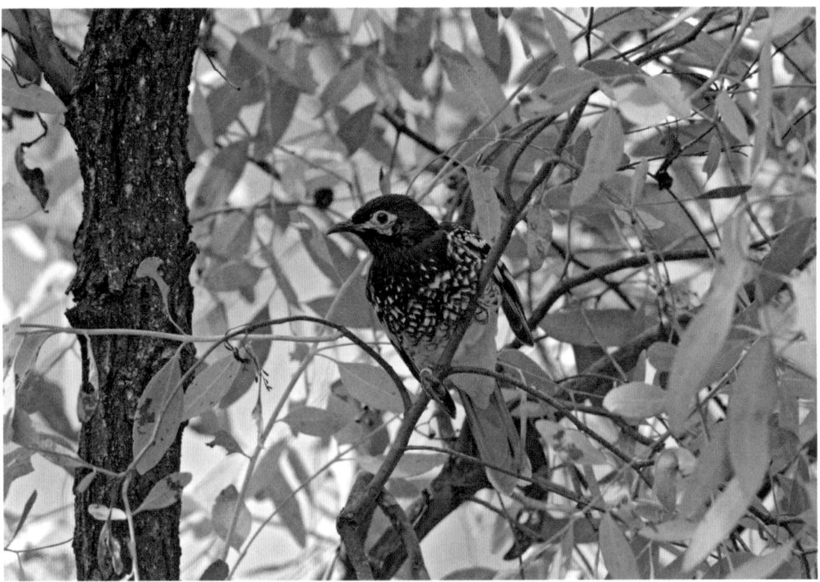

The regent honeyeater is critically endangered because of widespread clearing of ironbark forests.

project staff and volunteers. Thomas, a former secondary school science teacher, has devoted nearly twenty years to this community effort to protect and restore significant remnants of native woodland habitat in the Lurg Hills district near Benalla in central Victoria.

Although his achievements are remarkable, Thomas recounts them in a matter-of-fact kind of way, typical of those who have been born, lived and work in the bush:

> Over the past eighteen years, a colleague and I have worked with more than 140 landholders, 38 schools, plus .... more than 28,000 volunteers. Nearly 1400 hectares of habitat has been restored, more than 525,000 seedlings planted on 490 sites, 240 kilometres of fencing built, and 400 nesting boxes placed in trees – significant gains by any standard ... Achieving these goals on land that is also prized for farming requires working closely with farmers to gain their support and insights.

Thomas says threatened wildlife has responded to the improved conditions, with woodland birds moving into the planted areas after only five or six years, although most of the young trees are not large enough yet to support colonies of regent honeyeaters. Aggressive species such as noisy miners are losing ground to the shyer birds in the dense undergrowth shelters created by volunteers, while bird counts show a 250 per cent increase in the population of endangered grey-crowned babblers as the birds move through the corridors of bush that have been created, using them as 'stepping stones' to reach more fertile breeding habitats.

'In these days of escalating environmental problems we need to empower people, enable them to participate in positive success stories and demonstrate that they can make a difference,' he says.

> The growing number of volunteers, particularly young people from the cities, is a clear sign that we are succeeding here as well. They

come to lend a hand, but they also take away deeper ecological insights and practical learnings that feed into other projects elsewhere. The Regent honeyeater project is a great example of what can be achieved.

AS IS THE case for too many of Australia's birds, regent honeyeaters are critically endangered because of the loss of their box-ironbark forests. The birds feed mainly on nectar and other plant sugars from flowering eucalypts but they also catch insects and spiders, as well as native and cultivated fruits. The loss of these food sources because of land clearing has reduced their population to threat levels. Similar to other migratory birds, researchers say that regent honeyeaters have a tendency to follow definite routes to flowering trees at certain times of the year, and older birds in a flock will have detailed knowledge of where they previously found food. If the numbers of these leaders fall, however, their collective knowledge is lost, leaving the remaining birds uncertain of the migratory path to more food.

In 1995, with the species facing extinction in the wild, twenty regent honeyeaters in New South Wales were captured and cared for by curators at Taronga Park Zoo in Sydney. There the birds survived and bred prolifically, so much so that captive-reared birds have been successively released into the wild, many where Ray Thomas is based in Victoria. Monitoring of their release has revealed the birds have survived for several months before taking off from the release site. Thomas says the honeyeaters had already displayed all the appropriate behaviour of wild regent honeyeaters and had started nesting, with at least one bird rearing a fledgling. He says the success of releasing captive-bred birds, however, depends on the presence of suitable habitat and the birds locating it, so a lot of effort from volunteers and biologists has gone into protecting key areas, much of which is on private land and on stock routes, rather than in reserves.

Thomas has been involved with the zoo program from its inception and says there have been four releases of the Taronga-bred birds in recent years and that the process is now well established and refined:

> The released zoo birds quickly find their own food, interact with the wild Regents and, even more heartening, a number from previous releases returned to the same forest one or more years later to mix with the new cohort. In 2016, the number of birds released was raised to 77, more than double the previous number ... Many nesting attempts have been observed ... but in most cases the breeding success – that is, fledging young into the wild population – has been very low.

To try to find out what was happening, a few birds were radio tracked and there was extensive monitoring to find where they were nesting. Surveillance cameras were also installed to watch the attempts at nest building by the regents as well as other honeyeaters:

> The videos revealed a daunting number of threats to nesting, but also the tenacity of the Regents to try and try again after failing, with some building their nests in unusual positions such as on an open stump only half a metre off the ground! Several nests had been pulled apart although it wasn't possible to say if it was by the Regents themselves or by other competitive birds, or if it was after nesting had failed,

Thomas says in one of his regular newsletters to project members.

> Some Regent pairs were persistent enough to attempt nesting two, three or four times but many honeyeater nests, including those of Regents, were attacked by predators that included magpies, currawongs, kookaburras, goannas, ravens, squirrel gliders, sugar

> gliders, and even sparrows. Thinking laterally, we have other variables to manipulate, such as planting under-storey around remnant trees to boost the protective cover for woodland birds like the Regents ... Adding nectar-rich trees and shrubs to remnants also makes the habitat more productive overall and these actions combined can give Regents not just reduced competition, but also a richer food resource.

BIRDLIFE AUSTRALIA IS also fighting to save birds from extinction and it has a nation-wide army of supporters and thirty or more species-saving projects operating across the country. These range from site-specific, on-the-ground works to national surveys involving thousands of volunteers, all run by dedicated, experienced people passionate about protecting birds and their habitats. As mentioned earlier in this book, the organisation's chief executive, Paul Sullivan, called on members in August 2016 to help with the work being done to save woodland birds in the eastern states, such as the critically endangered swift parrot and the regent honeyeater:

> There are just 1,000 breeding pairs left of these beautiful Swift parrots, and fewer than 400 Regent honeyeaters. Birds like these are struggling to survive amid habitat loss from inappropriate development. They're constantly facing new threats to their habitats – and their very existence,

Sullivan says.

> The situation has become so critical that I want to fast-track a new Woodland Birds Conservation Action Plan to help these birds, and BirdLife Australia needs help. We will use our collective voice to lobby

> against habitat-destroying development such as the steel fabrication facility in the Hunter Economic Zone in New South Wales, home to many threatened birds; and protect and improve crucial habitat on private land through community education projects.

Along the lines of the Environmental Stewardship Program, BirdLife Australia will continue working with landowners to help them conserve habitat for woodland birds; undertake habitat restoration and revegetation projects; and increase community surveys and monitoring efforts. Sullivan believes these actions will not only help protect the swift parrot and regent honeyeater, but also thirty-eight other threatened woodland birds, as well as eighteen endangered ecological communities and numerous threatened flora species. BirdLife volunteers have been working to slow the swift parrot's bleak trajectory by planting hundreds of hectares of appropriate habitat, participating in annual surveys across south-eastern Australia and monitoring captive-released birds.

Sullivan refers to the 12,000 places throughout the world that have been identified as Important Bird and Biodiversity Areas or IBAs. One IBA, the Hunter Area in New South Wales, was chosen by BirdLife International as a success story. The Hunter biodiversity area is best known for its population of the critically endangered regent honeyeater and has been, in the recent past, home to 25 per cent of the world's population of this species; it was also the scene of the largest known regent honeyeater breeding event in modern times, while similarly supporting critically endangered swift parrots and a number of other declining woodland species.

One of the most important features of the Hunter area is its unfragmented forests, which exhibit a strong 'western influence' in their flora and fauna. Because they are closer to the coast than other similar forests, they receive more reliable rainfall, making the area a valuable refuge when forests further west experience drought. This feature makes them especially important to regent honeyeaters – yet this one intact area of bushland was earmarked for development by the local municipal council that dubbed it the 'Hunter Economic Zone'. The proposed development would have seen significant areas of bush cleared and it was only after a landmark court case that the council's permission to develop the area was declared invalid. A wealth of data collected by BirdLife Australia was crucial in determining the court's decision.

THEN THERE IS Bush Heritage Australia, a non-profit conservation organisation established by Bob Brown, one of the nation's best known environmental activists and a former Tasmanian senator and parliamentary leader of the Australian Greens. Brown founded Bush Heritage in 1991 after buying 241 hectares of native forest in Tasmania's Liffey Valley to save it from loggers. He used prize money from an environmental award he'd won as the deposit, and then ran a campaign to raise the remaining $200,000. The forest is now the Liffey River and Dry's Bluff reserves, part of the million hectares of private conservation reserves that Bush Heritage has set up across Australia. The reserves are managed in a similar way to national parks and the land is legally protected, with the intention of safeguarding it permanently.

Under the Bush Heritage scheme, partnerships are formed with other landowners to support conservation management on their properties so that, along with the thirty-eight reserves that the non-profit company directly owns, more than 6 million hectares of ecologically important and threatened landscapes across Australia are now protected. With more than 70 per cent of Australian land in private hands, Bush Heritage extends its reach by forming partnerships with other landowners while also working with Aboriginal groups, farmers, pastoralists and others to 'help identify conservation threats, plan strategies, source funding, and develop skills and resources needed for long-term sustainability'.

'From humble beginnings in Tasmania's Liffey Valley we now protect more than a hundred species of rare and threatened native animals, and thousands of species of plants across every state and territory in Australia,' says Bush Heritage chief executive Gerard O'Neill. He also refers to the 'ground-breaking' partnerships the organisation has developed with landholders as well as traditional owners, while emphasising a remarkable flagship scheme that was launched in 2015: a ten-year science plan aimed at expanding the research effort.

The decade-long plan seems remarkably ambitious but then it is starting from a strong base with the organisation already running fifty-five conservation research projects involving fifty scientists from fifteen universities. O'Neill says the aim is to double that number by 2025 through collaborative research, science fellowships and 'citizen science': 'We'll support young scientists ...while the organisation's growth will support 120 collaborative research projects aimed at halting biodiversity loss,' he says. 'As well, we intend to ... secure funding for Bush Heritage–led research through small $10,000–$50,000 per year grants so that by 2025 we'll aim to secure three small research grants per year.'

The United Nations General Assembly declared the years 2011 to 2020 the Decade on Biodiversity, with the goal of significantly reducing biodiversity loss.[14] The UN also created goals 'known as the Aichi Biodiversity Targets and, in Australia, they translate into ten specific goals, including setting aside an additional 60 million hectares of native habitat for biodiversity conservation,' O'Neill says. 'Bush Heritage Australia has set the ambitious goal of doubling the land we have secured by direct acquisition and partnerships from three to six million hectares to complement the government-managed national reserve system.'

Early in 2016, Bush Heritage was in the national spotlight with the news of the rediscovery in western Queensland of the night parrot (*Pezoporus occidentalis*), one of the world's rarest birds. Also grabbing national and world attention was an announcement that the organisation planned to establish a conservation property to protect the bird's environment by buying a 56,000 hectare slice of a large pastoral property where the bird was located. O'Neill describes discovery of the parrot as 'an incredibly exciting and important time in the history of conservation biology in Australia'. The planned land purchase of 56,000 hectares is intended to establish the Pullen Pullen Reserve to protect the night parrot population, estimated at twenty to forty birds (the parrot's name in the local Aboriginal language is Pullen Pullen). The reserve is said to be ideal night parrot habitat, rugged terrain with old-growth spinifex amid rocky ridges.

But Bush Heritage faces costly challenges to secure the long-term future of the species, having to take out a mortgage of $1.5 million to acquire the land, even though newspaper reports claimed it was already $3.5 million short of the $5 million it had planned to spend over three years on research, management and buying more property. The organisation is also involved in a dispute with another big nature reserve company, the Australian Wildlife Conservancy (AWC), over plans by the conservancy to build a predator-proof fence in the Diamantina National Park to protect bilbies and other endangered animals from feral cats and foxes. The federal government is providing $1.2 million towards what would be one of the largest investments in Queensland national parks. Ornithologists at Bush Heritage, however, fear that night parrots will be killed if they hit the fence during their night-time flights. In 2006, a park ranger discovered a dead night parrot in an area of the Diamantina Park fairly close to Pullen Pullen – it had been decapitated after striking a barbed-wire fence.

In a curious parallel with Bush Heritage, the Australian Wildlife Conservancy was also started in 1991 when its founder, Martin Copley, bought an area of land to protect endangered animals, birds and plants. The non-profit company now claims to be the largest private owner of land for conservation in Australia, with twenty-five properties protecting endangered wildlife across more than 3.25 million hectares in regions such as the Kimberley, Cape York, Lake Eyre and the Top End, stretching across the nation to the south-eastern coast and the south-western forests: 'The total AWC estate is nearly half the size of Tasmania or around the same size as Belgium,' the company website declares, adding that 519 bird species and 204 mammals are protected in the sanctuaries, including the largest remaining populations of threatened species such as the bilby, the numbat, the Gouldian finch and the bridled nail-tail wallaby.

> AWC sanctuaries contain an extraordinary diversity of habitats from the hottest deserts to the wettest rainforest as well as tall eucalypt woodlands, tropical savanna, extensive wetlands and grasslands. Around eighty staff manage our 3.25 million hectare estate and almost 80 per cent are based in the field (a much higher proportion than any other organisation in our sector). Across our estate, we manage the largest cat[-] and fox-free area on mainland Australia; the two largest feral herbivore-free areas in Australia, and the largest non-government fire program in Australia ...

THESE FEW PROJECTS, of course, are just some examples of the many ways various groups, and large numbers of individuals around Australia, are trying to counter the extinction crisis that has gripped the nation's wildlife. This is the reality, of course: Australia is facing an extinction crisis, and not just because of the short-sightedness of federal and state governments. Climate change is an even greater threat to the survival of all life on this planet.

But consider the mystery and wonder of birds: the magical qualities they possess, their constant presence in our lives, the music they fill our dawns and sunsets with. Imagine a world without these extraordinary creatures. Birds were flitting around this globe long before most of the animals that now share it existed – and a hundred million years before the first humans trod the earth. We have become the masters – and potential destroyers – of this planet. So it is our task to prevent the living world from disappearing into the abyss, taking with it these feathered angels and the marvel of their existence.

Epilogue

'Here's a Spot for a Home', They Said

The arrival of two swallows at our new house in 1980 was the start of my fascination with birds because it was the first chance I'd ever had to get an up-close-and-personal view of two small creatures intent on starting a new generation – an unforgettable experience. It led me to set out to learn more about birds and, later, to also interview the biologists who spend their lives studying them so I could write up their stories for publications around Australia. Increasingly disturbing reports about the state of Australian bird-life and the threats that climate change poses prompted me to write a book that I hoped would seve as a warning to readers about the dangers facing the world's birds – and to all us humans as well.

IT WAS THE end of November when the two visitors first arrived and fluttered around under the carport – a young couple inspecting the foundations of their new home. For days they worked, constructing their love nest from pellets of mud strengthened with bits of straw. About 90 millimetres across and just as deep, the nest these welcome

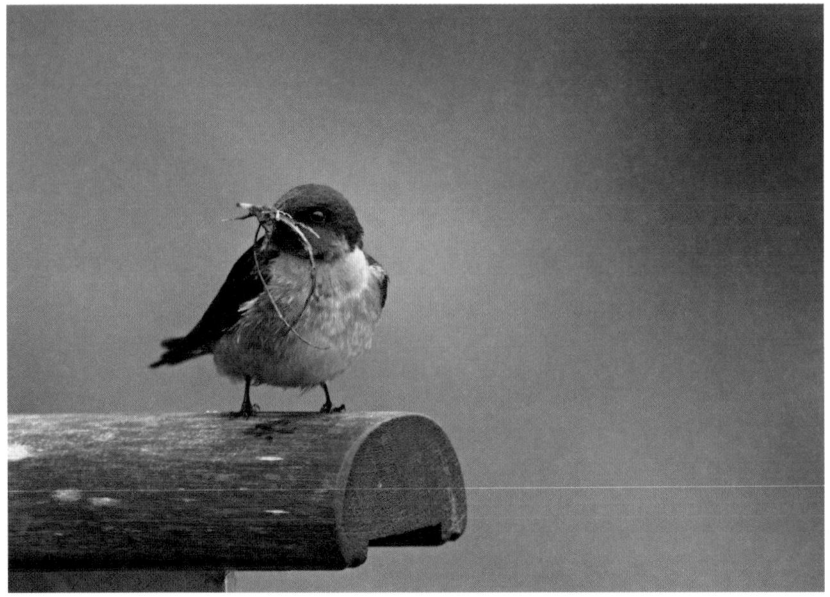

The welcome swallow provides an untiring meals-on-wings service for its young.

swallows built was cunningly placed just below the ceiling, sheltered from the weather and protected from feline predators prowling below.

The two birds took hours, swooping in and out with grass, hair and small feathers to line the nest. When all was ready, the female sat inside her cup-shaped shelter and waited. From time to time her mate paid a visit, gracefully swirling about her and hovering with his deeply forked tail and pointed wings spread as if he were a minute ballet dancer performing on air. Like his mate but slightly larger, he was metallic blue-black on top of the body, light grey below on the breast and belly, and rust-coloured on the forehead, throat and upper breast with a black bill, dark brown eyes and blackish legs and feet.

Once, when the female had left the nest to feed, I used a mirror to spy inside the soft and cleverly woven bedroom. Four eggs, each not much longer than a thumbnail, had been laid; they were white and spotted with red-brown dots. For more than two weeks the female kept the eggs warm. Then one morning, the week before Christmas, there was renewed activity around the nest as both birds swept continually in and out, like frock-coated waiters rushing to and fro in a busy restaurant.

Again I used the peeking mirror. This time, there were four naked, blind and squirming creatures in the nest: miniature pterodactyls with scaly heads and wings, entirely lacking the brown and black-feathered beauty of their parents.

In a matter of days, though, the tiny nestlings were covered with down and the efforts of their parents to fill the ever-gaping beaks of their offspring became even more frantic. The peremptory cries of the four inchoate, wide-open yellow mouths – 'Food!', 'Food!', 'More food!' – had its echo when human visitors came to stay and brought their young baby with them. Its shrieks of hunger generated the same anxiety, the same rush to offer succour among the adult humans as the young swallows' urgent twitterings created in their parents.

Swallows have to eat 400 times a day, or almost every four minutes, to maintain their energy but, with the demands of their tiny offspring increasing by the hour, the two grown-up birds seemed to spend all their time on the wing. I could see the swallows always caught their prey in flight using their incredible acrobatic flying skills (although the short rictal bristles that border the beak also help guide the insects into the bird's wide open mouth).

While the nestlings were very young their parents not only brought them their food but also regularly cleaned out the nest, taking the droppings away in their beaks. Soon, though, the little ones had been potty-trained: tiny feathered bottoms appeared frequently over the side of the nest, leaving a growing white mound on the concrete below.

Eventually, the adults seemed to decide it was time the youngsters stopped perching on the edge of the nest and began flying. They still swooped about the nest, but they no longer filled the open mouths on each flight. Instead they darted past with much twittering chatter, as if urging the ones on the edge to jump off and follow them.

Again I thought of the parallels in human families: the tension as teenagers begin their first steps towards independence. Of the banging bedroom door as the adolescent female flings herself away after a row with Mum or Dad: 'But why can't I stay out till 3 am? Everyone else does!' Like teenagers, though, the young swallows seemed reluctant to break with the security that the nest offered. They sat for hours on the edge, flapping their wings tentatively and peering down at the ground, no doubt awed by how far it was to fall. I estimated that an equivalent location for a teenager was 30 metres up in the air – and for many parents that might seem the best place for them.

Like teenagers, too, the young birds began to take considerable care in their appearance, each one meticulously grooming and preening its new feathers as if to suggest that something momentous was about to occur. The juveniles were duller and browner than their parents, the reddish-brown areas paler, with a buff-white forehead and throat and shorter tail streamers.

ALL THIS TIME the darting adults maintained their untiring meals-on-wings service. They also kept up a continual surveillance of the nest and the wellbeing of its occupants, even to the extent of making lightning sorties at me if I trespassed too close to the family home. Perhaps it was only instinct, yet the care and attention these small birds lavished on their young was a joy to see.

It brought to mind the observations of the nineteenth-century French naturalist Baron Georges Cuvier, who also studied a pair of swallows as they built a mud nest under the eaves of his home.

Cuvier was watching one day when the nest was invaded and taken over by a sparrow. The bullying interloper sat defiant in the nest, thrusting its beak angrily out of the entrance hole, keeping the rightful owners at bay. Finally, the swallows flew off. But they returned with an aroused host of neighbourhood swallows. With beaks full of the mud they use for nest-making, the birds converged on the invaded nest, smearing and daubing. As they veered off, Cuvier saw that the sparrow-occupied nest had been sealed shut: It had become the invader's tomb. The Frenchman said he felt that he'd had an extraordinary look into one of the fundamental meanings of life itself.

A significant figure in the natural sciences in the early nineteenth century, Cuvier helped establish the fields of comparative anatomy and palaeontology through his work comparing living animals with fossils. His four-volume *The Animal Kingdom (Le Règne Animal)* was published in 1817 and presented the results of his life's studies into the structure of living and fossil animals.

One of the first naturalists to fully describe the welcome swallow (*Hirundo neoxena*) was the great British observer John Gould. In his massive *The Birds of Australia*, Gould wrote that the species name and common name of the swallow was a reference to people welcoming its return as a herald of spring in southern parts of Australia. Other reports, however, suggest the name comes from the swallow's habit of building nests above doorways or on porches or, in my case, beneath the upper storey of a two-storey house – although when it does create a new home among humans it is not always welcome.

Biologists now accept that two subspecies of welcome swallows exist, with *Hirundo neoxena carteri* being slightly larger than *Hirundo neoxena neoxena*, even though the differences between the two are not obvious. The swallows that live in the eastern regions of Australia usually migrate north in winter while those on the western side, and in New Zealand, are mainly sedentary.

Flocks of swallows can become quite large, with up to 500 birds perching along powerlines or on fences to regroup. A birdwatcher in Perth says he once saw more than 200 arriving in waves at the Bayswater Bird Sanctuary. He told me how the massed flock of welcome swallows, tree martins, fairy martins and rainbow bee-eaters filled the air.

In the 1950s, welcome swallows began extending their range into New Zealand, and have more recently been recorded in New Guinea, New Caledonia and on other nearby island groups, such as the Chatham Islands and Auckland Island. Although the welcome swallow is the dominant species in Australia, its winter range in the north of the country overlaps with that of wintering barn swallows (*Hirundo rustica*), with the latter easily distinguished by their blue breast band. Barn swallows, now regularly seen from the Kimberley across to north-east and south-east Queensland, are also the world's most widespread member of the family, having migrated over the centuries across Europe, Asia, Africa and the Americas.

IN A REMARKABLE book called *A Single Swallow: Following an epic journey from South Africa to South Wales*, British author and birdwatcher Horatio Clare notes that, of all birds, the barn swallow carries 'the greatest weight of prophetic folklore';[1] that is, the swallow is believed to be capable of foretelling the future. Clare writes that Plutarch reported how swallows had nested under the prow of Cleopatra's flagship before the battle of Actium – an event seen as an omen of the disaster that then occurred. He also points out that barn swallows and humans have lived alongside each other for thousands of years: the earliest recorded instance was a 15,000-year-old nest in a cave in Derbyshire in England that had also been inhabited by a man. It also seems certain that welcome swallows have lived alongside Indigenous Australians for tens of thousands of years and may have played a part in their lore.

Horatio Clare and his brother, Alexander, were born in England but grew up on a hill farm in the Black Mountains of south Wales, where they were raised by their mother. She had divorced their father and had fallen in love with the mountains and with farming sheep. It was in those mountains that Horatio became a bird-lover and the keen observer who was entranced by the swallows that returned each April to their nests in the eaves of his family's barn.

In *A Single Swallow*, Clare describes how he decided to leave England and fly to South Africa so he could follow migrating barn swallows from their Cape Town wintering grounds all the way across Africa as they made their way back to Britain. This is a distance of some 10,000 kilometres. It was an impossible task for a human to try following a large flock of small birds, but it did make for a great story.

As with the swallows he tracks across Africa, Clare's journey takes him across two continents and fourteen countries – an epic and adventurous expedition for the human traveller, yet it is one that the swallows undertake twice every year. In explaining why he made the trip to South Africa and back, Clare says batteries and transmitters were too big at the time to be attached to swallows. 'The only way to follow them, therefore, was to go with them.'

He admits he was unlikely to keep up with any one swallow, given that they fly at 4 metres a second in low gear, 14 metres a second at top speed and, depending on wind, route and inclination, they can cover 300 kilometres a day. They can do the entire trip from South Africa back to Britain in twenty-seven days. In contrast, his own trip took him more than three months.

For me, at home and watching the swallows that were nesting under my house and hunting insects on a nearby football field, I noticed they fly low when feeding and travel less than a metre above the ground and up to 5 or 6 metres when it looks as if they are just flying for the sheer fun of being in the air. Clare says swallows prefer to fly into or across the wind because this allows them enough lift to hunt as they fly, feeding with no fear of stalling.

BACK AT THE swallows' nest under my carport, by the second week in January things had started to heat up: two of the young swallows suddenly took to the air. Whether it was their own doing or because the other siblings had pushed them off wasn't clear. But away they went, almost as fast and graceful as their parents, although for a time landing on a limb or back at the nest seemed fraught with difficulty. As for the two remaining fledglings in the nest, I had begun to wonder if they were suffering from failure to launch. Their parents continued to bring them food and, seeing this, one of the newly airborne siblings fluttered back into the nest and pushed the other two aside to claim the next parental offering – a prodigal son returned.

Soon after, I went past the nest and unthinkingly slapped hard at a mosquito. As if this was the signal they had been waiting for, the prodigal and his two tardy companions leapt into space in a great flapping of wings and excited twittering. I caught a glimpse of their first soaring flight and, while each came back a couple of times to perch on a ledge outside the carport, as if to have a last look at their old home, none of the young returned to the nest.

Later that year, however, the parents came back and set about refurbishing the nest in preparation for another brood. The same events occurred with the regularity of someone ticking off the days on a calendar. This time, however, there were six eggs in the nest and when six hatchlings appeared, the parents were never still for a moment as they rushed back and forth with food for the gaping mouths. As the youngsters grew and became increasingly heavier, whatever cement the parents had used to bind the nest to the brick wall of the carport began to give way. Fortunately, the young had all fledged and three had already taken to the air when the nest finally collapsed beneath the three remaining. As it crashed to the concrete, the tardy young swallows were forced into flight and off they all went, up and away.

I hoped the parents would not be deterred by this minor catastrophe but they must have decided the carport was not safe enough, possibly because of the nest's collapse – or maybe it was because Sox the cat had taken to watching them carefully from on top of the car roof. We never saw them again and, after our small aerial neighbours had finally left us, the front of the house seemed a quieter, lonelier place. We had some inkling of what the entire household would be like when the human fledglings decided, finally, to set out on their own.[2]

THAT IMAGE OF an empty nest was to stay with me as I researched this book and came to realise how threatened birds now are by the actions of so many humans. Habitat destruction and climate change loom like a mushroom cloud over the future of all life on this planet.

We need to contemplate the dreadful prospect that, unless we act now, tiny fledglings will never again occupy their parents' nests – that every nest will be forever empty.

Notes

Introduction

1 'Finding Australian Birds: A Field Guide to Birding Locations'; Tim Dolby and Rohan Clarke; CSIRO Publishing, 2014.

2 *Climate Change Adaptation Plan for Australian Birds*; Stephen Garnett and Donald Franklin (eds); CSIRO Publishing, 2014. (See also *The origin and the future of birds: Two.*)

3 *Systematics and Taxonomy of Australian Birds*; L. Christidis and W.E. Boles; CSIRO Publishing, 2008.

4 *The State of Australia's Birds*; BirdLife Australia, July 2015.

5 'Penguin population could drop 60 percent by end of the century'; Megan Cimino, Matthew Oliver, Patricia Robertson, Charles Robertson, Heather J. Lynch, Vincent S. Saba; *Scientific Reports* (*Nature*), 29 June 2016.

6 'Rapid climate-driven loss of breeding habitat for Arctic migratory birds'; Hannah S. Wauchope, Justine D. Shaw, Øystein Varpe, Elena G. Lappo, David Boertmann, Richard B. Lanctot, Richard A. Fuller; *Global Change Biology*, 19 July 2016.

7 'Biodiversity: The ravages of guns, nets and bulldozers'; Sean L. Maxwell, Richard A. Fuller, Thomas M. Brooks, James E.M. Watson; *Nature*, 10 August 2016.

Chapter 1 The Sixth Mass Extinction

1 *Spotlight on threatened birds*; BirdLife International: http://datazone.birdlife.org/sowb/spotthreatbirds

2 'Accelerated modern human-induced species losses: Entering the sixth mass extinction'; Gerardo Ceballos, Paul R. Ehrlich, Anthony D. Barnosky, Andrés García, Robert M. Pringle, Todd M. Palmer; *Science Advances*, June 2015. For estimates of bird numbers and their declining populations see http://www.amnh.org/ology/features/askascientist/question16.php

3 'Critically endangered swift parrot breeding ground in Tasmania illegally logged for firewood'; Emillie Gramenz; ABC News, 26 July 2016; www.abc.net.au/news/2016-07-29/swift-parrot-habitat-illegaly-logged.../7672504
4 Ask a Scientist; http://www.amnh.org/ology/features/askascientist/question16.php
5 *Climate change refugia for terrestrial biodiversity*; Stephen Williams et al.; National Climate Change Adaptation Research Facility, June 2013.
6 'Climate change could empty wildlife from Australia's rainforests; The Conversation', 30 April 2015.
7 'Australian Bird Index Launched'; Tanya Loos; Connecting Country: http://connectingcountry.org.au/07/australian-bird-index-launched/; 17 July 2015.
8 'Citizen science monitoring reveals a significant, ongoing decline of the endangered Carnaby's black-cockatoo (*Calyptorhynchus latirostris*)'; Mathew R. Williams, Colin J. Yates, William D. Stock, Geoff W. Barrett, Hugh C. Finn; *Oryx: The International Journal of Conservation*, 1 July 2015.
9 'Bushfires are pushing species towards extinction'; Tim Doherty, Emma Burgess, Martine Maron, Robert Davis; *The Conversation*, 11 February 2016.

Chapter 2 Catastrophic Collapse of Seabirds

1 'Population trend of the world's monitored seabirds, 1950–2010'; M. Paleczny, E. Hammill, V. Karpouz, D. Pauly; *PLOS ONE*, June 2015. See also 'Rapid climate-driven loss of breeding habitat for Arctic migratory birds', Hannah S. Wauchope, Justine D. Shaw, Øystein Varpe, Elena G. Lappo, David Boertmann, Richard B. Lanctot, Richard A. Fuller; *Global Change Biology*, 19 July 2016.
2 'Cross-hemisphere migration of a 25 g songbird'; Franz Bairlein, D. Ryan Norris, Rolf Nagel, Marc Bulte, Christian C. Voigt, James W. Fox, David J. T. Hussell, Heiko Schmaljohann; *Biology Letters*, 15 February 2012.
3 'Body shrinkage due to Arctic warming reduces red knot fitness in tropical wintering range'; Jan A. van Gils, Simeon Lisovski, Tamar Lok, Włodzimierz Meissner, Agnieszka Ożarowska, Jimmy de Fouw, Eldar Rakhimberdiev, Mikhail Y. Soloviev, Theunis Piersma, Marcel Klaassen; *Science*, May 2016.
4 'Migratory shorebirds of the East Asian–Australasian Flyway: Population estimates and internationally important sites'; M. Bamford, D. Watkins, W. Bancroft, G. Tischler, J. Wahl; *Wetlands International - Oceania*, 2008.
5 'World Migratory Bird Day'; Spike Millington; http://www.eaaflyway.net/, 10 May 2016.
6 'Protected areas and global conservation of migratory birds'; Claire A. Runge, James E.M. Watson, Stuart H.M. Butchart, Jeffrey O. Hanson, Hugh P. Possingham, Richard A. Fuller; *Science*, December 2015.

7 *Wildlife Conservation Plan for Migratory Shorebirds*; Australian Department of the Environment, August 2015.
8 'The marvel of migration – grey plover tracking'; BirdLife Australia, http://birdlife.org.au/campaigns/the-marvel-of-migration
9 To see images of the birds, their flight path and the transmitter go to http://birdlife.org.au/campaigns/the-marvel-of-migration
10 'The marvel of migration – grey plover tracking'; Birdlife Australia: http://birdlife.org.au/campaigns/the-marvel-of-migration
11 'The evolution of sex roles in birds is related to adult sex ratio'; András Liker, Robert P. Freckleton, Tamás Székely; *Nature Communications*, March 2013.
12 'Australia's waterbirds are disappearing – but nuclear physics can help save them'; Kate Brandis; *The Conversation*; 15 April 2016.

Chapter 3 Secret, Silent Killer of Sea Life

1 'Plastic pollution'; Australian Marine Conservation Society: http://www.marineconservation.org.au/pages/plastic-pollution.html.
2 'Intergenerational transfer of plastic debris by Short-tailed Shearwaters (*Ardenna tenuirostris*)'; Mark J. Carey; *Emu Austral Ornithology*, August 2011.
3 'The frequency of ingested plastic debris and its effects on body condition of Short-tailed Shearwater (*Puffinus tenuirostris*) pre-fledging chicks in Tasmania, Australia'; Hannah R. Cousin, Heidi J. Auman, Rachael Alderman, Patti Virtue; *Emu Austral Ornithology,* February 2015.
4 'Understanding the effects of marine debris on wildlife'; Britta Denise Hardesty et al. Prepared for Earthwatch Australia and co-funded by Shell Australia and the CSIRO's *Wealth from Oceans,* National Flagship program, August 2014.
5 'Threat of plastic pollution to seabirds is global, pervasive, and increasing'; Chris Wilcox, Erik Van Sebille, Britta Denise Hardesty; *PNAS*, September 2015.
6 'Chemical pollutants sorbed to ingested microbeads from personal care products accumulate in fish'; Peter Wardrop, Jeff Shimeta, Dayanthi Nugegoda, Paul D. Morrison, Ana Miranda, Min Tang, Bradley O. Clarke; *Environmental Science & Technology,* 10 March 2016. See also 'Microplastics'.
7 *Catalyst*; http://www.abc.net.au/catalyst/stories/4424996.htm, 15 March 2016.

Chapter 4 Ashmore Reef: A Tropical Paradise for Seabirds

1 'The status of breeding seabirds and herons at Ashmore Reef, off the Kimberley coast, Australia'; Rohan H. Clarke, Michael Carter, George Swann, Jim Thomson; *Journal of the Royal Society of Western Australia,* 94: 365–376, 2011.
2 'BP agrees to pay $18.7 billion to settle Deepwater Horizon oil spill claims'; Daniel Gilbert and Sarah Kent; *The Wall Street Journal*, 2 July 2015.

3 *The status of seabirds and shorebirds at Ashmore Reef and Cartier and Browse Islands: Monitoring program for the Montara Well release – Pre-impact Assessment and First Post-impact Field Survey*; Rohan H. Clarke; Federal Department of the Environment, June 2010. It is available at the Federal Department of the Environment website, www.environment.gov.au

Chapter 5 Traversing the Globe: The Bass Strait Mutton-Birds

1 'Trans-equatorial migration of Short-tailed Shearwaters revealed by geolocators'; Mark J. Carey, Richard A. Phillips, Janet R. Silk, Scott A. Shaffer; *Emu Austral Ornithology*, September 2014.

Chapter 6 Saving Australia's Threatened Species

1 National Threatened Species List of the vulnerable, endangered or critically endangered birds. See: http://www.environment.gov.au/cgi-bin/sprat/public/publicthreatenedlist.pl

2 *The Australian Government's Threatened Species Strategy*; Federal Department of the Environment, July 2015.

3 *Recovery Planning: Restoring Life to Our Threatened Species;* BirdLife Australia, the Australian Conservation Foundation and Environmental Justice Australia; July 2015.

4 *Threatened Species Strategy Action Plan 2015–16: 20 birds by 2020*; Federal Department of Environment, January 2016.

5 'Understanding the importance of small patches of habitat for conservation'; Ayesha Tulloch, James Watson, Jeremy Ringma, Megan Barnes, Richard Fuller; *Journal of Applied Ecology*, 26 October 2015.

6 *Living Forests Report*, 'Chapter 5: Saving forests at risk'; *World Wildlife Fund,* April, 2015.

7 'Queensland land clearing is undermining Australia's environmental progress'; Martine Maron et al.'; *The Conversation*, 22 February 2016.

8 'A fine balance: Saving Australia's unique wildlife in a contested land'; Rocio Ponce-Reyes et al.; *CSIRO Blog*, 12 January 2016. This blog is an edited version of a much longer report by these biologists, published as *Priority Threat Management for Imperilled Species of the Queensland Brigalow Belt,* see http://gisera.org.au/publications/tech_reports_papers/Brigalow-Belt-PTM-study.pdf

Chapter 7 Giving New Life to the Babbler

1 'What Determines Habitat Quality for a Declining Woodland Bird in a Fragmented Environment: The Grey-Crowned Babbler (*Pomatostomus temporalis*) in South-Eastern Australia?'; Kate P. Stevens, Greg J. Holland, Rohan H. Clarke, Raylene Cooke, Andrew F. Bennett; *PLOS ONE*, 22 June 2015.

2 *Australian Birds, Their Nests and Eggs*; Gordon Beruldsen; self-published, Kennmore Hills, Queensland, 2004. Brisbane ornithologist Gordon Beruldsen was not only an expert on the nests and eggs of Australian birds, he also wrote a series of books over more than thirty years on Australia's waterbirds, its large and small birds, and also one on raptors. He died in 2007 at the age of seventy-four.

3 'Demographic Effects of Habitat Restoration for the Grey-Crowned Babbler (*Pomatostomus temporalis*) in Victoria, Australia'; Peter A. Vesk, Doug Robinson, Rodney van der Ree, Caroline M. Wilson, Shirley Saywell, Michael A. McCarthy; *PLOS ONE*, 15 July 2015.

4 'Group size and composition in the Grey-crowned Babbler (*Pomatostomus temporalis*) in an urban environment'; Kathryn Teare Ada Lambert, David Geering, Hugh Ford; *Corella, Journal of the Australian Bird Study Association*, September 2013.

5 'Landscape restoration and revegetation'; Landscape Ecology Research Group website https://landscapeecologyresearch.wordpress.com/research-projects/landscape-restoration-and-revegetation-2/

Chapter 8 A Multi-Coloured Mob of Angels

1 'Guided by the light: What is going on with those huge urban lorikeet roosts?'; S. Daoud-Pit and D.N. Jones; *Landscape and Urban Planning*, 2015.

2 'Modelling the occurrence of rainbow lorikeets (*Trichoglossus haematodus*) in Melbourne'; Pavlina Shukuroglou and Michael A. McCarthy; *Austral Ecology*, April 2006.

3 'Distribution of tree-hollows and hollow preferences by parrots in an urban landscape'; Adrian Davis, Richard E. Major, Charlotte E. Taylor; *Emu Austral Ornithology*, August 2014.

Chapter 9 The East Coast Mafia: Masked and Dangerous

1 'Initial Changes in the Avian Communities of Remnant Eucalypt Woodlands following a reduction in the abundance of noisy miners'; Merilyn J. Grey, Michael F. Clarke, Richard H. Loyn; *Wildlife Research 24*; CSIRO Publishing 1997.

2 'Do miners affect bird assemblages in continuous savanna woodlands in north-eastern Australia?'; A.S. Kutt, E.P. Vanderduys, J.J. Perry, G.C. Perkins; *Austral Ecology*, November 2012.

3 'Habitat selection by a despotic passerine, the Bell Miner: When restoring habitat through lantana removal is not enough', Kathryn T.A. Lambert, Lalit Kumar, Nick Reid, Paul G. McDonald; *Ecological Management & Restoration*, January 2016.

4 'Stop the miners: You can help Australia's birds by planting native gardens'; Kathryn Teare Ada Lambert; *The Conversation*, 5 November 2015.
5 'Avifaunal disarray due to a single despotic species'; Martine Maron et al.; *Diversity and Distributions: A Journal of Conservation Biogeography*, December 2013.
6 'Avifaunal disarray from a single despotic species: Beating the bullies – managing aggressive Manorinas to restore bird assemblages'; Australian Centre for Ecological Analysis and Synthesis, February 2015. The centre, called ACEAS, [http://www.aceas.org.au/] is a virtual and physical facility within the Terrestrial Ecosystem Research Network 'for disciplinary and inter-disciplinary integration, synthesis and modelling of ecosystem data'.

Chapter 10 Magpies: Mozarts of the Bush (One)

1 'High levels of extra-group paternity in a population of Australian magpies, *Gymnorhina tibicen*: Evidence from microsatellite analysis'; J.M. Hughes, P.B. Mather, A. Toon, J. Ma, I. Rowley, E. Russell; *Molecular Ecology*, 2003.
2 *The Myth of Monogamy: Fidelity and infidelity in animals and people*; David P. Barash and Judith Eve Lipton; W. H. Freeman, 2001.
3 'Maintenance of a hybrid zone: The role of female mate choice'; Jane Hughes, Alicia Toon, Peter Mather, Corinna Lange; *The Auk: A quarterly journal of ornithology*, 4 October 2011.

Chapter 11 Magpies: Mozarts of the Bush (Two)

1 'Attacks on humans by Australian magpies (*Cracticus tibicen*): Territoriality, brood-defence or testosterone?'; Rowena M. Warne, Darryl N. Jones, Lee B. Astheime; *Emu Austral Ornithology*, November 2010.
2 *Bird Minds: Cognition and Behaviour of Australian Native Birds*; Gisela Kaplan; CSIRO Publishing, August 2015. Kaplan also published *Australian Magpie: Biology and Behaviour of an Unusual Songbird* in 2004; this is a great account of the extraordinary capabilities of the magpie, including its complex social behaviour and vocalisation.

Chapter 12 Selfish Genes and Cooperative Breeders

1 *The Future Eaters: An ecological history*; Tim Flannery; Grove Press, 2002.
2 *Cooperative Breeding & Sociality in Birds;* Percy FitzPatrick Institute of African Ornithology; Cape Town, South Africa.
3 'Multiple Benefits Drive Helping Behavior in a Cooperatively Breeding Bird: An Integrated Analysis'; Sjouke A. Kingma, Michelle L. Hall, Anne Peters; *The American Naturalist*, April 2011.

4 Go to: http://monash.edu/science-stories/story/follow-the-birds/

5 'Kin selection, not group augmentation, predicts helping in an obligate cooperatively breeding bird'; L.E. Browning, S.C. Patrick, L.A. Rollins, S.C. Griffith, A.F. Russell; *Proceedings of the Royal Society B*, July 2012.

6 'Experimental Evidence for Phonemic Contrasts in a Nonhuman Vocal System'; Sabrina Engesser, Jodie M.S. Crane, James L. Savage, Andrew F. Russell, Simon W. Townsend; *PLOS Biology*, 29 June 2015. See also 'Diversity and function of vocalisations in the cooperatively breeding Chestnut-crowned Babbler'; Julie M.S. Crane, James L. Savage, Andrew F. Russell; *Emu Austral Ornithology*, August 2016.

7 'Babbler bird calls "convey meaning"'; BBC News, 30 June 2015. To see the report and images of the babblers making the calls, go to the BBC website and type in 'Babbler bird calls convey meaning' or go to http://www.bbc.com/news/science-environment-33325854

Chapter 13 Lyrebirds: A Scratch and Scramble Life (One)

1 'A Little Flute Music: Mimicry, memory, and narrativity'; Vicki Powys, Hollis Taylor, Carol Probets; *Environmental Humanities*, vol. 3, 2013.

2 *The Life of Birds*; David Attenborough; *BBC Books*, 1998.

3 'Lyrebirds mimicking chainsaws: Fact or lie?'; Hollis Taylor; *The Conversation*, 3 February 2014.

4 'Where birdsong began'; *Catalyst*; http://www.abc.net.au/catalyst/stories/4194557.htm; 10 March 2015.

5 'Interactions between the superb lyrebird (*Menura novaehollandiae*) and fire in south-eastern Australia'; Daniel T. Nugent, Steven W. J. Leonard, Michael F. Clarke; *CSIRO Wildlife Research,* September 2014.

6 'Regional Variation in the Territorial Songs of Superb Lyrebirds in the Central Tablelands of New South Wales'; Vicki Powys; *Emu Austral Ornithology*, April 1995.

7 Further reports will be made available on the website http://www.flutelyrebird.com, which shows where the vocalisations have been recorded, along with a map of the geographic range of the flute-like songs 'from Allan's Water and beyond'. To date, the researchers' recordings cover more than a hundred lyrebird sites spanning 23,000 square kilometres of New South Wales.

Chapter 14 Lyrebirds: A Scratch and Scramble Life (Two)

1 *Australian Bird Names: A Complete Guide*; Jeannie Gray and Ian Fraser; CSIRO Publishing, May 2013.

2 *The Land of the Lyrebird: A story of early settlement in the Great Forest of South Gippsland*; Gordon & Gotch, 1920.
3 *Bird wonders of Australia*; Alec H. Chisholm; Angus & Robertson, 1934.
4 *The Dance of the Lyrebird* can be obtained by contacting the filmmakers at greenhillmedia@yahoo.com.au

Chapter 15 Corvids: The Smartest Birds of All

1 'Stone the crows! Are corvids our smartest export?'; Stephen Debus; *The Conversation*, 27 January 2012.
2 'Social learning spreads knowledge about dangerous humans among American crows'; Helen N. Cornell, John M. Marzluff, Shannon Pecoraro; *Proceedings of the Royal Society B*, June 2011.
3 'Avian brains and a new understanding of vertebrate brain evolution'; Erich D. Jarvis et al.; *Nature Reviews Neuroscience*, February 2005.
4 'The Mentality of Crows: Convergent evolution of intelligence in corvids and apes'; Nathan J. Emery and Nicola S. Clayton; *Science*, December 2004.
5 *Bird Minds: Cognition and Behaviour of Australian Native Birds*; Gisela Kaplan; CSIRO Publishing, August 2015.
6 'The social life of corvids'; Nicola S. Clayton and Nathan J. Emery; *Current Biology*, August 2007.
7 'Direct observations of pandanus-tool manufacture and use by a New Caledonian crow (*Corvus moneduloides*)'; G.R. Hunt and R.D. Gray; *Animal Cognition*, May 2004. To see videos of the crows in the Oxford experiments and read reports on the project go to http://users.ox.ac.uk/~kgroup/tools/tool_selection.shtml
8 For a full description of the van Dooren project, go to https://thomvandooren.org/2014/12/08/encountering-crows-living-with-wildlife-in-a-changing-world/. He also provides updates of his research at http://thomvandooren.org/encountering-crows/

Chapter 16 The Clever Birds People Like to Eat

1 'The Startling Intelligence of the Common Chicken'; Carolynn L. Smith and Sarah L. Zielinski; *Scientific American*, 29 January 2014.
2 'Identification of the Yellow Skin Gene Reveals a Hybrid Origin of the Domestic Chicken'; Jonas Eriksson et al.; *PLOS Genetics*, 29 February 2008.
3 'Who You Calling a Birdbrain? Chickens deserve more credit for their remarkable cognitive abilities'; Ruthanne Johnson; *All Animals Magazine*, May–June 2014.

4 *The Magic and Mystery of Birds: The surprising lives of birds and what they reveal about being human*; Noah Strycker; Souvenir Press, October 2014.
5 'Crafty chickens use complex clucking'; K-Lyn Smith and Chris Evans; *Australian Geographic Magazine,* 18 August 2010.
6 'Interview with Professor Chris Evans'; *Catalyst*; http://www.abc.net.au/catalyst/stories/2923730.htm, 10 June 2010.
7 'Chickens Are a Lot Smarter than I Originally Thought: Changes in student attitudes to chickens following a chicken training class'*;* Susan J. Hazel, Lisel O'Dwyer, Terry Ryan; *Animals*, 21 August 2015.
8 'Primitive Self-consciousness and Avian Cognition'; Andy Lamey; *The Monist*, July 2012.
9 *Defense of Animals: The second wave;* Peter Singer (ed.); *John Wiley & Sons*, May 2013. A lengthy YouTube video showing the life and intelligence of chickens (called 'The Private Life of Chickens) can be viewed at https://www.youtube.com/watch?v=1c06xOF4uQ8
10 'Laughs, cries and deception: birds' emotional lives are just as complicated as ours'; Gisela Kaplan; *The Conversation*, 7 December 2016.

Chapter 17 Songbirds: Australia's Gift to the World

1 'Song-selective auditory circuits in the vocal control system of the zebra finch'; A.J. Doupe and M. Kanishi; *PNAS*, December 1991.
2 'Where Birdsong Began'; *Catalyst*; http://www.abc.net.au/catalyst/stories/4194557.htm, 10 March, 2015.

Chapter 18 The Origins and the Future of Birds

1 'Soft-Tissue Vessels and Cellular Preservation in Tyrannosaurus rex'; Mary H. Schweitzer, Jennifer L. Wittmeyer, John R. Horner, Jan K. Toporski; *Science*, 25 Mar 2005. 'T. Rex Related to Chickens'; Jeanna Bryner; LiveScience.com, 12 April 2007.
2 'A Gondwanan origin of passerine birds supported by DNA sequences of the endemic New Zealand wrens'; Per G.P. Ericson, Les Christidis, Alan Cooper, Martin Irestedt, Jennifer Jackson, Ulf S. Johansson, Janette A. Norman; *Proceedings of the Royal Society B*, 7 February 2002.
3 'Tectonic collision and uplift of Wallacea triggered the global songbird radiation'; Robert G. Moyle, Carl H. Oliveros, Michael J. Andersen, Peter A. Hosner, et al.; *Nature Communications*, University of Kansas, Lawrence, 31 August 2016.
4 'A new time tree reveals Earth history's imprint on the evolution of modern birds'; Santiago Claramunt and Joel Cracraft; *Science Advances,* 11 December 2015.

5 'Whole-genome analyses resolve early branches in the tree of life of modern birds'; E.D. Jarvis, S. Mirarab, A.J. Aberer, B. Li, P. Houde, et al.; *Science*, 12 December 2014. Seven other papers in this edition of *Science* are also of note. The full set of papers in *Science* and the other journals can be accessed at: http://www.sciencemag.org/content/346/6215/1308
6 'A quantum leap in avian biology'; Leo Joseph and Katherine L. Buchanan; *Emu Austral Ornithology*, 9 February 2015.
7 'Comment on "Whole-genome analyses resolve early branches in the tree of life of modern birds"'; Kieren J. Mitchell, Alan Cooper, Matthew J. Phillips; *Science*, 25 September 2015.

Chapter 19 Tackling the Extinction Threat

1 'Great Barrier Reef bleaching is just one symptom of ecosystem collapse across Australia'; Dale Nimmo, David Lindenmayer, John Woinarski, Ralph MacNally, Shaun Cunningham; *The Conversation*, 3 May 2016.
2 *Australia's Biodiversity – A Summary*; The Wilderness Society, 10 December 2015. See also 'Targeting global conservation funding to limit immediate biodiversity declines'; Anthony Waldrona, Arne O. Mooers, et al.; *PNAS*, December 2012.
3 'Government offers hope by telling CSIRO to reinvest in climate research', Matthew England, *The Conversation*, 4 August 2016.
4 *Climate Change Adaptation Plan for Australian Birds*; Stephen T. Garnett and Donald C. Franklin (eds); CSIRO Publishing, 2014.
5 *John Gould's Extinct and Endangered Birds of Australia*; Sue Taylor; National Library of Australia, 2012.
6 'We can't save all wildlife, so conservation laws need to change'; Phillipa McCormack and Jan McDonald; *The Conversation*, 4 July 2016.
7 'Rethinking legal objectives for climate-adaptive conservation'; Jan McDonald, Phillipa C. McCormack, Aysha J. Fleming, et al.; *Ecology and Society*, vol. 21, no. 2, 2016.
8 *A review of biodiversity* legislation in NSW: Final report; Independent Biodiversity Legislation Review Panel, 18 December 2014
9 'The NSW government is choosing to undermine native vegetation and biodiversity'; Neil Perry; *The Conversation*, 9 May 2016.
10 Environmental Stewardship Programme, National Landcare Programme; http://www.nrm.gov.au/national/continuing-investment/environmental-stewardship
11 'Here's a Good News Conservation Story: Farmers are helping endangered ecosystems'; David Lindenmayer, Chloe Sato, Dan Florance, Emma Burns; *The Conversation*, 22 June 2016. See also *Learning from agri-environment schemes in*

Australia; Dean Ansell, Fiona Gibson, David Salt (eds); ANU Press, 2016. http://press.anu.edu.au/publications/learning-agri-environment-schemes-australia

12 *A Wild Success: A systematic review of bird recovery under the Endangered Species Act*; Kierán Suckling, Loyal A. Mehrhoff, Ryan Beam, Brett Hartl; Center for Biological Diversity, June 2016.

13 The Regent Honeyeater Project; http://regenthoneyeater.org.au/index.php

14 United Nations Decade on Biodiversity; https://www.cbd.int/2011-2020/

Epilogue: 'Here's a Spot for a Home', They Said

1 *A Single Swallow: Following an epic journey from South Africa to South Wales*; Horatio Claire; Vintage, 2009.

2 The website www.arkive.org/welcome-swallow/hirundo-neoxena/image-G138846.html has a detailed section on the welcome swallow. ARKive is a not-for-profit initiative of the charity Wildscreen. With the help of wildlife filmmakers and photographers, conservationists and scientists, the organisers have set out to create 'an awe-inspiring record of life on Earth'.

Index of birds